"'The Aging Athlete' will help you unlock _____ __ ____ ____ ____ ____ significantly impact your overall well-being. Its insights, logic, and practicality are outstanding. This book is meaningful, timeless, and profound."

—Dr. Jarrod Spencer, Sports Psychologist
Mind of the Athlete, LLC

"While the publishing and entertainment industry have extended their focus past an obsession with younger audiences, we are still in dire need of books that address issues of aging with grace and, why not, some sex appeal. The athletes interviewed for this book describe an aging process that can be enjoyed with passion, pride, and pizzazz. All of these extraordinary people with their memorable stories started out as people like you and me, and in the end they still are. All of them made mention of at least one person in their life who truly believed in them or simply modeled a positive lifestyle. With the blessing of some able coaching, they took on a period of elite physical performance, developing their gifts and working on themselves. What amazes is that despite the onset of age, they never stopped being physical or getting enjoyment from doing either professional, performance fitness or simply keeping themselves in shape through maintenance or recreational activities.

"If you know moments where the prospect of aging daunts you, if you sometimes worry about the quality of your life and health no matter your current age, read this book. It provides a sparkling perspective on believing in ourselves, realizing potential, and being committed to enjoying life's journey. I am grateful to Sifu Slim for his mix of determination and romanticism, that he never stops believing in people, in himself, and the pursuit of health and happiness. A great teacher, Sifu's fairness, modesty, and sense of humor shine through and keep us smiling till our work in this physical body is done."

—Tatjana Greiner
Editor and Performance Tango Dancer
San Francisco, Calif.

"I would have never guessed that so many former athletes aren't keeping themselves fit. I hope your book finds its way into their hands. Thanks for a great week of reading."

—J. E., Coeur d'Alene, Idaho

"When I stopped dancing my senior year in college, I got a job that was more than full-time. I gained about 25 pounds over the next year and a half. Pretty depressing. I'm glad you got this book out. This subject needs to be studied, especially as you suggest, from the standpoint of mindset."

—S. J., Braintree, Massachusetts

"… a highly provocative read. It is somehow counter-intuitive to think of great athletes becoming unfit in old age. The recent suit brought against the NFL by former players indicates that fitness and health can erode all too quickly. The aging pursuers of fitness featured in this book are the exceptions and not the rule. We can all learn from their own stories of perseverance."

—Tom Jones
Author of "Sports Competition for Adults Over 40"

Can We Learn from Former Athletes?

What can we learn from former top athletes that is especially relevant for our health and lifestyles? Even though most athletes are essentially performance minded rather than maintenance and wellness minded, it's still a compelling revelation why 90 percent of them don't continue a program to try and retain some of their skills and conditioning. Learning from the 10 percent who do stay fit and healthy is where we can all benefit.

"The Aging Athlete" chronicles the fitness and mindset of a group of retired and semi-retired athletes, of what's worked for them over the years since they stopped competing or serving in the armed forces.

Some of the top athletes include Billy Mills—1964 10,000m race gold medalist once considered the most famous living Native American; Ken Shamrock—former UFC heavyweight champion who was named the *World's Most Dangerous Man*; Sam "Bam" Cunningham who starred in the famous 1970 Civil Rights Football Game; and Allen Winder—a blue-eyed basketball player who was called upon to break the color barrier … in reverse.

THE AGING
ATHLETE

THE AGING
ATHLETE
ELITE ATHLETES REVEAL THEIR SECRETS FOR LIFE

INSPIRATIONAL
INTERVIEWS WITH
SOME OF THE FITTEST
SURVIVORS OF ELITE
ATHLETICISM

SIFU SLIM

Softcover ISBN: 978-0-9911829-3-0
eBook ISBN: 978-0-9911829-2-3

Printed in the United States of America

Interior Design: CreativePublishingDesign.com
Cover Artwork: RannDesign.com

COVER PHOTOS

Randy Beisler, no. 4 pick of 1966 NFL draft. High school 6'5, 218 pounds. Age 66, same height due to his weight training regimen, 248 pounds. "Five days per week I do fitness training in the gym, about two days per week I play doubles tennis."

PHOTO AND FACT WAIVER

All efforts have been made to honor the integrity and sometimes harsh honesty of the included athletes and the people and stories they recalled. If you notice something that may need correction, please contact us through the website. The photos were provided by the athletes and their families and they gave their permission to use the included photos. If you take exception to the use of any of the photos, please contact us.

OTHER BOOK BY SIFU SLIM

Sendentary Nation—The Answers Are Found in 1910

For the aging athletes who are still training and doing well and for the others who no longer can.

I'd like to express my gratitude to those athletes who were kind enough to share their stories and to those who have read and commented on this book. I thank them for their knowledge and experience in adding to our better understanding of the serious problem of well-being we're facing today.

Liability Waiver

The lifestyles advanced in these pages have worked for a number of people. These days, most people in the West spend most of their lives taking up static space—standing or sitting—not moving gracefully or vigorously in an anatomically friendly way. The compromise seeks to relieve the body of much of its sedentary reactions—most notably pain and dysfunction—and the mind of its stresses and pressures.

The stories found in this book are first-person accounts from aging athletes. Should you have any reservations about being able to travel through the pages and come to some sensible decisions that might benefit your own particular wellness, please put this book back now.

This is a book on motivation, self-mastery, and fitness. This book does not advocate rapid transformation. You should not go out and attempt to get fit and well in a week or a period that is too short for the reality of your current health condition. That said, if your health is currently compromised, you shouldn't wait until you are diagnosed with arthritis, nerve damage, gallstones, or Type 2 diabetes before you make some changes.

Waivers that say to check with your physician before undertaking any wellness changes are helpful and I suggest the same. Make sure your physician does a comprehensive evaluation and knows your complete history. See to that before making any dramatic changes in your activity level. If you aspire to get off the couch and begin a walking program by walking your child or grandchild to school, the best person to consult with before venturing out onto the road is the crossing guard.

Contents

Foreword

I was surprised and very pleased when asked if I might introduce you to "The Aging Athlete" because it's an excellent work that really doesn't need an introduction.

With the help of the motivated athletes whose stories appear in this book, Sifu Slim explains how an overly excessive amount of attention has been focused on all the physical aspects of sports and other styles of physical movement. In what could be seen as a worship of youth—by fans, stars, coaches, and even the athletes themselves—the immediate performance results gain the lion's share of the attention.

That attention mostly seeks to keep the elite athlete healthy and successful in his or her prime, a time when grace, strength, agility, and power predominate. This youthful spark and style is what makes sports exciting and thrilling to watch and play. Think of how Romanian gymnast Nadia Comaneci is remembered today based on what she did as a 14-year-old—six perfect tens at the 1976 Montreal Olympics. For many, she is still the world's little Nadia of her youth. Fortunately, Nadia has lived an active and exemplary life, still maintaining her fitness and spending a great deal of her time in giving back to the world.

In most cases, however, far less attention has been directed to what happens to the athlete after the lights go out and the adoration ends—the remaining 75 percent of life still to be lived. Sadly the picture is often a far cry from wellness and healthy behavior. As Mickey Mantle once said, "If I knew I was going to live this long I would have taken better care of myself." Mickey's father as well as others of his male relatives had died young, probably from dust they inhaled at work in lead and zinc mines. Mickey and his wife Merlyn and their four sons were reported to be alcoholics. Two of their sons died before mid-age and Mickey died at 63.

Not only does this book fill an important need in documenting what physically happens to many of our athletic heroes when the show is long over and the cheering has stopped, it also focuses on the inner mental experiences of those rare few, the 10 percent, who have discovered a new beginning after high level, youthful physical performance ends.

Useful life lessons in this book are revealed through the detailed discussions and recollections of nine high profile role models of perseverance. These men who had their time in the sun have chosen to adapt to a life of activity rather than bask along the banks of memory lane. While these nine stories and associated journeys appear extremely diverse, all share a common theme. All of these former athletes have conquered the typical frailties of aging by refusing to give in, by staying mentally strong. Their attitudes represent the highest possible order of what I would call mental performance which has led them to an ongoing pursuit of physical well-being as well.

Few of us ever experience the euphoria shared by the characters who share their insider knowledge in this book. Whether the experience stems from an NFL playoff win, Olympic upset victory, comedy basketball performance, or escaping from poverty on an Indian reservation, the story is the same. Careers and prison sentences end, leaving the participants with a whole new life to deal with. Some make it and live large. For others, a well-rounded second part of life seems too tall an order.

It's been said that athletes are the only people we ask to die twice (once in their retirement and once in their normal death). Over the years in my practice, I've seen the distressing truths of that statement. From a psychological perspective it's very difficult to cope with the silence and reversion back to "average" after all the hype and hoopla ends with elite level retirement. As a clinical and sports psychologist, I've seen how retirement can be devastating to those who are not ready for it. It quickly becomes obvious how few are prepared for it, especially at such an early age.

Starting with favorable genetics, to achieve at the highest possible level generally requires an almost super-human pursuit from an early point in one's life. That, combined with exemplary coaching and learning, puts athletes at their peak performance. When the game suddenly ends, what fills their lives is often depression, loneliness, or artificial attempts to replace the high. We may see an increase in the use of drugs, alcohol, domestic violence, and other forms of detrimental behavior.

Because it reads like a group of entertaining biographies, this book takes the reader in and, without being excessively preachy, drives home important points that have relevance today for everyone—former athletes as well as those who have had lives away from sports. It also serves to guide us with hands-on advice learned by this small percentage of peak performers who, despite any loss of identity and profession, still found a way to maintain their awareness to what's needed to pursue a second life strengthened and lengthened by physical and mental health.

Sports these days have become highly specialized and come with towering demands. The training for any sport is a year-round endeavor. In the old days, kids played many sports and chose one specific sport much later, often while in college. Pro athletes used to view training camp as a place to get into shape. In the past 20 to 30 years, the money available to elite level professional athletes and the improvement of training techniques only allows room for those willing to focus narrowly on one sport, and who specialize narrowly on one position.

If you want any chance of making it today, you are offered a training program that can become an overdose of single-minded concentration. This specialization can often lead to identity foreclosure as the athlete views himself or herself exclusively as an athlete. As a result, the devastation that occurs after a serious injury or retirement does double damage as the lost person struggles to find a new identity. This is like starting from zero on your own, now with possibly a severely limited drive and purpose to succeed. As they navigate around a virtually guaranteed pitfall, these aging athletes, who need more balance in their lives, tend to falter because of deficiencies in well-rounded lifestyle training.

Sifu Slim's book helps this rare class of athlete. But more importantly, it helps the 99.9 percent of the rest of us who might have competed recreationally in our youths, and then gave it up as we got older and as our lives became more sedentary.

Let me end by commenting briefly on the mental game, as this is the world I live in when I work with athletes. They visit me for help with their competitive edge, to embrace smarter strategies, or to deal with injuries or retirement. Physical aspects of sport and wellness are indeed essential, but what is easy to overlook is the puppet master of action—the brain. The brain plans and carries out our action steps. Humans rose to the top of the evolutionary heap not with sharper teeth or larger biceps, but with larger and more wrinkled frontal lobe gyri and sulci, those folds in the brain that increased cortical surface area and allowed us to better plan, strategize, and reason than our more beastly or venomous rivals. Proper desire and skilled focus always begins in the brain.

We often look only at the influence of the end product of physical activity. Rarely do we talk about the phenomenal mental consistency and focus required to eat healthy, exercise, and maintain the discipline that Sifu Slim and his featured athletic characters so abundantly possess. Just remember to include the mind and thoughts along with all the great activities you engage in as you pursue your own battles with health and wellness.

Through a collection of real life stories, this book demonstrates that there can be a much brighter future after sports and after youth for those who are willing to adopt the right attitude and engage in healthy and meaningful activities rather than giving up or giving in to a sedentary and inevitably unhealthy existence. In many ways, this book is a loud wake-up call. Because the reading was engaging, I feel the lessons came easily. Now I can use these skills of mindset and resolve, and even acceptance, in my own post-age 50 pursuit of health. As I do with you, the reader, I will recommend "The Aging Athlete" to my clients because they will benefit from it greatly. Our lives are made richer and healthier by learning from those who have been at the top and know what's needed to still function at their best.

John F. Murray, PhD
Clinical and Sports Psychologist
Palm Beach, Florida
JohnFMurray.com

Preface

*"Sifu, you should write a book called 'The Aging Athlete.'
It's a new field of study in orthopedics."*
—Dr. Bill Gallivan, fourth-generation orthopedic surgeon, former college rugby player and current martial artist, and father of five, plus one additional child currently living with his family.

Why I Wrote this Book

All of the included athletes came to this project because they felt they had something to share.

Sifu Slim asked the eldest aging athlete to come to this project: "Are you going to donate your body to science?"

Age 87 champion triathlete Charley French: "If anybody wants it, they can have it."

How many of the people you played with or trained with in your prime are still fit today? What if you heard the answer was "less than 10 percent"?

How many were practicing fitness even one week out of their performance activity, one week after "hanging up their cleats, ballet shoes, boots, or Speedos"? Why do you think a possible 90 percent of them stopped?

The answers are here for you to read. If you need inspiration, here it comes.

My quest began with a question to Randy Beisler, an exceptionally fit former offensive lineman from Gary, Indiana, who was the fourth pick in the 1966 NFL draft. "When you go to the reunions with the retired players from your era, how many of them are still in shape?"

"Less than 10 percent," said Randy, who was age 64 at the time when we met in Northern California in 2009. We had both just finished our own individual workouts.

Introduction

The Honor in Connecting with These Fine Fellows

I have long held a reverence for accomplished athletes and for those who simply pursue athletics. The abilities of some have, quite candidly, kept me in awe. I fully intended to gain interviews with aging female athletes for this first book. The universe allowed me to connect with a few, but due to scheduling, and even a severe illness, we could not put together the interviews. The intention will be to share the stories of aging female athletes in future books. All of the athletes featured in this first book on aging athletes were people I had never met before.

So, it was a situation in which I was contacting relatively well-known (at least among their peers) or very well-known athletes somewhat out of the blue. Sometimes I called with a referral, other times it was an e-mail through the spam filters of their websites. Once, with Brazilian Jiu-Jitsu Master Luis Heredia, I just walked into his place of business and challenged him to a 20-minute grappling battle on the mat. I win, he does three partial days of interviews. He wins, I mop the mat for a week wearing a sarong and, why not, a tropical island head scarf.

"Don't even dream something that preposterous," my inner voice told me. Don't even joke about that. For Pete's sake, the guy is a master. Don't challenge him to any live grappling on the mat. You couldn't afford the trip home from Hawaii on the airline's first-class stretcher seat.

But, if it came to that, I would have done it. I wouldn't have left the mat victorious, but maybe the master would have seen how serious I was about the project. I was a writer in search of a story and stories are often found in places of live fire. The only thing I could hope for was that I'd do better than writer and impersonator George Plimpton would have been capable of doing in his prime. For Pete's sake, I've done jiu-jitsu since 1997 and they don't call me Sifu Slim for nothing. But I'm a recreational jiu-jitsu guy; this guy goes at it with the best—he's big-time, this is his life … and meal ticket. But with guys like Master Luis, it's better to walk in there and just beam a martial arts beam, bow a few times, and hope for the best, which is what I did.

Luis said, "Sure," and became my first interviewed athlete.

I have to think that karma, honorable intentions, timing, and a bit of luck all were part of helping enroll aging athletes into the interview process. In one case—of hall of-fame swimmer Jeff Farrell (featured in a follow-up book)—my French fluency may have taken a somewhat reluctant, recently retired master's athlete, age 76, and instilled a bit of intrigue in him. Perhaps this was part of why this humble athlete at least came to see what I was about. Each chapter will mention how these athletes came to the project. The choosing of athletes and their motivations for agreeing are perhaps prefacing testaments to the later importance of their words. They all came because they felt they had something to share.

It was indeed an honor to have spent three to five hours with each of the athletes who shared stories that were sometimes dark or funny, and by rule were psychological releases. We can all use a bit of catharsis from time to time. The athletes all agreed to share deep parts of their past, present, and, in some cases, future. Robby Robinson is a very private person. He was still competing in bodybuilding at age 66—still at an incredibly fit and dedicated 205 pounds of ripped physique. Robby and football great Sam Cunningham both had unforgettable experiences being black athletes either in college or heading to college during the Civil Rights movement and the draft for the time of the Vietnam War. Both had stories of how they were able to remain healthy and alive while some of their friends and peers were coming home from Vietnam with mental or physical conditions or in body bags. When I called Robby for round two of our interview process, I acknowledged what had come out during my interview with Sam.

Sam is known as a decent and genuine person, always has been. I heard this directly from some of his friends and mentors. Sam has probably screwed up some things in his life and said things he wishes he had not, but he has mostly been a man who listened to his mentors, his parents, and his heart. He has never been one to do less than his best and has never been a maker of excuses. He was and still is a man who leads by example.

So, what I said was, "Robby, I was honored to have spent some time with Sam Cunningham on Saturday. You may know that Sam played football at USC and then the New England Patriots. I told Sam a bit about my conversation with you, and your upbringing in the Deep South. His response was, 'I'll tell you this, I grew up in Santa Barbara where racism was only a small factor, nothing like where Robby grew up. If I had grown up in the Deep South or somewhere like Chicago or the big cities where there were areas not conducive to a safe and productive life, it's likely I wouldn't be here having this conversation with you today.'"

The life and times of Sam Cunningham, who scored two touchdowns in the first interracial game in the University of Alabama's stadium, became another telling interview that went deep. And relaying that to Robby helped Robby's interview go deep. That's where stories of one's life eventually go. That's what a life of athleticism and training tends to do. To win or to endure, athletes have to marry their endless training with the art of digging deep. If I did my job as a chronicler of their stories, these pages will provide elements of that depth. You'll read about a so-called "bad kid" who was at times abandoned by his parents and grew up in foster homes before becoming "The World's Most Dangerous Man" in the UFC fight game and a caring coach to other kids and young adults who needed direction. You'll read about a man who grew up in a rough and tumble mining region and who was never given his due credit and his father's blessing until he finally found his world-class niche. He became his family's only extreme endurance athlete.

All of these fellows had to dig deep to attain their goals. In not one of these cases did success come easily. Each pedal stroke, max squat, swimming stroke, footstep, football drill, and punch to the heavy bag has a mindset component. The mind of the athlete is what was most engaging about this project. The mind and the history of each athlete's challenges were the driving force. We fans, colleagues, and followers want to know why. Why did they choose athleticism? Why did they choose the endless hours of training and the aches and pains of that life? Why did they choose the thrill of victory and the agony of defeat? And, most important, why are most of these specific aging athletes still training and maintaining fitness and wellness while the majority of their counterparts are not?

This subject would make a perfect research project for a sports medicine doctoral fellowship. In this book, rather than think of these questions in terms of a scientific study, let's check in with a look inside their hearts and minds. And let's see what comes up when we invite them to go deep down in their souls. The ultimate goal is to help people maintain good patterns and break bad ones so they can live full and happy lives.

Chapter 1

The World's Most Dangerous Man

Keeping the Dukes Up from Age 5

Your first group sport, if you're some of the only white kids in the neighborhood, turns out to be a playground fight. Your mother is a go-go dancer and waitress. It's a hard life but it's all you know. That is how the gifted and unbelievably strong athlete featured in this story experienced the beginning of his life

A lot of fighters come out of hard places. Others are just pure athletes who find their way into the ring. Some are neither. Larry Holmes falls into the first group. This former heavyweight champion boxer, who fell one victory short of tying Rocky Marciano's 49-fight perfect record, tells of being dirt poor growing up with a mother and 11 siblings. It wasn't so much that he was getting beaten up on a regular basis growing up in the '50s and '60s on the streets of Easton, Pennsylvania. He did, however, get thumped by his elder brothers for things like wanting his fair share of dinner. He was the fourth of 12 children and often had to fend for himself while growing up. This process of maturation happened quickly by necessity so he could help his family. He began working when he dropped out of school at age 13. When he finally became financially successful, he was able to express the pride that came with being able to make good money, forget that, excellent money, and do some wonderful things with it. All of his kids received a good education including some postgraduate degrees. By this time, his investments in income property had helped fix up the deteriorating city of Easton, Pennsylvania. Larry acknowledges his lack of formal education but states, "I have a PhD in common sense."

Holmes' unforgettable idol and forerunner was known as The Greatest—Cassius Clay, later Ali. Ali wasn't a street fighter, nor was he known as an all-around athlete. He was a decent runner, wood chopper, horseback rider, and fitness training athlete. He could sing and dance a bit, act and recite rap-like poetry, and he could jump rope with the best. His coordination, focus, and perseverance were incredible. A pivotal Muhammad Ali story from his youth involved a prized bike that was stolen when he was 12. He wanted to find and confront the person who had committed the theft but first, he reported it to a police officer who happened to be hanging out in a boxing gym. That officer also owned the gym and became Ali's first coach. Later, after proving himself the best in the amateurs, with an Olympic gold medal in Rome, he proved himself the best in professional boxing. Then he had to fight for his right not to kill or be killed in Vietnam, a place that had done him no wrong.

Boxing icon Rocky Marciano was an all-around athlete who grew up in Brockton, Massachusetts. He was born Rocco Francis

Marchegiano and both of his parents were immigrants from Sicily. Rocky's house was a stone's throw away from a local park where he honed his athletic skills and his likeable personality. He played offensive line and defensive linebacker for his high school's football team. Thinking he should take a chance on his first love, baseball, he once drove all the way to Fayetteville, North Carolina, to try out with the farm team for the Chicago Cubs. He had great hitting ability but no arm and was slow afoot. Amazingly, that poor throwing arm became the delivery mechanism for his knockout punch. He would retire at the appropriate time—at the end of his fighting prime—with a perfect record of 49 – 0. In the fighting game, Rocky stands out as an all-around athlete.

The athlete featured in the chapter below is cut from similar athletic cloth. While his first group sport was getting beaten up, he evolved into an all-around athlete who eventually decided to take up no-holds barred (NHB) fighting. You know, limited rules fighting, which involves fighting from any position—standing, on the ground, or even flying through the air with feet or fists flailing. This type of fighting became widely popular in the 1990s with all-out challenges to see who the best fighter was, given limited rules and sometimes no time limits or weight divisions. NHB fighting morphed into a safer and more equitable test of might and courage. It grew to eight weight classes, required the combatants use lightly padded MMA gloves on their hands, and required the referees to be more active so as to protect the fighters. Ken Shamrock learned submission fighting starting in 1989 and became the UFC heavyweight champion in 1994 at age 30. It was not too different than much of the daily fighting he engaged in while growing up, only now he was getting paid for his efforts and people sought him out for his high-profile persona.

Tale of The Tape
Ken Shamrock

Former UFC Heavyweight Champion and current Hall of Famer

Public Speaker, Director of a Non-Profit, and Youth Mentor

Born Kenneth Wayne Kilpatrick; February 11, 1964

Full name today: Kenneth Wayne Shamrock.

All-around athlete and graduate of the school of tough knocks who sort of fell into professional no-holds barred (NHB) fighting. UFC is one organization of NHB competitions. It stands for the Ultimate Fighter Championship.

Had a football tryout with the San Diego Chargers.

Age 17: 160–172 pounds. Benched over 300 pounds. For those of you who aren't aware, that's unbelievably strong. And his arms are on the long side, which makes it even more impressive because short arms of course aid in the bench press. Benched over 600 pounds at age 20.

Age 32: six ft., 205–220 lbs. This was in the early part of his UFC career. He admits a natural ability that was augmented by performance enhancing substances. But his number one strength is mindset. It's likely the only way to go from benching 300 to benching over 600 pounds is by first strengthening the mind. Pushing limits has always been Ken's greatest asset.

For MMA training, he regularly brought in some top NHB fighters. He would go all out with one training partner for 30 minutes, and then bring in a fresh new fighter for another 30, then one more for another 30 culminating in up to three hours of non-stop training. While he built substantial endurance and strength of mind doing this, he also admits to never being 100 percent for any fight. He says, "I was always hurt to some degree. Overtraining and resurgence of old injuries had a hand in that."

Age 49: six ft., 235 lbs. - He still was doing some NHB fighting as well as professional wrestling.

Has a titanium bar in his neck from a wrestling injury, having broken his neck at age 17.

Has metal brackets in his lower back. Knee operations have reduced his mobility. Even at over 230 pounds, his submission wrestling and NHB training partners have stated that his speed at shooting (shooting in for a takedown) was once the best in the gym, even better than the smaller (typically quicker) guys. He has also had a shoulder replacement operation.

Notable quote: "My fighting abilities have been reduced by age and injury. I'm about 60 percent of my former self. But, I still love this stuff. I love to compete. That's just how I'm wired. I've been fighting my whole life."

Father: The person he calls his father was Bob Shamrock, who died in 2010. Bob ran the boys' home where Ken lived in Susanville, California.

Mother: Diane Kilpatrick, died in 1995, worked as a waitress, a stripper, and a go-go dancer.

Ken's blood brothers, Richie and Robbie Kilpatrick, were both good athletes and tough kids. He also has a sister named Sandra.

Ken's adopted brother is Frank Shamrock, who retired as a top UFC fighter.

The Greatest Fight, a 2014 documentary by Darren Wilson, tells some of the key points of Ken's eventful life.

Website: LionsDenMinistries.net

I first got to meet Ken by phone. We had two detailed phone conversations before we eventually set up a meeting in Reno. I flew to Reno after one of perhaps the most moving days of my adult life. That morning, I had to say goodbye to my then bedridden mother who was in the final throes of life-ending cancer. That was to be the last time I saw her alive. Ken and his wife, Tonya, offered some kind words about what my family was going through. That meant a lot to me at such a sad time.

*Tonya and Ken Shamrock—
friends since their youth*

"Don't try this at home," was what I said to the camera as I sat down on the front lawn of a historic 1910 Craftsman home in Downtown Reno. Ken Shamrock had broken a handful of ankles with the very ankle lock he was to demonstrate on me and outweighed me by about 60 pounds. His arms were about the size of two of mine. My ankle, which had never been broken before, was in his hands. On the upside, he did seem in a good mood.

"This is the most effective move in the business. Once I hook your heel in my elbow, and I cross my leg over yours and squeeze so your knee and leg are locked down, there's no give. If I sink this in quickly, there's really no way out of this move. If you're not tapping before the pain sets in, it's already too late. Something's going to pop."

(As a man who had practiced jiu-jitsu for over a decade by that point, I knew what the move was about and how quickly I would want to tap out in submission. On my back, with Ken positioned at my raised legs, I turned to the camera and added …

If I'm on the ground, and a larger opponent is moving in on me, I have to use my legs. I can kick and I can try to tie him up, but from my back, I can't generate much power in my punch. I'm really defending. I can't easily grab my opponent's ankle—especially if I want to stay away from his punches. If he grabs my ankle, my ankle is basically a sitting duck if he knows ankle locks.)

"Speaking on that," Ken began, "when you walk into a jiu-jitsu school, the first thing they'll tell you when you go for a leg lock is, 'No, you can't do that here. They're too dangerous.' And the truth of the matter is because they don't know how to defend them. Leg locks are a perfect defense against a jiu-jitsu system because once the legs are wrapped around the waist, boom, there's all your leg lock positions. The jiu-jitsu schools are being very hypocritical because submissions are submissions no matter what they are. You can't kill anyone with a heel hook, but you can kill them with a choke. But chokes are legal and you do them every day."

(Author's note. Jiu-jitsu schools are part of the martial arts business. Boxing schools teach boxing and use those rules in running their business. In that same vein, jiu-jitsu schools have to keep their students healthy. Leg locks, while they don't kill you, can maim you for a long time. A number of the leg locks—knee bars and heel hooks—immobilize

you so quickly that you have to tap out before the pain starts. Otherwise it's too late and you can tear or break something. From the school's perspective, maimed students can't pay their bills. Chokes, while they can cause brain damage or death, generally take longer to sink in. That normally gives a student the time to tap out. But, as a jiu-jitsu practitioner who doesn't have a lot of upper body strength, leg locks have proved to be a favorite part of the game. The problem has been, in my entire time in jiu-jitsu schools, less than one percent of the instruction time has been spent teaching leg locks.)

"Bottom line, it's very political why leg locks are generally banned in jiu-jitsu competitions."

Ken, would it be accurate to describe you as a natural athlete first. And then, you found the combat sports?

"I think I was an athlete because I learned MMA fighting so fast. You know I started when I was 27. Before that I was a wrestler, I played college football, I boxed in tough man's competitions. You could say I really got into the mixed martial arts competitions late. When I was fighting for and defending the heavyweight title, I was in my thirties."

And you still look good. You must have good Irish genetics because you don't have any gray hair.

"You know I've been blessed and in the last 10 years, I have really lived properly. You know, good, clean health ... I never smoked. I rarely drink. My mindset now is in a good place. The first part of life it was trying to build who I was going to be and develop my family. The second part is taking all of those things that I have built and show other people who have come from my lifestyle that there is an opportunity to be able to pull yourself out of the gutter, out of bad situations, and do something positive. Then they can help others—it's like paying back, flipping the page, never forgetting to give back."

Passing on the good lessons. Helping others to follow in your footsteps.

(At this point we went inside the historic home and sat down for a conversation. As I always do to open the dialogue, I explained the premise of the book. During that intro, he politely asked if he could interrupt. What a nice guy. It may amaze some how polite athletes often are. I think of it this way, they have spent a lot of time in close quarters with teammates, coaches and trainers. The easiest way to go through all that, and life, is by being polite and using a kind word when you can.)

"I'm actually writing a column for Fight Medicine with a doctor. And it's about athletes and the aging athlete. It's about athletes' injuries after fighting and it's not even necessarily the injuries. It's the road they travelled for those many years and all of a sudden the road has stopped. And now, the excitement, the thing they did for every single day—made them who they were, made up their DNA—is now gone. Many turn to drugs, to women, alcohol … and some people turn to religion. But you know something has to fill that spot because it's an explosive and exciting life, especially if you're successful at it."

You mentioned "serotonin" in our phone conversation. You know, boxers, they didn't know what they were going through. Besides needing to earn money, Muhammad Ali had this situation with his many comebacks. So many fighters never retire in their prime. Yes, money is often the reason. But, is there something else that's going on in their minds? You mentioned serotonin [a feel-good hormone that elevates mood. The opposite feeling and reduced serotonin can occur during depression or depressive states]. How long have you known about that?

"I think I first found out about it because I actually took a medicine that helped serotonin production in the brain. And that's how I learned about it. It's that feeling you get and it's actually a false feeling. It's like cocaine or alcohol or anything else."

Tell me why you mean it's false?

"Because in reality, we are still who we are, we are still human beings."

It's making you feel a little superhuman so you can try to do superhuman things?

"Well, it makes you think there is no tomorrow. Like you are it, that there are no rules you have to play by. There is no after life. They don't realize that life goes on. And once we're done with what we do, then we basically come down to everybody else's level."

And you're signing autographs as "a former Ken Shamrock."

"You almost go below what normal respect is because people don't look at you at that same level anymore."

You're still a relatively young aging athlete. You're not some old coach who won back in the '50s. You are still recently moving into your new zone.

"You still have the ego. You still have that bravado. And it's basically being taken away from you because of health. And your mind hasn't caught up with your body. Your mind is still like a champion. And your body is way far away from that. For me, personally, I think it's probably the worst thing that happens to athletes. It's the mind and body disconnect and athletes are not being educated on what's going to happen."

What I offered to do for the Olympic athletes who are part of the military was go in and do a closing session where I'm not just giving a speech and wishing them well and telling them to work out. That's not gonna do anything. I want to get them involved in a program for about five weeks, maybe more, and bring guys like you in. Because they've seen you go from a top level to a dad level or a coach level ...

"Just another person walking the street and what's wrong with that?"

Ken, as world champion, 1994

Nothing ... What was your dream when you were a youngster?

"My dream starting at age 12 was to be an NFL football player. As life works out there are different paths that you travel. Because a door opens for you and it's exciting."

Did you have a lot of energy as a kid? Was there any hyperactivity?

"Yeah, I had anger issues, and was hyperactive. And I got in fights all the time and I got in trouble because of it. I had a real hard time controlling my temper. It was my adopted dad, Bob Shamrock, who taught me how to take that anger and turn it into something positive."

Bob Shamrock was a man who believed that respect worked both
ways. That was how he achieved results with the over 500 boys
he helped raise in his group home in Susanville, Calif.
Ken was his finest athlete and best fighter. Along the way,
Ken wound up becoming a youth mentor as well.

How did that happen?

"I had been in the juvenile system—boys' homes—for most of my young life so I had missed a lot of school. So I was way behind. I was embarrassed to be in special ed classes as a freshman in high school. So I signed up for football and I was hitting people and being very aggressive. At our first game, they had me playing cornerback. And there was a pass play that was the same I had seen in practice. My only thought was to hit this guy, to obliterate him. And the ball was in the air and I came running at him. Thank god I hit him the same time he caught the ball because I really wasn't timing it. I separated the ball from him and kept driving my feet even after I had him on the ground because I was so angry. Then the first thing to hit my mind was to head for the fence, to run. Because, the anger and feelings that I had at that time were always bad and I thought I should be punished. I stood up and I didn't know where to go. And then I heard the people cheering and screaming and my teammates were patting me on the back. Before this, every time I had that anger-emotion feeling it had come from me beating someone up."

How could you reprogram that into your brain?

"At first it didn't make any sense to me. But, eventually I learned that sports are a lot like life. In life, you have penalties. When you mess up, you think it's just you that's in trouble. But what about your mom, and your dad, and your brothers, and your cousins, and your girlfriend …?"

And teachers and mentors.

"All the people who put time and energy into helping you; you just let them down. Now, that team you are playing for and made that great hit for … What if there's a flag because you kicked the guy in the head? And a flag comes out and you get ejected. You cost your team a chance to win. You let the fans down because you disrespected your school and the other team's school. And you let your coach down because of all the time he put into you. Sports are just like life, you have to learn to manage your temper. Your temper is fine as long as you use it within the boundaries of the rules."

Are you young for your age? You know, young and playful?

"Yes, I'm still immature I guess in a sense because I really connect to kids and even my grandkids, one who is a toddler I watch a few times a week. I'm in a good spot right now. I think it's really important to you as you grow older to have those people around that you love and care about. It's really comforting when they can love and care about you back."

I have to share one bit about the difference in our physiques. I may have worked on my physicality as much as you. But, by age 16, I was still skinny. I kept thinking, when am I going to get more buffed?

"Well, when I was in high school, I weighed 160 and I benched 320. And I've always been that way. Later, I redshirted to try to put on more weight at college because I wasn't big enough to play college ball. I was lifting weights like crazy. Then, at age 20, I had a tremendous growth spurt and wound up weighing 220. At that point, I benched 605 on a regular bench, and I benched 535 in a bench press contest."

That's almost unbelievable. What happened to your speed when you got bigger and stronger?

"The bigger I got, the faster I got. I was also agile and flexible. I could do the splits. I was very gifted. It's just like when I started fighting. I went over to Japan and six months later I'm wearing the champion's belt. It's incredibly technical over there and I picked it up."

Did you concentrate on 10 main moves?

"I concentrated on one move and that was the heel hook. I could set it up from anywhere, ground, top, standing. It's like a guy who plays chess. You can't understand how he can think 10 moves ahead. When you get your setups and your submissions and it clicks, it's just like a master chess player."

So, in six months, you went from a beginner in technical MMA fighting to champion in Japan. Now, you're a world class athlete competing against other world class athletes who have much more experience in technical submission fighting. How did you make that transition?

"I think it's basically my childhood, the way I grew up."

*Ken, at age 40 after an all-out training session in the octagon—
the ring set-up used by NHB fighters. There is no running off
the mat to escape. You tap out, pass out, or are knocked out.*

Fighting for survival.

"Yeah, I fought through some pretty scary things. And now fighting was creating some opportunities. And I just kept moving forward. I started out living in an all-African American neighborhood in Macon, Georgia. I was fighting every day because of the color of my skin which I didn't know was the reason. But, as kids we start mimicking what our parents are doing. And we saw racial disagreements on TV so we learn from that. We don't even have reasons for it. I was the only white kid besides one other girl that was in my class. Every single day almost I was in a fight."

Was this the time when schools didn't send you home for fighting?

"There was nobody at home, my mom was a stripper, a go-go dancer. I didn't have a dad at that time, he was off struggling in his own ways. He was out of the picture. He was athletic. He was a boxer and he was pretty well put together, and he played football, too. So I think I got the athleticism from his side."

How is your family now?

"I'm very fortunate. I've got a good wife, good in-laws, I've got a good family surrounding me. My wife trusts me, she believes in me. She's always supported me. I've known Tonya since I was 13 and she was 10. Her parents ran the Shamrock boys' home in Susanville, California in Lassen County that my dad subsequently owned. So, I'm glad we finally got together at midlife and took our vows."

Could you walk me through the first decade of your life and describe your surroundings?

"I remember my first group physical sport. I was surrounded by a group of black kids. They were like 13, I was five. My brothers were six and seven. But only Richie was there. The girls were punching me and then I went to the ground and they started kicking me."

Basically killing you.

"I was down on the ground unable to protect myself. My brother, Richie, who was seven, grabbed a brick and threw it. The brick hit one girl in the side of the head, busted her wide open. Blood was everywhere. My brother grabbed me, and we began to run. The girls were stunned for a moment and then came running after us. We were running for our lives. I was partially being dragged. I remember this very clearly and I don't remember a lot from this era, but they literally looked like big giants running after us."

What a way to get introduced to group sports.

"Horrible fights became a normal part of my life and my brothers' lives. Also in kindergarten when I was in the bathroom, a group of kids my age came in and started teasing me. Before that, I used to cry. Then, I changed, and instead of letting kids see me cry I began to fight. So I started swinging at these kids. The next thing I know, I'm on the ground and they're kicking me in the head."

And your own kids have lived a completely different life.

"I was in fights starting at age five. I was in placement by 10 and was stabbed by 10. I did strong-arm robbery at 10. And I looked at my kids at age five and 10 and then my life and I asked myself how was that possible? Then you realize there are kids pushing drugs on the corner at 10 and carrying guns. Normal people living normal lives can't even fathom that. But the answer is that when you grow up on the street you become very mature, very fast or you're not gonna be there. And that's kind of how my life was."

And then you moved to Napa when your mother married.

"When she married the man who was in the military, Bob Nance, we started out in Napa. With our new name, my biological father couldn't even find us. But when we got there, we were so much more advanced in terms of being street tough than the other kids. But they again made fun of us because we were the new kids and we had southern drawls. Because of our Macon past, fighting and doing the street stuff with or against the kids in Napa, it was like a cake walk most of the time. And we Nance kids very quickly evolved into being the bad kids in Napa. Stealing cars, rims, radios."

What would you do with those things?

"It was easy to pawn stuff back in those days. And often we had someone who wanted those things and they would ask us to go steal the rims from a car they had seen. For that, they might give my brother Richie an eight-ball of coke. Or they would give us some money."

How did this end?

"I eventually wound up getting stabbed behind the 7-Eleven. I was 10 and I was with a couple of my boys and we got into a fight. This kid took a swing at me, I put my arm up, and blocked him. Then I hit him, he goes down, and then I started beating the crap out of him. Then he took off. I looked over and saw his knife sticking out of my forearm—my blocking arm. My ulna had stopped the knife. When I noticed the knife and pulled it out, it was almost surreal. Then I passed out when I took a look at a bunch of white bubbles in my cut-open arm. Everyone else ditched on out of there. When my boys saw the knife wound, they also took off."

Age 10?

"It's hard to imagine. But when you're on the streets and living without parents as young as age five, it becomes more possible to imagine. When you're left alone a lot, survival starts immediately. There was literally no past and no future. Everything is in the now."

Your life was R-rated compared to what we saw on TV growing up. I mean there were no knife fights or blood that we saw which related to kids on the TV shows.

"The worse thing you saw back then was Vietnam."

We're lucky we weren't born 10 years earlier.

"It's crazy, it's unbelievable to watch what we say is wrong and is bad and what we teach our kids and then watch what we as our government and the world says is okay to do."

We're going to send in some drones to wipe out a military base but along the way we're going to wipe out …

"A school across the street … It's a messed up world, it really is. The people who are in power …"

(At this point we talked a bit about his mother who has passed away. At the end of this moment, I asked the following.) Is there anything positive you can share about your mom?

"No. I didn't hate her, it's not like she did anything wrong to me other than not be a mother. My opinion is that she didn't know how."

Did you ever go to Christmas mass with your mom?

"She got me into church. She was going through a nasty divorce with Bob Nance. And my brothers and I were in placement [Ken was in a boys' home in St. Helena, Calif.] at the time and we came home for a home visit. And there was fighting and screaming and we weren't getting along. And she told me she'd gotten saved and she took me to church. That's when I was first introduced to the Lord. I was 11 years old. I later got baptized. This all felt good to me."

What helped you in the church life? Was it that people would finally listen to you and slow things down for you?

"What helped is that I wasn't being judged and considered different—the bad kid, the trailer park trash, the troubled youth that others should beware of. And I felt the Holy Spirit a little bit too and I wanted more of it. I kept striving to find something better than what I had known of life."

Let's talk about the UFC in 1993, you and Royce Gracie who would win the championship. You learned submissions very quickly in Japan in 1990 and '91. Then, in '93, at age 29, you meet up with a 27-year-old Brazilian Jiu-Jitsu master who comes from a lineage of 50 years of jiu-jitsu practitioners. They are known as Brazil's first family of jiu-jitsu. Besides some surfing and soccer, all those guys were doing was submission fighting and training. Now, you're in a match with him. It's the big time.

"He was good, there's no question about that. But he had an advantage. The gi [aka kimono], because he knew what to do with it. He used it as a weapon. I had never trained gi before. I had done my submission fights wearing shoes. For this UFC-1, they took my shoes away because they said it was a weapon. When I got choked by a gi choke, I remember thinking, that was a weapon. They took my shoes away which had provided grip. This also kept me from getting his leg—I would have had a better chance at heel-hooking him. What I was thinking was he just choked me with a rope ... how was that not a weapon? Because I'm strong, I can normally stop all of the other chokes, but the gi is different. It's as strong as a rope."

Yeah, that puts a lot of pressure and leverage on the veins, arteries, and throat.

"Tell me about it. So, instead of complaining about it, I went back and started studying submissions. I got videos. I watched them over and over. All of the old Gracie footage. At that time it was hard to find this type of thing. And I went to the Machado's [other Brazilian Jiu-Jitsu practitioners who married into the Gracie family] school in L.A. and rolled with them. Jean-Jacques Machado was amazing, he didn't tap me out but he was amazing. A couple of the other guys tapped me out. We were wearing gis. Once I understood the gi, I decided that not wearing a gi was now an advantage for me. And one year later, I fought Royce again and it was a different story."

Is that the fight in which you trained for endurance?
"Yes."

And you were ready to go for three hours?
"That's right."

How did you train for endurance?
"I did submission training whereby every half hour I brought a fresh guy in. I grappled for three hours with fresh guys on me."

So you're doing muscle and cardio endurance without running hills.

"All grappling. I needed to be able to know I could roll with him for three hours. I did that for three months leading up to the fight."

And you cut down to 205?

"202."

And how did you feel at that weight with all of that endurance?

"I felt like superman. Then, a day before the fight, they cut the time limit down to 30 minutes because of TV—Pay Per View. But I didn't change my strategy one bit. I controlled his hips by blocking them every time he tried to turn. I'd block the hips and hit him … mostly in the body because I didn't want to extend my arms and risk getting arm-barred. My strategy was, if I hit him enough times in the body, within three hours, he is going to wear down. If you watch it, at the end of the fight, he couldn't even walk out of the ring. And that was only 36 minutes."

I thought they said 30?

"The original time limit was 30 but then his brother, Rorian, [pronounced 'Horian,' one of the founders of the UFC] yells out, 'Three more minutes.' And I said, 'Okay.' That's when they stood us up. That's when I blasted him. He went to throw a kick and I knew he was gonna shoot. I didn't back up like most guys do. I just sunk my hips in and his foot came in and slid down and as it slid down I hit him as he was falling in."

So it wasn't a knockout punch but …

"I glazed him and still blew him up. If I'd had hit him solid, that would have been it. He wouldn't have fought again."

As it was, he didn't fight again for what ...?

"Ten years." [It turns out it was 11 years later at UFC 60]

Ten years. And what did his brothers and his dad say about the UFC at this time?

"Basically they say that that's not the sport they wanted. The whole thing got to be too political. Basically what had happened is that everybody was catching up to them. That's the bottom line. And it was a smart play by the Gracies because other fighters were catching up."

[In the meantime, the Gracies and all of their friends and cousins—and even their enemies—were opening up jiu-jitsu schools all over the world ... mostly based on Royce's fame in the octagon. The smaller fighter who had defeated much bigger opponents.]

Along your route to the next few UFCs you suffered injuries that prohibited you from fighting or from doing as well as you wanted. Over the course of your career that spanned two decades, how often, for focus, for training, for being in perfect health ... what percentage of the time were you at 100 percent?

"I don't think I was ever 100 percent. Maybe some guys do get there, you know, where everything is clicking, I don't think I had that. I did a lot of hard training, a lot of uneducated training. Most of my injuries happened in training. I tend to go for it in life, and that includes my training. When it's on, it's on."

What was one of the new styles you learned in your training?

"I took Muay Thai in Japan to combine with my grappling. I actually had a Muay Thai fight against Frank Logan who was a former Muay Thai kickboxing champion."

Was this a battle with knees to the face?

"No, he broke his hand on my forehead and then leg-kicked me. Once he couldn't punch me any more, he concentrated on the leg kicks and after a number of them, they swelled up and he dropped me. I had to go to the locker room later where they drilled holes in my swollen leg to allow the blood to drain out."

Leg kicks are brutal.

"Yeah, they're brutal. But that's when I put that bit of knowledge away. Later I decided that that was the style that would mix very well with MMA."

How did you start your training center, The Lion's Den?

"In 1991, I rented a place in Lodi, California. I had a little money from fighting in Japan and I rented a really small place and got some mats. I tried to put together a team. I brought in my brother Frank, Guy Mezger [who later co-wrote The Complete Idiot's Guide to Kickboxing], Jerry Bohlander [later a Napa County, California sheriff], and held tryouts there to find other good fighters. I brought in Maurice Smith [who in 2013 was still fighting at age 51] to teach us stand-up and we taught him ground fighting. Lots of good fighters trained there and we had some dominant years in the UFC."

So there was no other grappling gym around at the time?

"No one had even heard of it. Not in 1991."

Yeah, the first time I got into jiu-jitsu was in 1997 in Sacramento. And the gym had probably been around for a year or so by that time.

"I had to start a gym and bring in other good fighters so I could have people to train with. That's the reason I formed The Lion's Den. In the early '90s, as far as martial arts gyms, there was not as much to choose from: usually only judo or karate."

How did you put together your repertoire of moves? I know how hard it is to memorize new moves and put them into your arsenal.

"I had limited time because I was in my 30s and I had to use what I could remember easily—this is using what worked for me. If you are studying a bunch of disciplines, you can't master them all. You have to use what works—what comes easy for you."

What was one of the best things you learned?

"From great boxers, I learned that your legs, your feet, have to get you to where your opponent is. The punching ability comes from the feet. Which, when you look back to my wrestling background, makes sense. In wrestling, you shoot through your opponent. But your legs get you there. The same thing in boxing—you punch through your opponent and it's your legs that get you there."

Tell us about your wrestling.

"I broke my neck wrestling one month shy of my 18th birthday. Most people cut weight, I always tried to put weight on for wrestling. At 170 pounds, I was wrestling at the 185 weight class. I felt I could beat the larger guys with speed. I had an advantage, I was faster than they were and I could bench 320 pounds. In my senior year, I had qualified for states and was training over the break in January 1982 and they had cleaned the mats and had not taped them back together. I picked up a bigger kid to take him down. The mat slipped and we fell. He landed on my neck and it broke."

So you were incapacitated, not able to move?

"Yeah, and I started to atrophy and lose weight. During the recovery I went down to 140 pounds because I couldn't train, I couldn't lift."

How soon after this were you able to do contact sports again?

"I had to get a release from Dr. Cate in Redding, California. I was never supposed to do contact sports again. But Dr. Cate was one of the first people to repair the neck by going in through the front. They said my life was probably going to be completely different now but I had fun with it. I didn't worry about it. They put a metal halo on me to immobilize the neck."

Did that stop you?

"Heck no, I even got in a fight with the halo drilled into my skull. They had to teach me how to walk. Of course, as the toughest kid in the house, now that I had dropped weight and had this thing on my head, some of them thought they could take advantage of me. This kid at the group home called me 'head of metal.' He was a big, fat guy about 260 pounds. I picked him up and slammed him. The bolts from the halo tore out of my skull."

You mean blood was coming out the side of your head …?

"It was nasty. When the bolts tore out, my head sounded like a freakin' bomb went off... *boing!* That sent me back to the hospital."

That incident and then the knife in the arm incident, are those the two wildest things that happened to you physically?

"No, I've had a lot of stuff. At age 19, I was a peer counselor at the group home. I had a car crash at four in the morning going straight off a 30 mph turn doing 130 mph. The car flew through the air. A metal cattle fence post came up through the back seat and my friend, who was sitting in the back, almost caught that between the legs. He looked down and said, 'I almost became a human popsicle stick.' The turn was maybe 100 yards from a house so we landed in the front yard of the home. We got out of the car and saw that all of the underneath—the wheels, the rims—was shot. The engine was turned sideways, all the bolts were broken. But the body of the car was good and we were fine."

So what happened?

"I learned that the guy in the house had come out and saw the car. He called the cops. My dad had a good relationship with the cops. I had gone skiing with a couple of the cops and had a reputation as a good athlete who was coming back from open neck surgery. So, we were just making the turn on Waynefield Road to walk back to the group home and here comes this friend of the family in his cop car. And we had been drinking. My friend, the cop picks us up, gets us home, and says to my dad, 'Take him inside, I'll take his statement later.' He had the car towed. The only thing I got from it was reckless driving."

You guys took off in flight like the Dukes of Hazzard.

"I remember landing. It's the worst sound in the world. Things are bending and tweaking, then there's silence. There's smoke everywhere. If my friend had had his seatbelt on, he would have been impaled. Instead he was slammed up against the side of the car. If he would have been killed or disabled, that would have completely changed my life … And I also wrecked on a motorcycle going around that same corner. I was making a turn and a deer came out across the road. And, like an idiot, I hit the front brake and went right over the handlebars. And I just relaxed. I had this, like, ability to know what to do."

Maybe you were taught in a prior life. Perhaps as a human cannon ball in the circus ...

"And I was at Eagle Lake one time. And they had these docks with the big aluminum tanks on the bottom. Normally, they have a chain tying them down so they don't float away. And there was one with a big metal post on it. Anyway, there were six or seven of us and we swam out to it and flipped it upside down. The metal post was now holding the dock down by digging into the lakebed. Anyway, me and my brother, Robbie, got underneath this thing and told the others to get on the side of this thing and said we'd lift it to get it right side up again. So they get on there but we're not thinking of the physics of this thing. At some point they have to get off. So they get it tilted up and I get under there with my shoulder and I'm underwater. All of a sudden, this thing got really heavy. And I started going down and I'm underwater. And my brother is like dead-lifting it. And right before it basically pins me underwater, he pulls it sideways. And as he pulls it, the thing lands on his leg and slices his leg open and he has a six-inch gash on his leg. If he doesn't pull it, I'm pinned underwater with the post in my shoulder."

Yikes! ... so you said in the interviews there was someone who is doing a film on your life?

"Yeah, there's a guy named Darren Wilson who is doing a docudrama on my life."

What else are you taking part in these days?

"Besides a lot of family time—which is four generations of folks right now—I'm doing motivational speaking. I do some where I use my Christian walk, and some where I don't bring up the religious side. With Tonya, my wife, and some other people's assistance, I run Lion's Den Ministries. It is a Christian, faith-based ministry run under a nonprofit."

[The website explains that the organization's activities include: Prayer Support, Athletic Events, Group Homes, Correctional/Juvenile Facility Outreach, Health Outreach, Church/Christian Events - Speaking Engagements, and more.]

This is a video capture of us when we started talking about the insanity of government behavior in respect to geopolitics and war. It drove us into a perplexing Zen moment.

It's good you are able to travel and put back. How do you raise money for your ministry?

"We raise money for group homes and other organizations in need of support. Frequently, people contact me and my organization because of who I am, not just because what I believe. For example, we were just contacted by a church in Indiana that wanted me to come out and participate in a two-week drive they have. They are trying to attract people outside the church. Because of my tough-guy image and success in overcoming the obstacles of my youth, they thought I could reach people and help them make a change in their lives."

So in these interviews, I like to ask the aging athletes how they are doing in respect to health. From what you have told me about the fighting and accidents you have been involved in, I'd say you have to consider yourself a lucky person.

"Well, I heal well. I've broken my nose seven times—all in fights. I've had various cuts on my face. I've had open-neck surgery on my spine twice. The second time was to install a titanium bar. I had an ACL replacement in my left knee—they replaced it with my patella tendon. It is still a nagging problem. I've got brackets in my lower back—this is an ongoing problem. I had my right shoulder replaced and it works great."

So, Ken. We've had two phone conversations where you were open to listening to me attempt to talk some sense into you about moving towards being a less combative-arts-oriented athlete. All of your surgeries seemed to have gone well.

"Yes, I'm very fortunate."

Do you think that the charmed life that you have had—in terms of always bouncing back—should be honored by maybe being more sensible for the next 40 years?

"Absolutely." (We both broke up at this point.)

So, if you were your own coach, what would you tell yourself about the ego? You love the athleticism and the combat … you already know how the ego works. You've done well at your fighting career. How do you tell yourself to go into a different realm—the next experience for Ken?

"I can't speak for everyone, but I think you have to live your life the way you want to live your life. As long as you are not hurting anyone."

But you are responsible now to a lot of people who love you.

"Absolutely. But I believe that love from others shouldn't have a price on it. It shouldn't have to cost you anything. That love comes from a place of purity. But I wouldn't go to them and say, 'I love you so you can't do this anymore.' That's like putting a price tag on it. And I think a lot of women do that with husbands. And they get to a certain point and the wife says, 'I don't want you to do that anymore.'"

What about a senior division in MMA? Like you and retired MMA master Bas Rutten doing a match but not trying to kill each other?

"That's kind of what I'm doing now with my fights. I'm trying to fight guys from my era. And I'm still working out regularly. That's where I am right now."

You know the 90/10 rule that I have come to learn—that less than 10 percent of former military, or athletes from high school, college, the pros, etc., even ballet stars, are not doing fitness on a regular basis. Yet, you and I are. Why are you and I wired the way we are?

"Your personal story, Sifu, may be because you were smaller of stature. That made you have more drive to succeed. For me it was more being a wayward kid. I was told I was never going to make it, that I was going to wind up in prison. In my mind, I was thinking,

'No one is ever going to be able to tell me that I'm not going to be able to do that.'"

You were proving people wrong.

"Yeah. Now, at this point in my life, I don't want anyone to be able to forget me. I don't want to be lying in bed. I don't want to have to be walking with a crutch. For me, I think it's unfair for an athlete who has made their living with fans, fans who have spent money to come and see them, and have put them on a pedestal … And then the athlete keeps doing appearances and keeps reaching out and being part of the fans, making money on the fans. For the athletes not to hold themselves up in a higher part of respect … to walk in 50 pounds overweight and sign autographs. To go out and do motivational speaking 50 pounds overweight. It's almost as if when a fan sees that, you break their heart, you've taken some air out of their sail."

It's not good for either side.

"It hurts both of them. To me it's like how did you go from all this pride and wanting to be the best at what you do to quitting, to literally just stopping, giving up almost. You see what happens to them: how quickly they get old, how quickly they're in a hospital, and how quickly the body fails them. And it's like, why?"

One of the things I've come to learn is that they're disconnected to wellness and maintenance. They're these high-performance athletes doing high-performance drills, but they don't know how to go into recreation and maintenance. They did all of this hard stuff, maybe banged up their knees and got a few concussions, and then …

"You stop. It's almost like if you had never done it you'd be better off. But if you train for 25 or 30 years and then you just stop, your body isn't used to that."

Atrophy happens quickly. When you broke your neck in high school—you went from 171 to 140-something in a matter of weeks.

"And I had to fight back to get healthy and put weight back on. I remember there was this one kid named Mike Anderson who was in the group home. He was running track. I had just gotten my halo off, I'm 140 pounds. And I was still a tough kid—this wasn't going to be my swan song. And Mike was talking about how he could run faster than me."

There's nothing like a challenge.

"And how. So I said, 'No, you can't.' I was super competitive. So Bob Shamrock said, 'There's one way to settle it, you boys can run from here to town,' which was just about three miles round trip. I was with him up until we were just about into town, and he made the turn first, and I made the turn about 100 yards behind him. And I was struggling the whole time but my will would not let me quit. And I got about halfway back to the group home and my body shut down—I literally could not move. And he was already home. But I started putting one foot in front of the other and walked home. There was a car following us with some of the younger boys in it. And they offered me a ride home but I wouldn't quit. It took me a long time to get back home because I was throwing up and beat, but I made it. And when I got there, I shook his hand and, in front of all of these kids who thought I was the tough guy, I said, 'You're the better man, you won.'"

§ § §

When we finished the interview, I felt an incredible amount of honor and pride in the warmth we both had experienced. It was spectacular to have been blessed with an over three-hour interview with the World's Most Dangerous Man. And it was more friendly and more enjoyable than I could have ever expected. He knew I was writing this book on spec. And he still took the time from his busy schedule to come and share his very moving life story. That was very important to me and I trust it was for Ken as well. Ken was open, humble, honest, and friendly.

What probably really bonded us was the fact that both of us were young at heart. It also helped that I had studied some of the same art forms he has and I had shed some 15 years of sweat on the grappling mat. As I spectator, I had followed his sport more closely than I had been following any other sport over that time period of my life. What I take away from learning about him is that Ken has always lived life in the moment. He has lived through so many momentous experiences that he said he honestly cannot even remember half of them. A book of the true details and interactions of his life—with all of the events—would almost be like reading an encyclopedia on the battles faced in small-town USA.

Ken's battles continue. He told me he has to deal with his own skeletons while also attempting to live a good family life. Through his nonprofit ministry, he remains dedicated to making a difference in the lives of troubled youths. What you get from spending time with him is that he is open for discussions, he's open to share wisdom, but eventually, he has to get back to the current goal he has in mind. Armed with his unstoppable will,

Ken will be taking on some further battles tomorrow. Still tough, yet smiling with the relief that he's already succeeded in making it through five decades of keeping up his dukes.

Chapter 2

The Guarded Life From the Deep South

"Out of the night that covers me, black as the pit from pole to pole, I thank whatever gods may be for my unconquerable soul. In the fell clutch of circumstance I have not winced nor cried aloud.

"Under the bludgeoning of chance my head is bloody, but unbowed. Beyond this place of wrath and tears looms but the Horror of the shade, and yet the menace of the years finds and shall find me unafraid. It matters not how strait the gate, how charged with punishments the scroll, I am the master of my fate, I am the captain of my soul."

—"Invictus" from the Book
of Verses by William Ernest Henley

Working on self-mastery is the plight of the driven man, woman, and child. We decide to move forward, mastering skills and overcoming obstacles. There is simply no other way. For the author

---

43

of the poem listed above, one technique that had to be mastered was the ability to hobble about. Otherwise, the ground he would have covered would have been limited to the far reaches of his bed. The English writer, poet, and editor William Ernest Henley, was born in Gloucester, England in 1849. A tall, well-built man, he was an amputee victim of tuberculosis. Henley had a sharp editorial eye and was highly regarded by his close friend, Robert Louis Stevenson, who credited Henley as the inspiration for the peg-legged pirate Long John Silver in "Treasure Island." Henley died in Woking, England in 1903. His stirring poem "Invictus" became one of his most beloved and well known works.

One might envision "the naked place" as somewhere to go for wine, woman, and intimate frolicking. Actually, the word "gymnasium" is derived from the Greek word "γυμνός," meaning naked, and the gymnasium is thus the place to be naked.

In the Hellenic world between 480 and 323 B.C., it was customary for Greek men to compete in athletic events stripped to the buff. That was also a time in history when Greek women could live as free, liberated souls. They wore revealing attire, competed in athletics, and even participated in nude ceremonies. A big problem for the non-gentry, and non-upwardly mobile class of men, aka the poor guys, was war conscription. Attrition had drastically reduced their ranks, which left more women than men.

The rest of that story may lie buried for eternity in the ash heap of Athens. Bodybuilding was a popular pastime. The sculptures from this period represent gods as having beautiful bodies. Thus, you could be more godlike if you created your own body beautiful. People also presumably used the gymnasium as a means to sweat out any sexual frustrations and as well as to refine their athletic ability for competitions held to honor the gods, especially the phallic god Priapos to whom men prayed for more women.

The pedigree of bodybuilding, using weight resistance techniques, can also be traced to India in the 11th century, 1001 to 1100. During that time muscle training people made use of Nals, which were circular weights made of stone. This design had no bar between the weights. Nals were lifted using handles carved in each individual stone. The Indian people also developed a barbell made of Babhul wood, which was used because of its strength, durability, and dimensional accuracy. It was called the Sumtola, which means equal weight. Carving holes at equal distance from each end and is how the dumbbell was conceived. Although they may not have realized it at the time, this allowed for progressive resistance training and ultimately, the rippling muscles on display in the magazines of today like Ironman, Flux, and others.

Modern bodybuilding began with Sandow, the Magnificent, born as Friedrich Müller. This proponent of building bodies is justly deemed the father of bodybuilding, which today is a multi-billion dollar industry.

In the city of Königsberg, Prussia, now Kallingrad in the Russian Federation, Friedrich was born in 1867. For ages, the Prussians seemed to be fighting one country or another. Young Müller was having none of it and decided to use his young and able body to dodge the draft. Of course that required a fast name change and out of the hat he pulled Eugen Sandow. Because of an inability to deal with his dysfunctional family, he ran off with a traveling circus where he became an acrobat and developed a magnificent physique. Along the road, Sandow, the Magnificent and Florenz Ziegfeld crossed paths in 1893. Ziegfeld, a theatrical producer, signed Sandow to a contract. Thereon, it was blast off to international fame and glory, until his beautiful body was laid to rest in 1925.

His legacy spawned a plethora of musclemen from Arnold, "The Austrian Oak" Schwarzenegger, a seven-time Mr. Olympia winner, to Robby, "The Black Prince" Robinson, whose accomplishments include: Mr. Masters Olympia, Mr. America, Mr. International, Mr. World, and Mr. Universe (a number of these victories were multiple times). Like his poetic predecessors, Robby, who has penned poems since he was a child, had to face a number of challenges on his path to self-mastery. One was verbal expression—he was born with a speech impediment that can still affect him today.

Robby was especially known for his abs and back.

Tale of The Tape
Robby, "The Black Prince" Robinson

Professional bodybuilder and Personal Health and Fitness Coach

Born in Damascus, Georgia, in the Deep South, on May 24, 1946.

He was called Robert Leo as a boy. Real name: Robert Lee Robinson, Jr.

Son of Robert J. Robinson, Sr., a sawmill worker and logger.

Son of Lucille Lewis Robinson, who ran a juke joint.

Height: 5'7"

Weight at age 18: 185

Weight at his peak in his early 30s: 215

Weight at age 64: 185

Personality traits: Quiet, focused, keeps it simple, a learner of lessons. Steady in the face of trouble.

Book: "The Black Prince, My Life in Bodybuilding: Muscle vs. Hustle"

Website: RobbyRobinson.net

Notable quote: "My English teacher flunked me. As my punishment for failing, every day the entire school year I had to recite the poem *Invictus*, by William Ernest Henley. That taught me discipline." Also of note: "I've never even been inside a McDonald's."

Pivotal moments of self control: Not turning and engaging in fights of words and fists when other non-black competitors lashed out at him with racial slurs in the Deep South. This was to be Robby's M.O. as he did well in his amateur competitions in the 1960s and '70s. Instead of fighting back, he kept things cool and walked away with trophies and still holds the amateur record for having competed in some 300 competitions.

I had long been a fan of Robby's, it was quite a joy to finally get to speak with him. He responded to my email and we set up some times to do Skype conversations. Because of his busy schedule of training his clients, together with his personal time for diet, rest, and his own training, we had to spread the online meetings over three sessions. I got an energetic charge before and after each one of those. In fact, I was literally jazzed for the entire week. There were countless bits of wisdom Robby was willing to share and there was a lot of softness in the man's resonating voice.

What was your birth name and where did your family come from?

"Robert Lee Robinson, Jr. The majority of our family came from Georgia. My grandfather owned a huge farm in Dolton, Georgia. The house was built high up over the ground. In those days adults told you what they wanted and children didn't ask questions. It just wasn't allowed. People talked on the porch in the evenings. I spent a lot of time under the porch listening. That is how I learned about the world and life."

What's your mom's full name, and where did your parents meet?

"In the neighborhood everybody called her 'Charlie May.' Her name was Lucille Lewis Robinson. More than likely, my parents met in Damascus, Georgia. A friend of my mom introduced her to my father. He was six feet, 200 to 220 pounds, and all muscle. My mom was 5'7" and also had a great body. They didn't work out, but they looked as if they had. Their genes emerged into all of us. We all had great bodies. My sisters were all shapely, small waists and big chests and big butts. The boys were all very muscular and chiseled. Even today my grandkids and even my great grandkids are all muscular."

How did your parents support your family?

"Our homes were juke joints. People could come, stay, eat, and drink—emphasis on the drinking and partying. It was like a not-so-legal hotel with peach alcohol we made in buckets from rotten peaches. So, we kids basically grew up in a family of boot-leggers. My mother ran the juke joint. People would also come to our house in the woods to buy 'juice'—bootleg liquor. We were open 24/7, 365 days a year. This is how the family made most of its money to keep us going. There were a lot of mouths to feed."

A juke joint. I wonder if that's where a juke box came from?

(It turned out the terms are related. The term juke box relates to the music played at a juke joint—a place of merriment, dancing, and gambling.)

People have to get by somehow ... This was the era of sharecrop-pers, both black and white. Vast numbers of these folks had no savings whatsoever, they were indebted to the landowners. To run away from the debt was illegal. The KKK was also lurking.

"That's right. There wasn't much of a chance to get out from under that if you worked the land of someone else. There was not a whole lot of employment for blacks in those days. In our region the work was primarily logging. I remember my father worked in the sawmill long hours, usually seven days a week, moving logs and cutting wood. When I first became aware of his physique, I was amazed at how muscular he was. As a young kid growing up I could see that I was muscular too. By the time I was nine years old, I was able to do chin ups, pull ups, dips, squats, you name it. I just kind of started doing those exercises out in the woods. I later learned some more of that by watching Jack LaLanne on TV. Jack gave me a great foundation for health, nutrition, and being physically fit. Jack LaLanne and my mom gave me a solid male and female foundation."

Similar things happened to me. I started watching Jack LaLanne in 1967. I'd do the exercises right next to the kitchen while my mom was cooking. I thought Jack was brilliant because he didn't need machines.

"Jack is something else. He was an early bodybuilder. Like him, I was almost always into bodybuilding. And as a kid, I just spent a lot of time being physically active."

Did you ever go to the sawmill?

"Yeah, if my dad couldn't make it back for dinner, my mom would send me with his meal. It was amazing to watch him move wood and feed it into the saw. He had it down like an art. All the men at the job admired him; all the women in the neighborhood loved him. My mom had to keep him on a leash. He was a good looking guy with sharp features. As I look back there could have been some race mixing in our family either with my parents or with the ancestors before them. It did not affect me, but it did come out in my brothers and sisters. Their hair was straighter, their skin was lighter, and they had smaller lips and noses. Their eyes were different than mine. My brother, Jerry, and I, and my mom were darker skinned."

When you were in your 20s, did the word "wellness" mean anything to you?

"Yes, because I grew up on a farm. I was raised on a place that had some fields but was mostly in the woods and that's where I spent most of my time as a kid—in the woods. Everything I knew came from that farm. This is going to sound strange, but the first time I went to a grocery market I was in my late teens."

When your mom and dad went into town to buy things that didn't grow on the farm, did you go with them to see what the town was all about?

"Well, I don't even remember my parents ever going to a grocery mart. On the property where we lived when I was in my teens, we raised chickens, hogs, and had a smokehouse. We had a big garden and fruit trees. That's how I ate until I went into the military service."

I'm sort of anti-coffee and caffeine for me and for most people, but I know people who say it works for them. How about the use of caffeine in your life?

"Back in the early '80s, I trained with guys who got Columbian Gold, which was a coffee they would drink before they trained. I found out for myself real quick when I was doing this that I was not able to get to sleep at night. Even if I have a coffee in the middle of the day it will have me charged all day and all night. I'm not saying not to have it. I'm saying go ahead, have it occasionally, but I don't think it should be something you consume every single day and definitely not all day long."

When did you graduate from high school and what do you remember from that time?

"I graduated in 1965 from Lincoln High School in Tallahassee, Florida. From that general time, I remember everybody being totally depressed and very sad at the time of the Kennedy assassination and afterwards. I think that my mom and my family felt that we as a race didn't have a chance after that. My mom felt that President Kennedy was our savior. That was the information I got from listening to older people talk in their conversations, when I was a kid."

How many brothers and sisters did you have and how many are still alive?

"There were 14 of us. I had seven brothers and six sisters. In the boys I was the sixth boy. My brothers Willy and Jerry and my older sister Sally-Ann are still alive. The others are all gone."

How did you get along with your siblings?

"I was a momma's boy. I spent more of my time with my mom. I didn't spend that much time with my brothers and sisters. My mom and I were the darkest members in our family. If you're the darkest one in the family, you're not going to be in a good place in those times. It was the white and black conflict that goes on even to this day."

What was an average day for you when you were on the farm?

"There were animals to be fed, wood chopping, and other farm activities before school. We had breakfast at 6:00 or 7:00 and were out of the house by 7:00 or 7:30. It was a mile or two to walk to school. I was always by myself. I had a speech impediment, I stuttered. It was just horrible. I was picked on by my brothers and sisters and in school and basically withdrew to myself because of it. I didn't even walk with my siblings to school—I stuck by myself. Again, I was the darkest one. In my culture you were separated from white people very early on. I never let it bother me. I never had an attitude about it and if the white people did, that was their problem. I didn't have a problem with it, I knew it was going to be tough."

How did you spend your time?

"I spent 90 percent of my time by myself, mostly in the woods when I wasn't near the porch, with my dog. His name was Five Cents, like the nickel. He was my best friend and partner. Soon as I got home from school he and I would hit the woods deep in the southern swamps, hunt, fish, trap, and just be alone to dream and imagine. I knew I was a person of color and the world was not going to be easy on me. I knew that I would have to work hard, and whatever I did, I knew I had to be a success. I spent a lot of time dreaming about it."

Could you share a bit about racism?

"As I mentioned, I even felt it at home, from my brothers and sisters. Because of my dark color, a lot of kids at school didn't know they were my brothers and sisters. When I look back on it now and look at the time we grew up, I kind of understand because the world out there was not ready to be good to me. For people of color during that time, it was likely you were going to have some problems with that. Racism was a problem all over the world. In our black culture, it seems to be all over the world. In the former slave cultures, the inferiority was inflicted in your mindset starting from the slave owners back in the day."

That's a lot to overcome.

"That's what I thought. I grew up in that exact environment. So you already kind of knew where you were. It was set aside because the slave owners, the people who had the black people, were the ones who put us on the side. They had a house for themselves, they were the ones allowed to have the family and the babies. That is just how it was."

That's a tough thing to overcome. Who was teaching you, was your dad around?

"I learned a lot from my pa. He was a very religious person and spent a lot of time in church. In my culture, church life was law. He was a very quiet man, but a big disciplinarian. It rubbed off on me. You didn't want to get into trouble because you knew exactly what was going to happen. I was attached to my mom. I put myself in positions to succeed so she would be proud."

Would it be accurate to say you are a deep person who is very driven?

"If I do something, I have to succeed, to do better than someone else. It is always my goal to get better. I leave a mark for someone else to go after. When I grew up, I saw a lot of illness, sickness, and death. I remember that so many people were complaining and unhappy. I didn't want to be that way. I wanted to attain a certain level of healthiness. The only way to achieve that was to maintain a healthy lifestyle, and keep up a physical regime. It all started with my mom who was an incredibly great cook. The meals were always on time. They were always healthy, straight from the garden. I've followed that throughout my whole life. I have never had a McDonald's shake, fries, and burger, never even been inside of a McDonald's. I think if you eat healthy and work out, it's definitely going to extend your life and make it a better one."

Tell me about school, your teachers, and what subjects you enjoyed.

"I went to Lincoln High school. It was small, about 100 students in my class. I had a lot of positive role models. Mrs. Peacock, my history teacher, inspired me. I love history. I think that history is enchanting. You grow up knowing things and end up being a part of history. I love to read and spent a lot of time reading. I was a super athlete, but sometimes behind in my classes. My English teacher flunked me. As my punishment for failing, every day the entire school year, I had to recite the poem *Invictus*, *by William Ernest Henley*. That taught me discipline. I got serious about sports and training. I spent almost no time chasing girls. I was too focused."

Did you go to the prom?

"I was at the dance. I went by myself and hung back along the wall. I had my mind on training at that time."

When you played sports in high school you were 5'7"?

"I'm probably about 5'7" and one half, and to be running back you want to come in about 5'7"or 5'8". That gives you a good low center of gravity to turn, cut, and plow into people. I'm not that big. I have very small joints. My ankles are small, my wrists and elbows are small—all the joint areas are extremely small. When the muscles come into play and are pumped up, it makes me look bigger. So the bigger the muscles and the smaller the joint areas are, the more it creates the illusion. Despite what you see in the photos, I am actually not a very big guy."

Not a big guy, what …? Have you trained people with my build—slim like Gilligan?

"The majority of the people I train and work with are not actually bodybuilders. They basically want themselves in shape for when they go on vacation. They definitely want themselves to look good for themselves and they want to be healthy."

What were some of the highlights of your athletic career in high school?
"I was an all-star fullback on the football team and all-star in track. I wanted to be the next Bob Hayes. I ran ten 100-yard dashes each day."

("Bullet" Bob Hayes was a running back and wide receiver and track star for Florida A & M University and later a record-setting pro football player. He is the only athlete to win both an Olympic gold medal and a Super Bowl ring. He and Robby share the first two names, Robert Lee.)

How do you think you developed a vision at such a young age?
"My mom was my role model. She had a huge influence on me. I learned some important stuff from my pa, but I didn't really spend a lot of time communicating with him. But I got what he was about and what he wanted for me. I always talked with my mom more than anyone else."

What happened right after graduation?
"I was playing football in summer practice at Florida A&M University when I was drafted into the Vietnam War. This was soon after high school, in 1965. I did not want to go. I had been defending myself in my own country. As Muhammad Ali would come to say, the Viet Cong had done nothing to me. During that time, whites and blacks were escaping to Canada. My mom took me by the hair and said, 'Listen, I don't want you to go to jail.' She took me to the bus station. I got on that bus and ended up at Fort Benning, Georgia. If it weren't for her, I'd have probably ended up in prison."

Did you have to go overseas for your military career?
"Right after I graduated from Advanced Infantry Training as a mortar man, I went to Airborne Training with the 182nd. Then

my name was called to go to Vietnam. I didn't want to go. I wasn't ready to die. Before you were deployed, you were allowed a 7-day leave. I actually overstayed my time and it forced them to come get me. The MPs showed up and took me back. Because of going AWOL, I missed the crucial jungle training that was needed for Vietnam. At this point, they shipped me to train in the Dominican Republic. When that was done, my two years were coming up—it was like only four months before the end so they kept me in the U.S. and I wound up missing the Vietnam conflict completely."

Sometimes the clouds part or you part the clouds and things work out.

"The only damage I got was partial loss of hearing from the many months doing mortar training. But, since I'm still alive and well, my experience in the War—basically not participating in hostile activity and getting shot at—was a major blessing. I returned back to Tallahassee and worked for a book packing company. I had gotten married before entering the Army. When I got home I soon became a father of two daughters and a son. I was thankful for having a good job, especially not having a college education."

You were raising a family, did that give you time to do physical training?

"I was an amateur bodybuilder, training for Mr. America, Mr. Florida, and Mr. Southeast United States. I had to be at my job at 4:35 a.m., and work until 3:00 p.m. The job was very taxing and extremely stressful. I developed my own little system. I'd go home to eat and spend time with my wife and kids. Then it was off to the gym to train for about two and a half hours. Then I'd go back home spend some more time with the family. My crew would work with me at the gym, and on Saturday mornings we'd go to the different competitions. I had everything down to a science."

At what point did you decide to officially become a bodybuilder?
"Actually that started in high school. In those days if you were bodybuilding, you were considered gay, a punk, or a sissy. I didn't care. I did it anyway. I was like a manchild. I was straight out muscular. When I got serious about it, I didn't get involved with girlfriends or any sexual behavior. I was just a pure athlete. I wanted to be the best at what I was doing. I knew that if I took care of myself and did weight training that everything was going to work out exactly to the vision in my head."

Were you doing amateur competitions in high school?
"Oh yeah, I was probably around 17. My first one was Mr. United States. I was competing in Alabama and in the heart of Georgia, in places where blacks did not want to be caught hanging around. There was always the possibility of something happening to me. But, I just kind of blocked it out of my mind. I loved the competitions, but I didn't win the overall. I would win all the best body portions, to the point where I would piss off a lot of the guys. It got to where the sponsors would ask me not to compete because a lot of the other guys wouldn't show up. Those competitions helped me develop my mindset about weight training and bodybuilding. Competing at such a young age is how I hold the record with 300 amateur competitions."

Have you been back to your high school in the past 20 years?
"They've asked me back for the past 20 years but I haven't gone. They erected a statue in tribute to me."

Clothed? I mention that because the statue they erected of an athlete out front of the Los Angeles Memorial Coliseum had required water polo athlete Terry Schroeder to model for the statue—nude.

"Yeah, the statue is clothed." (Laughs)

What did you do to get started in professional bodybuilding?

"I moved to Los Angeles."

Robby with some of the crew at Venice Beach:
Ed Corney and Arnold Schwarzenegger

How did that happen?

"I knew I was going to have to work harder and find a way to enjoy working harder. So I worked hard. I did well in my amateur competitions which resulted in a letter from Joe Weider [the leading business mind behind professional bodybuilding] asking me to come out to California. Some of my friends and family didn't think I should go. I think there is a lot of anger and bitterness in my culture. To me it's just a huge waste of time."

This was your chance so you had to take it.

"I just feel like if you find something in yourself to drive you to get you out of a situation or to keep you focused on what you love, then do it. Don't let the world come down on you, and go out there and do something. If you let the anger get at you then you just spend the rest of your life angry and alone and blaming everyone around you because you didn't do something for yourself. I feel like that is a waste of time. I heard people say to me, 'You're just lucky and you made it.' Well, I was lucky because I worked hard and because I was willing to take a chance. That is what I did. In 1975, I had that job at the local newspaper in Tallahassee that I could fall back on, and just a little bit of money saved away in case I failed."

Under a 1000 dollars?

"Way under that because I had a family at the time."

Where was your family when you went to California?

"They were in Tallahassee. At that point I had three kids and a wife in Tallahassee. But, because I wanted to achieve being a better person and doing something with myself, I took a chance. My wife didn't want to come along for it so we had to go our separate ways. First thing I did was give them most of my money and made sure all the bills were paid, and then I left for L.A. Everybody, even her friends were saying, 'He isn't gonna make it.' In my culture there is a lot of that kind of thing, that negative way of being. They would say a lot of things to make you feel bad, to make you not believe in yourself. But I just said to myself I'm going to come out here and give it my best shot and if I don't make it, I'm going to keep trying. I wasn't going to go back to Tallahassee and give them the opportunity to say, 'Hey, I told you.'"

That would have made a great video clip—you packing your stuff and talking about your departure with some clips of the naysayers warning you.

"Yeah. When I got to Venice Beach, I trained hard. But in 1975, there was no way for me to make a living at it in that area—California. People like Arnold had cornered the market. I had to go to Europe to earn money. I lived most of the year in Holland—in Haarlem and in Amsterdam. I was able make a living doing seminars and coaching. I ended up buying a home in Amsterdam, which I still have. I would come home to compete, do magazine covers, photo shoots, articles, and then return to Europe."

You were welcomed over in Europe?

"I don't know why, but they just love me in Europe. I think bodybuilding is considered an art there. Europeans are very interested in shape and form. I was able to find a niche and get consistent work there. I was the first black from America to create a line of promoters and sponsors. I became the big guy, which allowed me to really make a living."

Do you recall when you started finding out who you really were as a person?

"I think it hit me in about 2005 when I won my first Master's in Mr. Olympian."

(I laughed) Are you serious? You were 53 when you found yourself?

(Laughs) "I learned that I wanted to get out of bodybuilding. I needed something else to feel whole. To fill that void, I had been writing, reading, keeping notes, and watching National Geographic specials. I started funneling that energy into creating a master class to teach people around the world the art of bodybuilding and health and nutrition. I also explain herbs and how to use them to increase vitamin and protein levels. The master classes have been very successful. I'm now booked from January to December."

That's good news. It would also be interesting to hear about the tough times, the hard days. Did you ever come across people who wanted a piece of you?

"In the early days, a lot of guys who lost their trophies to me had it out for me. It was, 'Don't you let the sun catch you down here, boy, or we're gonna kill you.'"

Sounds pretty bad?

"It was. Who would want to hear, 'Get out of town before sundown'? I found it was best not to say anything at all. It's just the ignorant bigot talking. Mouthing off at them makes it worse. I was always very calm in control. Anger does nothing for you; it's a waste of energy. Calmness is a source of energy and empowerment. It always wins out."

In terms of wellness, how fit were the people you were competing against, and how well are the ones who are still alive today?

"I think a majority of them are not in a good place. Many of them were overdoing their steroids, etc., and not taking care of themselves. You can't mix those substances with junk food and other things like drugs and alcohol or partying. My good health has a lot to do with better eating and healthier habits. Back in the day you found very few accidents or injuries in physical training, though. There are many more today and I'd say more so now because of overdoing the steroids. The way some of the guys are using steroids, they are liable to have kidney failure and heart problems. The smart ones of us—a group around Weider, Arnold, and the core group—we mostly only used steroids eight weeks before a competition. We all went to the same doctor who was the doctor [Joe] Weider recommended."

What is the difference between your look and Arnold at his best?
"When I came in in 1975, Arnold was getting ready to retire. We trained alongside each other for the 1975 Mr. Olympia. I had more muscle in the abdomen, and smaller joints than Arnold. The time right before he began his Hollywood career was the best he ever looked, because he was training balls to the wall."

What about when he came back in 1980, after "Conan, the Barbarian"? The word is the competition judges gave him the Olympia title instead of Mike Mentzer and others who deserved it more.
"No disrespect, I like Arnold, but I think he should have just stayed retired. After Hollywood, it set a bad blip for him to come back to bodybuilding. He didn't deserve to win that one."

I've been studying the workouts that go for shorter training time and less frequent training intervals. The muscle overload program like Super Slo and the rest. Have you done something similar, like the Mike Mentzer workout? Would that type of workout be a good compromise for busy people who are trying to get fit?
"I'm a big fan of Mike. I appreciated his attitude. He knew what he wanted to achieve and he did his best to put his system out there. I definitely use a lot of his teachings. But I believe you've got to have

more variety. Do it slow and intense like he did, and then more reps and longer workouts with more sets to balance it out. I would say the first few sets go for speed, not weight, to get the blood pumping for that muscle. Then go to the slow set with a little heavier weight. Speed plays a role in muscle tissue size, and, above all, muscle fullness. The muscle needs variety. It is just like eating. The more you become in tune with yourself, the better things become."

Are there some key things you'd like to share about diet?
"People don't drink enough water. If you're going to eat turkey, eat dark meat. A 16-ounce steak is enough for a full week. Break everything down to ounces; 2 ounces of broccoli, 4 ounces of beef, 4 ounces of turkey meat, 2 jars of split pea soup. That is how I break things down so my body will look like a piece of art."

Did you have a coach?
"I never had a coach. I've always thought you have to learn from yourself. I'm a big reader—I love to read. I read everything. And I write poetry. In fact I used to go to a bar and recite poetry. People would cheer me on. I am always trying to reinvent myself. I have a journal, a diary about my life from when I was a little boy in Tallahassee until now. It's 40 books of that writing and some poetry. It contains my thoughts and sayings about growing up."

Did you pick up Jack LaLanne's books or Arnold's books?
"I definitely read Jack's books. I always thought he was just such a great motivator. I didn't read any of Arnold's books because I pretty much knew all of the stories (Laughs). We grew up together back in that Golden Era of bodybuilding. Jack LaLanne was more of a father figure for me. He was more of somebody you wanted to be like."

How good a singer are you at karaoke?

(Laughs) "I used to occasionally go in, alone with my sunglasses and my hat on. It has been a long while. I used to love to sing though. I grew up with my father and mother running this juke joint and my brothers and sisters were like the Martha and the Vandellas of our time. We sang for people and we got paid enough money to go to our school and have school lunches. I love music. I love to sing and I still do it when I'm alone and clean my house."

I loved 1970's music.

"I like that too. I also like Rick James, Tina Maria, Isaac Hayes, Barry White, George Michael, and these days Justin Timberlake, all of the musicians really. Another one is Janet Jackson. I basically have a long play list of stuff I listen to a lot of the time when I'm at the gym. I'll be playing music and singing to myself."

Robby in his 60s, looking ready to sing for "Soul Train"

Have you met any of these singers?

"Isaac Hayes and Barry White, and I had a chance to see Tina Maria and Rick James."

Did they ever get you to sing with them?

"No, if I sing I use it to serenade the woman I'm with. That's about it."

What are the steps and time commitments for self-mastery?

"Find something in yourself to drive you. Always try to find something to learn that empowers. I was baptized very young and grew up in the church. Definitely meditation and prayer, but mainly just have a belief. I was angry when I was younger, especially with the identification of the racism. I knew I was going to have to work harder. The anger and bitterness of my culture is a huge waste of time. If you let anger get to you, you'll spend the rest of your life angry, alone, and blaming everyone around you. A lot of the other kids, my siblings, did that."

A bodybuilder once told me it takes six months to get big and six years to learn how to get big. Is that true?

"Some of them never learn. It starts with building a foundation. Some of these guys are inflating it with four to six thousand calories a day. That is a lot of calories. You have to store a certain amount. I eat about 2,900 per day. You have to hydrate a certain amount. A lot of the high calorie people are mostly putting on body fat. The body cannot be forced to grow. It takes time."

How do you think the mindset and challenges of Robby Robinson can help the everyday guy?

"The only thing I can think of is that I'm just driven by life, by what I grew up with. I watched my mom building a Buddhist garden. She worked in that garden day in and day out to bring people from all cultures, black and white, together under one roof."

What would you rank yourself on things like focus, kindness, happiness, things such as that?

"I'm not perfect, but always try to learn from mistakes. Being nice to people should bring a smile to your face and it slows down the aging process. It's important to be nice and kind to yourself, but definitely confront yourself. Confrontation with yourself is empowering. It is very important to look another human in the eye and apologize. I'm a very happy person."

How do you compare sex and sleep, at 25 and today at 67?

"I'm a big believer in sleep. If you don't rest the body, it can't recover. Your immune system will not be healthy. You're not going to have the energy you need to thrive. Letting a woman know that she is appreciated is great. Sex is one of the most powerful feelings. It takes you to completely another world and it's drug free. It is one of the most amazing moments you can have, especially if you love that woman. It is a drug in itself. You don't need marijuana."

What is the secret to raising kids?

"Giving them a sense of right and wrong, being honest with them and letting them know the importance of truth. Teach them responsibility."

Are any of your kids into fitness, and do they call you on occasion?

"We talk about two or three times a week on the phone. We have gotten closer over the years. My children are all muscular. My son, who is about my same height as me, and one of my daughters, are into fitness. I really do think it's just a genetic thing. I now have 10 grandchildren, six great grandchildren, and a few great-great grandchildren. So I'm a great-great grandfather now. It is interesting to be living and be a great-great grandfather. To myself I'm thinking, I'm too young for that."

Are you a loner who trusts his own intuition?

"Oh yeah, strong intuition. I always believed that the mind gives a clear vision. If you listen to yourself the guidance is almost infinite. When I didn't listen to my intuition, problems arose. When I didn't listen it was like going against a godlike spiritual essence. When I listened it was empowering and synchronistic. Everything worked out."

You mentioned your unwillingness to verbalize for decades. Am I hitting you for your story at the best point in your life to share it?

"That's true. Earlier, I would have said I wasn't interested. When I was in Haarlem, in Holland, I got a chance to visit a museum and saw paintings and works of art by Michelangelo and Vincent Van Gogh. I thought, damn they put a lot of work into that. It made me think my body was a canvas and dumbbells were my brushes. I wanted to create an incredible piece of art with my physique."

A detailed story of Robby's life is featured in his book

Can you describe your feelings as you are aging?

"I feel vibrant. I feel vibrant and alive. I can't wait for the day to come. I want to put my work out there and inspire people from England to Afghanistan. I have high expectations of myself. I'm starting to pretty much put things together getting more organized so that people can have a better understanding of me and my belief system."

What would you like your epitaph to read?

"Robby is cool."

§ § §

Robby is more than cool. Despite growing up in the Deep South, where racial discrimination was rampant, vitriolic, and hateful, he wished his oppressors well. When bodybuilding was considered gay and sissy, he paid little heed. When other teenagers were chasing girls and having fun, Robby formed a vision to carve a masterpiece from his body. Robby was called upon by Joe Weider, a powerful figure behind the money in professional bodybuilding and supplementation. When Robby needed a job in his early days in California, he was rarely called upon to be a spokesperson for professional bodybuilding as was Arnold.

Instead, he could be found in the Weider warehouse in Santa Monica, doing a job similar to what he was doing in Tallahassee, boxing up supplements to be shipped out to stores and customers. Robby, the black champion, was doing menial labor to survive.

When America would not have him, perhaps because of his color and his partial speech impediment, he went to Europe and became beloved. By the power of his will, this gentle giant of a man became "The Back Prince." Robby is a prince of a man and it's an honor to include part of his story in this book. Sharing three long conversations with him was very therapeutic and it enhanced the way I think about a number of things—especially fitness training and perseverance. We should all remember to recite a verse or two to the troubled members of our friends and family. We can do it in our heads if they're not paying any heed. "We are the masters of our fate, we are the captains of our soul."

If we do that repeatedly, we may grow to realize we are the invictus, the unconquered.

Chapter 3

The "Blue-Eyed Soul Brother"... Who Broke the Color Barrier in Reverse

"We were part of something that America needed at one time, America needed Joe Louis. America needed Arnold Palmer. America needed Sammy Davis Jr. and Louis Armstrong."

—Meadowlark Lemon, the Clown Prince of Basketball, 2003 inductee into the Naismith Basketball Hall of Fame, and famed showman for the Harlem Globetrotters

Some will have it that the first basketball game ever played was inspired by Jaguar-Man, the chief god of the Olmecs, an ancient Mexican people who may have played the first game in 1513. Basketball has come a long way since. At least now it's played with a ball made of rubber composites. The Olmecs were more cerebral. They used the decapitated skulls of their enemies.

In 1892, the Canadian doctor James Naismith civilized the game using a leather ball and two peach baskets. The game is the ballet of sports and is played everywhere in the world; perhaps more seriously but never more entertainingly than when orchestrated by Meadowlark Lemon of the Harlem Globetrotters. This determined kid from the poor streets of the Deep South learned to play with a cut onion sack tied to a hoop-shaped coat hanger nailed to a tree—and a carnation milk tin can, his first basketball.

Talk about ageless athletes, Meadowlark has claimed his age is between 50 and 150. That certainly never diminished his cognitive capacity—or his schedule. He is and has always been committed to excellence and to those in need of a laugh or some fundraising. Along the way, Meadow (his real name, as his dad's before him) caught news and saw the high-flying flair of Allen Winder, the "Blue-Eyed Soul Brother," a nickname given to him by Bruce Jenner on an NBC Sports World Special. Meadowlark, the "Clown Prince of Basketball," holds the record in foresight by recruiting Allen as the first white dude to play for the Bucketeers, an all-black comedy b-ball team which formed in 1979.

At the time, Allen was a college student-athlete who was open to a change in scenery and a different way of entertaining the crowds. For this hyper-programmed junior in college, it was time to take things more lightheartedly and see a bit of the world on the Bucketeers travelling team's lemon-yellow soul bus followed close behind by the California Coasters' bus—the team that served as their opponents most shows. Allen—in a way not foreign to dedicated athletic philosophers like baseball icon and Normandy Landing veteran Yogi Berra or UCLA legendary coach and mentor John Wooden—has his own long list of sayings. Two of his favorite "Winderisms," as he calls them go, "Speak to that which is not as though it were, and it will be," and "Happy cows give better milk."

I was delighted to chew the cud with a guy whom I wouldn't dare foul on a basketball court or, he warns, "Go head-to-head in a game of Trivial Pursuit!" I launch back that in 1980 he would have dominated me along the low post of Trivial Pursuit. But today I say to the big windman, "Bring it on."

For this, the longest of the interviews thus far completed, it was no piece of angel food cake to enlist Meadowlark's first Caucasoid into the life-story sharing process. For one thing: Who the heck am I? I'm just some guy calling Blue Eyes out of the blue. After a plethora of interesting emails and some relationship-building phone calls, he began to warm to the process. Now, which has amazed me, he even wants to hang out—virtually, for now. I only wish we were trustafarians (trust fund recipients) or olden days investors in Google so we could spend our time fishing, talking just to fill dead air space, helping non-profits, and doing what we both excel at, mentoring kids.

The big question is what happens when we finally meet person to person, how are we going to handle the pecking order? I've never had a buddy who is 6'9". And this one has an elevator that goes all the way to the top—the mental penthouse suite. So here's what I have put together in my mind on how to handle such a colossus of wit and vertebrae. He's big, I'm a bit younger. He's a bigger target, I'm somewhat fragile. He's so competent—perhaps overly qualified for most jobs; I'm a guy who doesn't hanker to working 9 to 5 (which has become 7 to 9 in so many corporate settings) in the same space every day. I have no skills in basketball; he has very little background in martial arts. If he'll keep laughing at my haughty repartee, we'll see how that plays out. We'll be sure to film it so you can access and assess our reality show.

The one and only Blue-Eyed Soul Brother

Tale of The Tape
Allen Winder

*Basketball player, former corporate executive,
and current Director of Operations for
Meadowlark Lemon Ministries.*

Born January 26, 1957, Texas City, Texas.

Father: Aaron Riley Winder, went by A.R., b. August 21, 1923 in Shawnee, Oklahoma.

Mother: Dorothy Lea McKay, born October 7, 1924. Grew up on a farm in Arp, Texas, with nine siblings. Both parents were educators with masters degrees.

Sisters: Sue, eight years older, has an M.A. in Education. Nancy is two years older and has an M.A. in Education as well.

Age 18: 6'9", 230 lbs

Age 56: 6'9", was 250 lbs, lost 25 pounds during the time we worked on his chapter. This was the first aging athlete whose fitness transformed during the writing of their chapter story. Allen shared,

"This process with you, Sifu, put the focus on my health and fitness. That was important and I thank you for it."

A man of many talents: music, video, communication and analytical skills, many sports. Ranks high in the art of reason and the ethic of pushing himself.

Famous Incidents: In one game, he dunked a few times on a legend of the basketball world—Wilt Chamberlain. Later assisted in taking a billion-dollar software company public. Rang the bell to open the NASDAQ in 2003.

Two more quotes (aka Winderisms): "Plan your work and work your plan" and, "Do the right job right the first time."

Health Setback: Allen says: "I maintained a very rigorous and disciplined exercise schedule up until I was 46, then I experienced 'The Perfect Storm' of multiple diagnoses, physical and mental. First I was hit with Freiberg's Disease and nerve damage in my feet. It really put a damper on that aspect of my very active life.

"I am a very positive guy by nature, but it still bums me out that I can't run, cut, or play a real game of hoops with my youngest son Christian who lives for basketball. My two eldest kids—Garrett and Elissa—knew me to be very active, playing hoops, hiking, water and snow skiing ... We had my son Christian and my daughter Zoe in my forties and I was always highly motivated by thinking about one-on-one matches with them up into my eighties. Then I was diagnosed with bipolar disorder. This is a much over-diagnosed disease, but not in my case—it was textbook. Chronic short term memory loss was also diagnosed."

Websites: AdubStudios.net and MeadowlarkLemon.org

———

Here's our first email exchange.

Me to Allen:

I'd like to discuss interviewing you for The Aging Athlete Project: The aging athletes—aged 45 to 100—for the book are folks who are likeable, interesting, still fit, and available for a brief Skype or in-person interview. Sifu

Allen's response:

Intrigued. Bullet out a few things for me:

Where did you get my name?

What is the vision/intention of the book?

My response:

Allen ... As you requested, responses to your bullets.

Where did you get my name?

From reading about you on the web. Started with Meadowlark's website and spent a few hours on you and a few former Harlem Globetrotters. You're the only one I've contacted.

What is the vision/intention of the book?

To help aging athletes and regular folks understand the mindset it takes to pursue lifelong fitness/wellness/physical activity. Fitness = Health. Euphoria comes from the Greek word euphoros, to be well. That's the way to go through life, high on wellness. Exhilarated through endorphins, etc., not popping pills unnecessarily.

Allen recalled in a previous conversation that I said our interview would have the vibe of two kids hanging out in their tree house like the little dudes in the film "Stand By Me."

"That was a pivotal moment, Sifu, because in my mind, that was the moment I agreed to do this ..."

Here are some of the key exchanges of our interview.

Before we get started on your personal life experience—including your athletic career of course—it might be nice to begin with a little bit about your family's heritage and any wisdom that may have been passed down because this interview is based on mindset. We're trying to figure out how you developed your mindset.

"Sure, my dad's dad was born in 1891 in Bowie, Texas, and my dad's mom's side came over from Romania, and then traveled down to Texas from Canada by wagon. I'm sixth generation Texan on my mom's side, predating Texas becoming a state. My third great grandfather moved there right after the battle of the Alamo and Texas' Independence from Mexico. My mom's family history in America goes back to the 1700s. My fifth great grandfather, Ezra Alexander, actually signed the North Carolina Mecklenburg Declaration of Independence in 1775 that preceded the 1776 Declaration of Independence."

Besides the airport, I haven't set foot in Texas. I somehow consider that almost un-American.

"I'd be the right person to give you a tour. I was born in Texas City, Texas. It just doesn't get more Texan than that. (We both laughed)

It sounds like you have a long family history of folks who were doing progressive things?

"My dad had a framed quote on his office wall, wherever we moved it was always there. It was the title of a Norman Vincent Peale book, it simply said, 'The Power of Positive Thinking.' That's the way I was raised, and I'm sure that is what influenced many of my quotes, my Winderisms, which I pass down to my four beautiful kids. Their names are Elissa, Garrett, Christian, and Zoe. I could talk hours about each one of them. They ground me and humble me at the same time. They are all very special and very talented in their own, very individual way. I love them all dearly."

Can you remember anything that was a big challenge your father had to deal with in his life?

"Well, the Depression and World War II, of course. He enlisted in the army when he was 19, on December 7th, 1942, one year to the day after the bombing of Pearl Harbor. He was a master sergeant airplane mechanic with the 82nd Airborne, the Screaming Eagles, assigned to the gliders that landed at Normandy ahead of the coastal assault. Early on, he would never talk about the war. We did learn he had spinal meningitis in France and spent a few weeks in a recovery hospital. During that time, the soldier in the bed beside him listened to the song 'Mairzy doats and dozy doats and liddle lamzy divey,' over and over again. After that, he was never again able to listen to that song."

Was he a solidly built guy? And how tall was he?

"He wasn't light, he was six foot. He played basketball and tennis, and he rode a bike up until he was 82. He passed at 86."

Sounds like an active chap.

"He walked every day and played golf often. He and I played golf almost every day when I took some time off and stayed with him at his home in Houston for six weeks in 2004. What an incredible experience in many ways. Not often does a son have the honor of spending 24/7 with his dad, for six weeks later in life. We took care of each other during that time in some ways. I was very fortunate. He was never sick and never in the hospital after the war up until six weeks before he died."

Where did you get your size?

"That's always been an unanswered question. As you know, I picked up genealogy as a hobby from my mom. I don't have actual heights and weights, but I do have pictures from four generations back and no one was excessively taller than others."

Is there anything you can share about your grandparents?

"On my mom's side it was 'Granddad' and my dad's dad was 'Grandpa.' Unfortunately I never knew my grandmother on my mom's side. She died when my mom was 18. I remember going into the watermelon fields with my granddad on an old dilapidated wagon pulled by his two mules. I can hear him ... 'Heeya, Betty, 'Heeya, Sue,' then a *Click, click* out of the right side of his mouth avoiding spitting out his Luden's Cough Drop. He always carried them with him and it was another treat for me when he would hand me one when I'd fetch a bucket of water from his well. He never had running water in the house. Finding a yellow-meated watermelon, instead of red, was always a treasure. He was a very quiet man. He lived to be 90. He died when I was a freshman at the University of Houston."

People today don't realize how recent was the absence of running water in lots of rural America. And, it made it interesting in winter just to get water.

"Sure did. On the other side, Grandpa died when I was in the first grade. That was the first time I saw my dad cry. The second was the day I left for college. Grandpa taught me how to milk a cow. After my grandpa's death, my grandma, 'Granny,' moved into town. My dad inherited the old home place that he came home to after the war, and he ran cattle there for years. I spent most of my Saturdays working on the farm, plowing and planting coastal Bermuda grazing grass, building and repairing acres of barbed wire fence, and tending to the livestock. Pulling calves, bottle feeding calves at the crack of dawn, giving shots to cure the scours. We ate lunch with my granny every Saturday. She and I were very close. She died when I was in eighth grade. I remember my grandpa as a kind man. He rolled his own cigarettes. Kind of a strange memory, but that was how people rolled back in the day—so to speak. What I saw and learned from my grandpa, granddad, my mom and dad, and my sisters were kindness, family values, and a strong work ethic."

Did you get into basketball at a young age?

"The earliest times I remember was when I was about ten. My dad put up a hoop on our slanted driveway in Texas City. I remember it was pretty challenging to shoot. Things were on an angle and you had to be very precise with every shot. I really started playing basketball more seriously in sixth grade."

What prompted that?

"That's when we moved to Arlington, Texas. We had a back-entrance garage, so you'd drive down the driveway, then encounter a huge open space—all cement—where you'd turn around to go into the garage. So that was my court, it was perfect. Everybody would come over, and my dad actually handmade the first backboard there out of plywood. Again, one had to be very precise avoiding the eves that held our Christmas lights that lit up the court beginning the day after Thanksgiving. At first I was worried about the ball hitting the eves, then, as years went by, I had to worry about my head hitting the eves!"

I've never had that problem. Touching the rim is something I'm planning for a future life.

"Who knows, you may come back as me ... We later replaced it with a store-bought backboard. Dad bought me some spotlights, you know, those clamp lights. I'd put them up on the fence and we'd play all day and all night into the morning. We'd play in the winter as well. Heck, we'd play anytime."

Who were some of the people who influenced your early athletic development?

"My dad, of course, then coaches. Dad never put pressure on me to practice or play basketball, but if I ever asked him to play, he never said no. I guess another of my biggest influences was a guy named Jim Prichard, who was the assistant coach at Arlington High School. In eighth and ninth grade he picked me up at the bell to go play basketball at the high school gym with the big boys. He'd talk to me about life and who I would be when I wore the green and white. As far as work ethic goes, as far as what drove me, some of it could be my bipolar condition. I was achieving at a high level in schoolwork and in athletics. I didn't know I was bipolar until much later in life—in my mid-forties. It was actually another of many epiphanies for me explaining life as I knew it. I then realized what kept me up, alert, and a bit manic as that term was explained to me."

What a life-changing discovery.

"That is a very misunderstood mental disorder, and it's frequently over-diagnosed—but not in my case."

Allen Winder (afro! with ball), skies over Bill Cartwright #24 (NBA 1979-1995) in the"Finals" game at the Bluebonnet Classic Finals in 1976. UH beat USF in this game 84-63.

What did you think you had before you were diagnosed? I mean did you have a hard time living with yourself?

"Well, I guess I have been bipolar all my life—so it was just 'me.' I knew no other way. I realized I had some issues at times, but I mostly reaped the benefits of the disease for years and lived more on the north side of the bipolar line. I believe a great deal of my success in basketball and later in business is attributable to me just having more stamina and thinking faster. My mind did race at times."

It helps to have a speedy mind. People in business sometimes don't have confidence if you don't have a quick reply.

"Sounds accurate. As far as did I have a hard time living with myself, let me set this up a little with some history of my crash, what I refer to as my 'dark times.' Dark as in being confused, and more disheartening, dark as in my behavior. During the '90s things were incredible. I built a software company that partnered with a billion dollar privately owned software company, which eventually hired me to run a marketing sector worldwide. I was fortunate at that time to be given a large number of stock options. We went public in the late '90s. My stock went through the roof. Built my dream house, married, and added two more loves to my life. We were a very legitimate software company providing software to half of the Fortune 500.

"Then the dot-com crash hit and it was death by association. I took a year off, then was brought on as the COO of a dot-com in Las Vegas that actually had a great business model. Steve Winn, a governor, and one of the top executives at Dell were on the board. The CEO was the former CFO of Texas Instruments. How could I turn down an offer to have the opportunity to be a turnaround artist with that crew?"

That kind of offer doesn't come around every day.

"This was when I was in my mid-40s. Some kind of switch was thrown. We had moved to San Jose and I was running around the world and going coast to coast rebuilding and reorganizing after a merger of two large entities. At that time I was the VP of the Americas and had direct line responsibility of a $300 million dollar P&L, a 700-employee organization within a very large corporation. My scope of geography and responsibility stretched from the Arctic Ocean to Argentina. I was basically hired into a shell, trying to put together a competent executive and management team while holding my fingers and toes in the leaking dike dealt to me at the same time. It was simply too much with the limited resources and lack of leadership I found when I hit the ground there."

Business and jobs in general can pull you in and never let go of your time and attention. Can't be the best things for our health and family time.

"No doubt about it. I guess that's when the illnesses' symptoms began to show. My infant daughter was in and out of the hospital and I was never there. I left the company for personal reasons. This was somewhat the beginning of my dark times. After I crashed, I remember wondering, 'How could this be happening to me?' Also, you don't realize exactly what you're doing while in a depressed or manic state. It was like I was on the outside looking into my life and not being able to control some of the things I was doing and exhibiting behavioral traits that were contrary to my personality and polar opposites of who I knew I was."

Uncontrollable behavior, we all get to experience that. But, the bipolar switch is definitely something altogether different.

"This was off the charts for me. I acted in a way that hurt several that I loved the most. The shame and guilt of the path of destruction overwhelmed me. Did 'I' do these things? Or did the disease kidnap me and place me in a state of mind that fostered these actions. I felt like I had no say, no choice. It felt as though choice was taken away from me. When I came out of the fog and was thinking straight, I remember being aware of the thought that the real me would never have done those things. I would never even think of those things nor think I even had the ability to do those things ... but I now must live with, and attempt to mend, the consequences of my actions during that time."

Allen, it's really helpful to me and will undoubtedly be of value to the readers to hear this. When we are honest about life, it's cleansing. Dirt can be cleansing.

"That's a good one, Sifu. I later realized that I couldn't place my shame, or forgiveness, on others. I was responsible for my actions during the manic or depressed times because it was my physical being that was doing those things. Then I asked myself the inevitable question, 'Am I responsible for the behaviors if I'm not responsible for having the illness that drove those behaviors?'"

We can all relate to losing our grip on our own behavior. You were in a situation beyond your control.

"I had to educate myself on the facts of the disease and begin the inward healing and forgiveness process. I encountered those who were untrained in the condition or refused to understand or accept it. I still do to this day. I had to grasp this concept before I could heal. I had to learn to forgive myself even if those closest to me refused to. Some still refuse to and that hurts me more than you will ever know. I had to really learn to love myself again. One must love oneself to be loved. How could anyone love you if you don't love yourself?"

Maybe if you make sacrifices and people see an expression of your heart, they will love you no matter how you love yourself.

"That's a good point. I still have so many regrets, Sifu, for some of the things that went down personally that were the symptoms of bipolar. As I said, I do take full responsibility for those, though. I have to. And you have to forgive those who don't or are too busy to understand. I hope that you, and all who read this chapter understand there is a difference between physical and mental wellness and awareness."

I'm considering your work and family life. What you are suggesting is that life was a bear. Anything done in excess always catches up with us. Life is best lived with a balanced approach. It's not always easy, but that is the goal.

"That all makes sense, but sometimes things keep piling on and eventually consume you."

Did the bipolar condition increase in intensity over time?

"I never realized it was a problem until put into a situation where I had to over-think my own capacity. So I was over-thinking a bunch of concepts, sales, marketing, software development ... The doctor who diagnosed me said, 'We usually find this earlier, or younger than you because a person runs out of money.' Since money wasn't an issue at the time, my condition continued to spiral. I guess if I had gotten into financial trouble earlier things would have been much different, right?"

It was probably overwhelming your system. But your manic side just kept on doing.

"Sounds correct."

So, let's go back to how your brain cells were firing and retaining things. When was the first time you took an academic test where you knew you were testing high?

"My mom made me take all kinds of achievement tests. I think it started in junior high. I always scored high. School was not that easy to sit through. Sometimes it was just boring. I didn't have to study that hard. I could just read something and retain it. For all kinds of reasons that gift has somewhat subsided."

Allen with his son, Christian.
"I was hitting the weight room every day at the time
of this photo. I was stronger in my 40s than
I was as a college or pro athlete."

How old were you when you realized what mastering something was all about?

"I don't even think I thought about it in those terms. I always did set goals. Long and short term. I had learned over time that if I did my best, if I worked hard, if I worked smart, everything else would fall into place. It wasn't like I was focused on mastering something or the art of mastery. With basketball, I'd see a move or think one up. Then I said, okay, I'm going to do that. Then I'd go into the backyard and practice it all day and all night sometimes, until I got it."

Sounds like mastering parts of the game?

"You can master, or at least get down the road on mastering anything you put your mind on as long as you have the desire and drive. Same with my business career. I always knew I needed patience as well but that didn't come naturally ... Still doesn't."

How about physicality and physical training in your youth? Besides games and playing, did you put up a chin-up bar or a mini tramp or anything to work on specific skills or fitness skills that you thought would develop you as an athlete?

"OK, here's how the 'physicality,' as you called it, turned into a mindset of maturing my body physically—some by chance, some by gifts given to me, and some by hard-targeted work. I remember one day when I was in eighth grade, out of the blue my dad put me in the car and said we were going to go buy a 10-speed bicycle for me."

That was a big day in my life, but in my case I basically did it with a type of vision board—I had magazine cutouts on my wall. I worked hard with my dad on the farm and, finally, we drove to the bike shop and picked it out. That bike is still around, rusting on the East Coast.

"In my case, it wasn't Christmas or my birthday—just a regular day. That had never happened before. He must have been insightful because I rode the tires off that thing. I believe I owe a lot of my leg strength, jumping abilities, and my eventual success on the court to my dad's surprise bicycle."

Maybe your dad had a secret vision board and he knew you should be a jumping master.

(Laughs) "In junior high and high school, playing sports, football, basketball, and doing track, but mostly playing hoops all the time, gave me stamina."

It's not easy for someone your size to run and do drills for hours.

"I luckily found that by doing it every day, I was able to keep the stamina from my youth. So stamina was never as big an issue as it frequently is for someone my size."

Was the growth spurt hard on you?

"As far as height, weight, strength, and body mass, it was a roller coaster ride. I was always a head taller than anyone in my class throughout K-12. I had mono when I was 11 and had to stay home for an extended period of time. I gained a lot of weight and carried that through my sixth grade year."

Now I know I should have been doing more kissing. I could have used the weight in junior high.

(Laughs from both sides)

"My metabolism changed in seventh grade and I became increasingly skinny and awkward, almost like I couldn't walk and chew gum at the same time. It was pretty embarrassing being the big guy and not being able to live up to others' expectations. Although that pressure could have been from within. That continued until the summer between my eighth and ninth grade when something just happened. You see now why I treasure my magic first 10 speed."

I get it. Magical mastery with a vision. What happened then?

"From that crazy summer and on for several years I was doing things on and off the court that started getting some attention around the neighborhood, school, city, state, and, eventually, nationwide. I started jumping higher, running faster, making quicker moves with more ease than those around me. Stuff a guy who would eventually become 6'9" dude usually can't do. Coordination just hit me along with a few more athletic attributes. I think that was the first time I got a taste of crowd approval and appreciation."

Athletes talk about the accolades and how that drives them to new heights.

"It was like a drug I guess—very motivating. It wasn't like a Clark-Kent-discovering-Superman-powers epiphany, but close. It was a conscious self-awareness that took place. The skinny, smart nerd who played sports because he was taller than everyone else turned into a guy who started appreciating his new gifts. I guess the status and attention just came with it, which I can't say I minded. Can I put it that way? I'm sounding a bit 'I'm all that,' but I want you to know that I was consciously humbled by the whole ordeal."

Ah-men to that. Happens to me every time I start flexing in the mirror next to my 1975 Arnold poster ... Very humbling.

"Sifu ... (Laughs) I did begin at that point to do 'quickness drills for quick muscle fibers,' as it was explained to me, like jumping rope and doing deep dips before jumping on the bench-press benches, back and forth very quickly. Back-forth-back-forth, hundreds of them. Out of the blue came satisfaction and reinforcement of my work ethic. My mom would bring in the morning paper when she woke me up for school and there I was, front page. And all the benefits, like eating free at the local BK and Taco Bell, and praise that came with it. It didn't get to my head because I was still questioning and pinching myself of this new reality I was in—sometimes thrown in, sometimes simply perceived in because everyone was cheering for me and expected nothing less. Which drove me more, you know?"

You were 240 in college?

"Yeah. 6'9", 240. I'm at 250 now, but these days it's not all muscle. For me, and my growth, it just happened. You don't always think about it when you're growing up, you're just big and you can hold your own."

1977, Allen, baseline on left, no. 25 for the University of Houston at the Rainbow Classic in Hawaii (athlete's collection)

Did you have good jumping abilities when you were younger?

"Pretty good. In junior high, I ran the 440, the mile relay, and high jumped. A little under 6 foot was my best Fozberry flop. I was dunking in seventh or eighth grade, although awkwardly."

How did you increase your jumping skills?

"My 14-year-old son actually asked me that question this week. I told him it boils down to two words—discipline and dedication. I have been teaching him jumping drills and setting goals with him, he has them framed on his wall. As for me, besides riding the tires off my bike, I worked on it. I wore ankle weights everywhere back in the day. I mentioned the workouts jumping back and forth over benches, making a deep dip as I jumped. I also jumped rope a great deal and, of course, played lots of hoops. Jumping, I mean really jumping, is a state of mind. You have to believe and expect to jump. You have to visualize yourself jumping, dunking—heck, I visualized and dreamed all the time that I could fly. One has to channel one's energy to the lower extremities, then blast off! It's like when you mix baking soda with water, cork the bottle and shake it. The pent up energy lights the fuse and the cork soars."

David Mars, no. 5, Allen, to his left in a fro,
and their teammates in 1978. University of Houston won
this post-NIT-tournament championship. (athlete's collection)

This should be in the handbook of jumping.

"All of the good jumpers, I imagine, go through the same thing. It's not just a physical, athletic move. I remember when I first understood the concept of hang time and the first time I experienced it. Meaning I could jump high enough where I could look down, see my feet and the cement below them. It felt like time stopped for a couple of counts, and that I stopped in the air like a cartoon."

Flying, catching big air. If humans could only fly.

"I used to try to jump over the hood of my car in the backyard. At first, I'd jump as far as I could across, then slide the rest. I ate it a couple of times catching a foot. I remember the first time I cleared it except for a butt bump on the other side. Fun memory. With my friends, this hood jumping became a standard on Friday nights in a parking lot on the drag."

Gives new meaning to the amusement of bumper cars. Could you summarize your hoop career?

"Sure. It went by pretty fast. It was in most respects the time of my life. I played for the University of Houston for three years and left during my junior year, because I was just flat out tired of playing basketball and wanted to pursue life outside of hoops. It shocked more than a few, but I had played about every day since I was a kid and was burned out."

A sports psychologist told me about a limitation athletes have. Some people in this field talk about total minutes one has to perform at a high level. They speak of emotional and physical minutes. My guess is many pro athletes, especially the older ones, just seem to possess an abundance of those minutes.

"That makes sense. People like Wilt Chamberlain and Meadowlark seem to fit that model."

The top player on my school's college team my freshman year wound up getting benched by the coach and missed several weeks. Some of these situations may be simply an example of subconsciously or consciously creating a behavior which gets you benched so you can find some recovery time. What do you think of that?

"In my case, my personality may have become less of my normal, fun self. The culture in college was quite different. It just wasn't fun to play anymore. I knew it was time to hang up the Chucks [Chuck Taylor's b-ball shoes], concentrate on life, and pursue a career in business. Interestingly, fate came knocking on my door. Almost immediately after I hung up the Chucks, I did a 180 back to hoops when I got 'the call.' I was in business school at the University of Texas at the time, where I eventually returned to finish up my degree."

I'm guessing this was the call that originated from someone who knew how to liven things up and put smiles on people's faces—including his teammates?

"That's exactly it. A guy who worked for Meadowlark Lemon called and told me quite candidly that Meadowlark wanted me to guard Wilt Chamberlain on an NBC Sports World Special. Wilt had recently retired from the Lakers. Meadow was launching a new all-black comedian basketball team like the Harlem Globetrotters. I was tired of playing hoops, but who can refuse an invitation from Meadowlark Lemon, the Clown Prince of Basketball."

Amazing. Business school sounds dull to many of us and not a super fun place to go after ending your time entertaining the crowds. But, now you're being offered a chance to yuck it up with some really fun folks.

"That rocked my world. And, can you imagine the chance to guard The Big Dipper? I mean, many basketball historians consider him the best player of all time."

I'm not a b-ball historian, but Wilt tops my list.

"Here's a little known fact. Wilt Chamberlain started his professional basketball career out of Kansas with the Globetrotters under Meadowlark. Meadowlark used to call him 'My big little brother.' I was to be on the 'opposing' team—which of course was all white, like the Washington Generals. I went to training camp and was in intense 8-hour sessions learning the tricks and the choreography of the show—and going one-on-one with one of my idols. At that point in my life I could put my elbows on the rim. I had fun with Wilt those few days. I was in awe—Wilt and Meadowlark had been on photos on my wall all my life and now I had the opportunity to post up Wilt! I got lucky a few times and out-quicked him and dunked on him. I think that's what got Meadowlark's attention."

As they would say in "In Living Color"—d-a-n-g!

"Meadowlark got this wild hair and called me into his office one day, 1600 Avenue of the Stars in Los Angeles, and asked me if I wanted to make sports history and become the first white player to play comedian basketball alongside him, Wilt Chamberlain, Marques Haynes, Jump'n Jackie Jackson, and others on the all-black team—Meadowlark Lemon's Bucketeers. 'Break the color barrier in reverse,' he said with his grin. I asked him if I had to wear those funky hats and uniforms. He replied, 'Yes, you do.' So ... I did."

How did Meadow know about you before? You were basically a young retiree.

"It had to be fate, karma, that kind of thing. There was some computer printout and verification from some that were close to both camps, mine and Meadow's from what I understand."

What do you mean? What printouts?

"Printout, like a scouting sheet of available persons to consider to guard Wilt on an NBC sports special. Anyhow, there I was, headed to tryout the training camp."

Allen being interviewed by Bruce Jenner, the 1976 Decathlon Olympic Champion and, more recently, the Star of E! reality series "Keeping Up with the Kardashians" (athlete's collection)

What an opportunity.

"It was almost too good to be true. I was in my early 20s and didn't really understand what 'breaking the color barrier in reverse' meant. But that's what we did. After breaking that barrier, there were several things to deal with on the team, in the media and at a few arenas. Some were just in fun, some were not. Nothing like Jesse Owens or Jackie Robinson, by any means, but it was uncomfortable now and then."

Could you share a memorable event from those times?

"Well, there was this one interview on Sports World in 1980. Bruce Jenner was working for the show and he pulled me aside for an interview. He wound up pinning me with the nickname 'The Blue-Eyed Soul Brother'—and it stuck. While I was playing for the Bucketeers, I became this odd-to-me phenomenon in basketball and some family entertainment circles for a couple of years. This had me appearing in talk shows and TV specials. Things like the "Tonight Show," Good Morning this and that, and a few other shows on NBC and HBO. It was a fun ride and I remember those years fondly."

Where's Waldo? Do I have to tell you? (athlete's collection)

Why do you think you were picked to be the first white Bucketeer?

"Sifu ... Really? You saw the HBO interview! [he said, chuck-ling]. Good looks, charm, Texas accent ... You know I'm kidd'n right? I don't know. Maybe a part of it was my personality, maybe because I was playing around all the time, you know, cutting up and having a good time. I always knew a bunch of stuff to do with the ball. I chattered and laughed a lot under pressure. I was always comfortable and relaxed on a basketball court. I guess Meadowlark saw that in me and liked it."

The following is what Allen Winder, at age 23, said back in 1980 on an HBO interview, after spending time on the road with the Bucketeers. The interview in its entirety is on YouTube.

"It's beautiful the way Meadowlark treats us all. He makes me feel right at home. I don't know, if I get an offer from the NBA—and there's been some talk of that—I believe I'd stay right here where I am. [It's about] the family that exists right here on this bus, in the gym, and in the locker room."

That is an interesting thing. You're being treated pretty well by the blacks who had been having a tough time in white America.

"Sure. It was a great learning experience for both sides of the racial coin. I had great friends and roommates on both buses."

Did they make you sit in the back?

(Laughing) "Nah, but there was some jealously and resentment at first. For every player who made the Bucketeers, there was a player who didn't, and they either ended up leaving or playing on our opposing team. So obviously everyone knew the player that would have made the Bucks if it wasn't for me. There were some ill feelings that were sometimes pretty intense. There were a few guys who just didn't really agree or want me to be on the team. At first the ones who opposed me being on the Bucketeers thought I was there for reasons other than my basketball skills. That didn't last long. I brought that to a head in a single afternoon pickup game with those guys. My play was able to take the air out of that argument pretty quick."

Actions tend to speak louder than words. You were the novelty. Tell me about the DubClub.

"That's my family. Zoe (Zobug) is my youngest. Now, she is unbelievable! Cute, funny, smart, fun … Zoe was a baby when her mother and I divorced and like her older brother, Garrett, she really didn't know any other way. Zoe and I have always said, 'Winder starts with a "W" (DubYa).' So we're affectionately known as the DubClub!"

"My son Christian, aka Cdub. He's a blessing
from above, even though he beats me in H-O-R-S-E!"

Who is your current best friend?

"Well, that's an easy one. My absolute best friend and love of my life is my wife, Kayla. She and I have been through so much together in the last eight years and neither can imagine life without the other. She's something else, Sifu. Get this, she got her BS in psychology and was a thesis away from her Masters in Clinical Psychology when she decided to pursue a career in nursing. She had been in health care for 15 years so I guess her real passion rose to the top of her list. With incredible resolve, she started working towards that new goal and graduated last May with highest honors which included two national honor societies while carrying a 4.0 most of her college career. She's now a really, really smart RN! (laughs) That just reinforced what I have known for a long time, even before she did, that she can accomplish anything that she puts her mind, heart, and soul into. I'm so proud of her. I've never had a friend like her. She, like our friendship, is certainly one of a kind."

The DubClub: Allen, Christian, Kayla, Zoe,
and "the girls"—Boots and Huggles

Could you share a bit about your life, given the difficulties you've had to deal with?

"Compared to my past, I now live a pretty simple life—but not simple as in undemanding, simple as in somewhat uncomplicated. I have stepped out of a world where you were measured by the size of your home and millions in the bank."

The material world and the notion of success, what a discussion that makes ...

"You bet. But, I have stepped out of most of that world and all of the pressures that come with chasing that status. Don't get me wrong, overachieving is still in my DNA, it's just channeled differently today. I'm still a very proud dude, but at this time in my life I am fulfilled in a much deeper, different way than in the past. I said earlier that when someone asked me who I am, I would respond with my accomplishments."

The business résumé approach—happens all the time.

"Today, it's different. I would respond with the essence of who I believe I am as defined by where and how I spend my time and energy."

To many, that would be what mastering life is all about.

"Sure. I try to take advantage of my experiences and knowledge from the past using my current cognitive abilities. I spend a great deal of thought and time on my family as well as overlooked sectors of our society that I quite frankly had overlooked previously in my life. I now take the time to teach and try to make a difference around me and make other lives a little better. Working with kids, the disabled, the elderly, and teens within our military families worldwide are where I concentrate much of my energy and talents. This is where a big part of my heart is. I believe that my current behavioral and personality traits, the essence of who I am, this all originates and is fostered by my time together with anyone associated with these groups. Now this is what I'm currently all about."

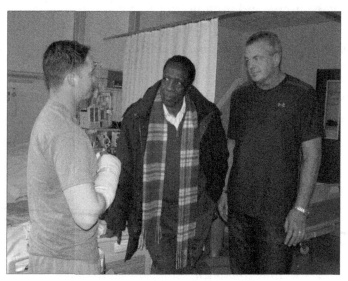

Meadowlark and Allen visiting with a wounded warrior
at Landstuhl Hospital, Germany

What about your basketball abilities now?

"My basketball abilities are somewhat on the inside wishing they could get out. My mind says and desires to do things that my body simply can't deliver. Due to Freiberg's disease in my left foot and nerve damage in both feet and legs, I am limited as to what I can do on the court."

Aging for the athlete is not always a walk in the park.

"Yeah. My ability to jump, run, cut, and make quick moves— which used to define me on the court and brought me much success—simply aren't there. My shot is, though. And I still retain the knowledge and ability to teach, coach, and clearly transfer and relate my knowledge at many levels as I did at the recent Camp Meadowlark for Military Teens in Europe over the holidays. My son, Cdub, is clearly improving, which delights me as well. The other young players I coach impress me as well and are a joy to coach. As I said, my abilities are still on the inside and I'm pretty good at explaining quick and powerful moves, tricks of the trade and how to use and optimize your legs, arms, butt, and mind."

In that order? (we both laughed)
"Never underestimate the power of the butt ..."

Tell me about your fitness regimen.
"You're not going to believe this, but my trainer is a very famous and respected member of the President's Council on Physical Fitness and Sports, Denise Austin. You might have heard of her? Well, that fixed-at-age-35-year-old joins me in my living room every day on the big screen. Kayla has done her 10-minute intense 'Hit the Spot' workout series since her twenties. She had Denise's 'Hit The Spot' abs, arms, legs, etc. on old VHS tapes made in the '90s. I converted them to digital. I plug in her DVDs and do a couple of intense but low-impact, 10-minute workouts every day. They really do make a difference. Muscle memory is a great friend of mine, thank God! Other than that, I do still shoot hoops, golf some, and try to walk as much as Freiberg lets me."

How about a last comment to end our "tree house" conversation? [Again, we had spoken for over five hours and shared a great deal. Lots of catharsis took place from both sides. Most of my lengthier statements were not included. This chapter had to be edited down more than any aging athlete interview transcript to date.]

"Of this 'tree house' talk I can say, it really held my interest and put me in an introspective and somewhat healing place. Not many people can do that to me, especially for this length of time. I have never in my entire life had a two-hour, much less a five-hour conversation. I can see where your core is and understand more about you than you think, my new friend, I totally do. Your physical and psychological gifts are amazing. Your compliments are nonstop and you wear your kindness and feelings on your sleeve, and I respect that. I teach my kids that a simple act of kindness, a simple compliment takes what—10 seconds? Those 10 seconds can make someone's day. It's amazing how many people in this world don't take the time to pass out a simple compliment, but they are often quick and eager to take them. There are too many takers in this world and not enough givers, and you certainly are a giver, Sifu.

"You're gifted in the way that you're intellectual but somewhat transparent and vulnerable. You are also very empathetic—like litmus paper—sucking out one's thoughts, determining whether they are red or blue, then talking one through it based on your find-ings. I know you get it, that's why I love ya! Through this process you've taught me that I shouldn't look back other than to learn and draw on my experiences. That life isn't about peaks and valleys necessarily. Or maybe it's a redefinition of those terms ... Meaning that peaks don't necessarily have to be measured by big houses or millions in the bank. That peaks can be a time of happiness in a downsized, more calm and contented environment—which is what I found with Kayla and what I needed to survive. I hope we can do something like this again. You've really brought me to a place where it's okay to stay for a while. You're at the top of my list of people I want to know more about and be friends with. I love yah, always will. It's time to climb down the ladder, dude …

"Peace out."

§ § §

That ended my long, inspiring "tree house" conversation with Allen Winder. I can say that we were blessed that together we came to a new space in time. It's a good space, a space of honor and healing. It was the well-being and clearing that comes with honest catharsis and new introspection. Despite his tremendous athletic abilities, and his later rise to success in the corporate world, the big man admits he eventually crashed and burned. I am a big proponent of downtime and proper sleep—including naps—so I asked Allen how much of this he was getting when he crashed.

I wasn't surprised when he revealed he was accepting more and more responsibility and doing less and less of what we consider wellness activities. He was "on" all of the time. Then came the crash. During episodes, bipolar can turn a person into being excessively emotionally charged and out of control. He needed help. His brain chemistry had forced the issue.

His struggle to overcome depression associated with bipolar disorder ended a way of life as he knew it. He has been in the restructuring, re-awareness stage for some time. Now, Allen is the Director of Operations for Meadowlark Lemon Ministries. He does most of his work pro-bono using his business acumen developed over many years running large organizations. He also continues his passion of graphic design and videography through Adub Studios, a graphic design and video production company which is geared to help nonprofits. He loves spending time raising and playing with his kids Christian and Zoe and stays close to his older two children Elissa and Garrett. Allen still puts on his do-rag or reversed hat and gets down with his guitar.

He told me he's happy and he's loved by his kids and his partner, Kayla. His father and mother have passed on. Now, he lives out the integrity they taught him—do right by others, do good deeds, and believe in yourself.

I believe Allen shared the story of his true essence and, despite being wired differently in a number of ways, we shared an equal relationship for the duration of the interview. Then the initial connection continued to warm and we became friends. His sweetheart mentioned that we were having a bromance, which is defined as a relationship or friendship between two hetero males. That was a hoot. Truth is, she was spot-on. If we were neighbors, we'd be having barbecues and good old times. Catch you on the flip side. Out. (I'd stick a photo of the two of us here but we have yet to meet. Ours has been a virtual bromance.)

*Meadowlark Lemon and Allen, autograph signing
at Rammstein Mall in Germany, 2014*

Chapter 4

The Heart Runs to Spread the Word

"The first peace, which is the most important, is that which comes within the souls of people when they realize their relationship, their oneness, with the universe and all its powers, and when they realize that at the center of the universe dwells the Great Spirit, and that this center is really everywhere, it is within each of us."

—Black Elk, Oglala Sioux holy man and medicine man
(Born 1863, Little Powder River, Wyoming,
died 1950, age 87, Pine Ridge, South Dakota)

Some people grow up in a safe and loving household. They have an obvious support group and enjoy a time of relative peace and bounty. They get three squares a day, do their homework, interact and share in the nurturing kinship with their parents and siblings, and eventually say goodbye to them when they head off for college or to seek their fortune. For other kids, things aren't so soft and peachy. They carry a key (if their house has a lock), pace the streets and travel the roads alone. They fend for themselves. We are all different. We come from different places. The details of our home life are never exactly the same.

Sociologists teach that we are products of our environments. They also hold that our ancestry also has a profound effect on us. The lives of our forbears were different from ours in many ways, but what touched them has a way of touching us. If they were raised poor or hungry, we may feel their painful moments and cravings. If they were abusive, we may still feel the abuse. One friend shared a story about her family's karma. "My grandpa's side goes back to the European kings in the 17th and 18th century. A past-life regression therapist told me I was still being affected by it. My karma in relationships and at work has had its share of deplorable moments."

Bad karma can take generations to clear. Some shamans and spirit-world healers offer sessions of karma clearing. We can also sit with these medicine people to do some karma relating, which teaches that you don't always have to clear things completely; you can sometimes just honor and accept them. What if you come from a tribe that once lived in freedom on the eastern part of North America and wound up decimated and impoverished living within the confines of reservations far away from your ancestors' region? What do you do then?

As for karmic energy, perhaps, if your intentions were worthy, you could run circles through the karma—adeptly grabbing only what you want and attempting to elude what stings. Perhaps there's even a propulsion speed at which you circle and cause the bad karma to fall by the way side. At that juncture, you develop your own destiny, turning negatives into positives. Your former naysayers not only eat their words but become your advocates. At the end of a path like that, you could even be left with a prized gold medal and a calling to right some wrongs and spread wisdom, good cheer, and maybe even a bit of good fortune. You could choose to put back into a society that once challenged you at nearly every step before it allowed you to do great things. Karma it forward, pay it forward, do right by those who need as many pick-me-ups as you once needed.

The following is part of the story related to me over three deep and endearing conversations with Billy Mills, a soft-spoken, yet direct point maker who is Lakota Sioux Indian of English descent. Several aging athletes had schedules that required me to wait until the time was right to meet them for an in-person interview. Billy was a six-months wait. He's good on the phone, and he comes across gracefully and engagingly on video. But, once you meet him, you realize how important it is to spend time with him in person, to feel his physical presence. Though, I'd still buy his DVDs and books.

Because of his fame and hard work on benevolent causes, Billy has met with every U.S. president (except Bush, the second) since John F. Kennedy. A traveling public speaker and campaigner for global understanding, Billy is an aging athlete who is no longer able to do the sport for which he was once celebrated as the finest in the world. Billy has been blessed with an eventful life. He grew up poor on a South Dakota reservation and was orphaned at age 12. Even though he suffered from Type 2 diabetes which started before college, and faced predation of American-born racism even while honorably serving in the U.S. Marines, Billy dug deep into his spiritual center, found his jets, and came from several lengths back to win a gold medal in the 1964 Tokyo Olympics.

For many decades, his quest has been to bestow gifts of the heart and mind to those he encounters. You could call him a traveling medicine man whose medicine is directly rooted in his presence and, his essence. His victory in the Olympics was considered an upset even though Billy had predicted he was going to win. He blasted through the final 50 meters of the Olympic 10,000-meters race at a velocity that drove the color commentator to rise to the occasion. Dick Bank grabbed the microphone from the lead commentator and called out, "Look at Mills, look at Mills …" Utter astonishment caused Bank's voice to go shrill before briefly laughing himself into near delirium. A voice we appreciate today on YouTube as an integral part of Billy's momentous, unprecedented moment of thrilling victory was not appreciated by the T.V. network. Bank was fired for unprofessionalism.

Billy also tells of a Japanese official who shook him at the end of the race. Billy couldn't understand what he was saying. He finally learned the official was asking in Japanese translated to "Who are you?"

So, the karma cleared, the Great Spirits with Billy—he made it. He made it past poverty, past the early deaths of both his parents, past substantial blood sugar problems, and past racism from both sides of his ethnic lineage. In his final 50 meters, feeling the blood sugar dropping, running-on-fumes, Billy stunned the world. But he didn't stop there. He is still going full bore today and is passing on his gift to all who listen.

For those who wanted to keep Billy and his struggling native people down, his life's successful path has also been an upset. Besides his resonating voice that ranks up there with the likes of Burl Ives ("Rudolph, the Red-Nosed Rein Deer's" narrator), after our several conversations I found his most defining feature to be that in his plight, Billy has been unstoppable.

In his 20s, Billy finally found his own family support. His wife, Pat, an abstract impressionist artist who has been by his side since college, is as big in his life as he is in the world of coaching and motivation.

Tale of The Tape
William Mervin "Billy" Mills

Olympic Champion, Author, Public Speaker

At the time of this book's publication, Billy is most likely the most famous living Native American on the planet.

He certainly put in the miles on the paths and tracks to win races; now he puts on flight and automobile miles to get to where his message and wisdom are needed.

Born June 30, 1938, Pine Ridge Indian Reservation, South Dakota.

Oglala Lakota tribal given name: Makata Taka Hela, which means "Respects The Earth."

Age 18: 5'11", 155 lbs.

Age 75: 5'11", 205 lbs.

Second Native American, after Jim Thorpe, to win an Olympic gold medal.

1964, Tokyo Olympics, 10,000 meters. The only American (from North, Central, or South America) to have won the Olympic 10,000-meter event. He won the race by running it nearly fifty seconds faster than he had ever run it, breaking the Olympic record. His time: 28:24:04.

Started out as a boxer, and ran to train for boxing. Later moved to running.

Injuries to the knees now prevent him from running.

He was a first lieutenant in the U.S. Marine Corps Reserves during the 1964 Olympics.

Member of the National Track and Field Hall of Fame and the U.S. Olympic Hall of Fame.

Co-Author of "Wokini: A Lakota Journey to Happiness and Self-Understanding." Published in 1990, this was a book that made a profound impact on Native people world wide.

His life story is featured in the 1983 film "Running Brave."

Setbacks: Poverty, parents dying young, racism, hypoglycemia, Type 2 diabetes. After the Olympics: downhill skiing injuries. During his earlier days, the white people called him an Indian and the Lakota called him an Iyeska, a half-breed. They no longer do.

The most fun part of the interview: calling a 75-year-old "Billy."

Notable Quote: "When you are given a gift, you begin to wonder 'What's it for?' One of the most powerful virtues in the Native American world is that of giving back. So I've tried to choreograph my life giving back."

Personal Connection: We both worked at the same financial firm in Sacramento. Billy left in 1984; I started in 1987. I did not know of our former common place of work until he shared that with me in 2013. In the late 1980s, I was a runner with the Fair Oaks Running Club; Billy has lived in Fair Oaks, California since the 1980s but had ceased running by that point. I first met Billy in person in September of 2013.

1964 Olympics

Billy Mills crosses the finish line in the 10,000 m
U.S. Marine Corps photo

Billy on a speaking tour, 2012

At the end of our last discussion, I asked Billy whether he was ever going to become a runner again.

"You know, probably not. 50 percent of both medial meniscus bones are gone. It happened while skiing. I was in my early 30s. And when I had my first surgery, I was still young enough to attempt to make the Olympic team. My wife is a good skier. I told her I would ski with her if she would golf with me. Now she beats me in golf and I can't ski."

Once the knees are gone, it's a tough go.

"50 percent of the medial, 75 percent of the lateral meniscus, soft tissue damage to hip ... so I do a lot of stretching. I don't call it yoga, but they are yoga-type stretching maneuvers. I use the roller a lot, I also use the big ball [physio ball]."

He points to the steps leading upstairs in his beautiful home outside of Sacramento.

"If I do that routine in the morning, I come bouncing down the steps—no problem. But, if I don't do that, I come down having to use the railing. What a difference. At age 75, if I stretch—good news."

Do you do any muscle building exercises?

"I do a little bit of weight lifting, but I go in cycles. You get automatic atrophy when you've had that type of problem with the knees. So I'll go to the gym for a few months, then take a break for a few months. But the major factor as a 75-year-old is stretching ... the benefits are overwhelmingly noticeable."

How many times a day?

"Sometimes twice. Sometimes I'll go in intervals: 15 minutes and then some more a bit later."

From what you have told me, you didn't stop physical activity after your running career. You went from running to skiing to golf and some other things?

"That's right."

What is your advice to people who come out of the military, ballet, dancing on Broadway, or professional athletics who may not know how to recreate? What do you tell people who end their time as a high-performance athlete and need to get into recreational endeavors?

"I think you have to separate the difference between sport and fitness. A sport doesn't always make you fit, but fitness will make you a better athlete. So you just analyze what you did to be the great athlete that you might have been and transfer that into a less intense version. That approach will help you lead a more quality lifestyle. That's not only the nutrition, it's not only the stretching, some weight lifting, but just as powerful is your internal side, the spiritual, and your frame of mind. If you do that, you can be blessed."

What do you say to the people who say, "I'm burnt out on the gym. My coaches used to push us so hard on the field and now I just want to sit around and think?" I tell them about recreation and dancing. I tell them about hiking. How do you get high-performance athletes who were never recreational athletes into recreational sports or activities?

"That is an incredibly difficult task. I quit competing as a world-class athlete when I was very young. I was 26 years old. I quit with maybe the best 10 years ahead of me. I had a world record, I had a gold medal. And, as of now, I am the only person from the Americas to have won that event. When I came out of professional athletics, whether it was the insurance business, whether it was pursuing another entrepreneurial effort, people just automatically expected me to excel at the same level now as I did in sport. They wanted the gold medal in this new venture. If you make the mistake for trying to achieve for other people, then you're in for a hard, unhappy experience."

You're suggesting that we should maintain the theme of doing right for ourselves. Looking out for and treating ourselves right.

"I was blessed that whatever I was going to do, I was going to try to excel at it and I was going to try to empower myself through empowering other people. If you do it the right way, it can be very easy. You can be a school teacher, you can be a fitness expert, you can work in the police force, whatever it might be. A lot of times in America, we equate money with success instead of the internal, a peaceful mind and that internal strength within you which brings happiness."

The spiritual quest … the quest for meaning.

"Indeed. I sought out a real strong spiritual base within myself to seek happiness. Then I choreographed my whole life to those people who helped to empower me as an athlete. I'm blessed in this great country of ours to be able to help my Running Strong for American Indian Youth group. We've probably raised in the last 27 years $125 million in cash and in kind for poverty pockets of America. All made possible by the compassion of people. We've also helped champion runner Kip Keno and his wife, Phyllis, with their program Bread and Water for Africa, in Kenya that involved a children's home. We helped to create the program."

What a way to give back, Billy. What does this do for you?

"It's all about returning the gift. And it keeps me moving. The more you get involved, the more healthy you have to be with your own self—your body, your mind, your spirit. As a Native American, the more powerful I want to be spiritually, the more I have to be in control of myself. I have to be more healthy, eat more healthfully, and be able to do things effectively from a physical standpoint. The body, the mind, the spirit have to be fit and all fit together. Everything has to work together."

Which is the most important?

"You have to address them all. So often we neglect the body. For me as an athlete, it was a very easy transition to normal life, but not at first. I still wanted to get another gold medal. In my mind, I felt I could have won seven, eight, nine, 10, 12, or 15. My wife said, 'You got one, so just let it go, be happy.' With that I made the transition into trying to empower other people through my journey and my life experiences."

So that's what your speaking tour is all about?

"Yes, this past year I was on the road, traveling about 300 days. I've been doing the speaking tours to some extent since the early 1960s. But for the last 15 years, I've done it full time. But the most powerful thing I can do to help others is to empower myself— physically. If I went to bad food, I could be a diabetic destroying the body. When you go into the zone of low blood sugar—you are constantly fighting with weight. You start ballooning up because you have to have food, so you start eating. But I have to discipline myself. When I'm starting to go low on blood sugar, I have to be sure I take the right foods. But still, I fluctuate in weight. But the stretching, proper nutrition … what a difference that makes. If I didn't do the stretching, I would be in sad shape."

Who motivated you in your later years?

"Here's one eventful moment that involved a family member, my Auntie who was 100 years and four months old at the time.

There was a moment when she reached up on her tippy toes and gave me a hug and I finally asked her what she did to stay so fit. She said, 'Well, I walked all the time. I never won any races.'

"In her 90s, she entered in a race for which they had flown in several men who were in their late 80s. And they were running and race walking and they were winning these medals in their age group. Auntie didn't have the five dollars, so she walked on the sidewalk, in her street shoes. And she came in and crossed near the finish. I was waiting for her at the finish line. Once we arrived I said, 'Auntie, you should have entered the race.' She responded, 'Oh, I raced with them. Race walking.' When I said, 'Did I get here late?' she responded, 'They'll be coming.' They were maybe 600 yards behind her. And she beat these two elite race walkers. This shows you that you don't have to have the Tour de France outfits. You just have to have a pair of shoes and some comfortable slacks and go out for a walk."

Never underestimate the willpower nor the foot power of the living ancient. What was your biggest setback with your running?

"The only real blemish to my record was not winning an individual NCAA title. I think a big part of this was my hypoglycemia, which wasn't diagnosed until 11 months before the Olympics. I think if I had known how to deal with hypoglycemia and Type 2 diabetes, I would have won a couple. But that's the past. This total exhaustion I kept experiencing turned out to be the cycle of low blood sugar, not fatigue from running. And I couldn't properly explain it to the coach. The coach would send me to the doctor. The doctor couldn't find anything wrong with me. They would say things like: low self-esteem, orphaned, minority, poverty. And they said I would have to learn to deal with those issues. But all it really was was hypoglycemia, borderline diabetic."

So what did you do?

"I changed the diet. Before knowing this, my breakfast frequently was oatmeal with brown sugar and raisins, milk, a glass of orange juice, one toast with butter and a little bit of jam. Doing this would guarantee going into the diabetic range. Once in that range, I'd drop drastically into the low blood sugar range. So, in an attempt to be more level in my energy, I went on what I call an indigenous diet."

What did that consist of?

"One day I'd eat something that was on the ground, which meant you had to kill it to eat it. Deer, antelope, elk, buffalo, beef. The next day you'd eat something from the water, for example fish. The next day, something from the air—a pheasant, a duck, a goose, or even chicken. So, that's the ground, the water, the air. The next day you ate something from the live food source that grew in the ground or from a tree that had roots in the ground. So every fourth day was totally a vegetarian-type day. This was the one day you didn't have to kill something to eat. Every one of these vegetarian days, I tried to eat according to a five-color code and take a minimum of five to 10 helpings over the course of the day. And the color code had to be from the live food source. Go to the produce department and look at the five color codes. Grains, vegetables, fruits, nuts, legumes. I didn't know what a legume was until I was in college, but I knew my color code. This actually wound up producing a very high-quality meal."

Did you get your blood sugar tested before you changed your diet?

"No. I had made some changes before they tested me in 1963, the year before the Olympics. The highest I tested in the blood glucose tolerance test was almost 200. By U.S. standards, if you go over 200, you're diabetic. But before this, in 1962, I had started the new diet on my own, trying to follow this color code. They gave me the test at the time I had graduated from college and had taken a commission in the Marine Corps."

So, even with your improved diet, you were still testing out as a near-diabetic?

"Yeah, it had a harmful effect on me. Initially I was at the top academically and physically, but then, as I was going through Officer's Candidate School, I began to deteriorate. As I began to deteriorate physically, I had a hard time focusing for the exams. One wondered how this man with this tremendous potential as an officer could start to fall apart."

So you hadn't done any blood tests in college?

"No. But afterwards, they finally had me do a glucose tolerance test."

Over three hours? (I said this knowing that Carlton Fredericks, who had a prominent dietary radio show in New York at this time [1960s and beyond], had campaigned for longer duration glucose tests.)

"Six hours. And that's when I tested 198 or 199. They called it borderline diabetic, but I went very low over the course of the six hours. I can't recall how low, but I was shaking, clammy sweat, vision problems ..."

What did the doctor suggest?

"At the time, the doctor put me on a high-protein diet. And even that helped. But still, at the time, in college and the first year in the Marine Corps, I had been eating every four hours before a competition. And if you're hypoglycemic, you have to eat every two-and-a-half to three hours. Gradually I started realizing that. But I came to the full realization only after I retired from running. I was learning by hit and miss. And I learned a lot before races."

Can you recall a specific example?

"I remember San Diego, 1965, where I set the world record for the 5,000-meter race. I was low before the race and got a Hershey bar. I ate the Hershey bar five minutes before the race. And I remember in Tokyo in 1964, I was fairly comfortable with the race, very confident that I could win. But I was going low in blood sugar then too. And I had an Asian apple two hours before I ran. Who knows, if I hadn't had that, I may not have won."

Amazing. I completely understand the low-blood-sugar scenario. Now, if we can, Billy, I'd like to move to the motivational, spiritual side. Could you take us back to your early years?

"The event that has affected me my entire life was that my mom died. I was eight years old. I prayed with my dad, I went to church with him. As he was seeking his form of redemption, he was mentoring me, I think without even knowing it. My thought was that he was grasping to try to redeem himself as a man."

What did you learn from him at this time?

"My mom had died, which was hard on me. My dad told me I had broken wings. And he said, 'If you do these things, Son, someday you'll have wings of an eagle.' He said I had to let go of the hurt, the hate, the jealously. He said, 'The jealousy blinds you. You don't see the good in our culture, you don't see it in other cultures, other people, and you have a whole lot of self pity. He said, 'You have to look deeper because way down deep is where the dreams lie. It's the pursuit of a dream that heals you.'"

Billy's father in the 1930s

It's as though the great spirits were speaking through your father.
"That's probably it. Here was a man who had little background in philosophy and religion, so to speak. But he became quite helpful to my spiritual path. He would say, 'You have to find your dream, Son.' And he would repeat that for the next four years until I was 12, and then he died. He would say, 'Here's where to find your dreams: sports, drama, music, creative writing, academia, working with the elderly, anything constructive that you can enjoy. I hope you try sports, Son.'

I wonder if he knew something was inside you and that it was running?
"That is what it sounded like. I thought he meant for me to become an athlete. Then he died. And in this life journey where I continued to feel very alone, I started taking some of the thoughts

he gave me. I have long said that my dad gave me philosophy. I was the only person to whom he read poems. I have an actual copy of one of the poems, because I refer to it every once in a while. It's called 'Abou Ben Adhem.'"

(Billy later showed me his copy of the poem.)

> *Abou Ben Adhem (may his tribe increase!)*
> *Awoke one night from a deep dream of peace,*
> *And saw, within the moonlight in his room,*
> *Making it rich, and like a lily in bloom,*
> *An Angel writing in a book of gold:*
>
> *Exceeding peace had made Ben Adhem bold,*
> *And to the Presence in the room he said,*
> *"What writest thou?" The Vision raised its head,*
> *And with a look made of all sweet accord*
> *Answered, "The names of those who love the Lord."*
>
> *"And is mine one?" said Abou. "Nay, not so,"*
> *Replied the Angel. Abou spoke more low,*
> *But cheerily still; and said, "I pray thee, then,*
> *Write me as one who loves his fellow men."*
>
> *The Angel wrote, and vanished. The next night*
> *It came again with a great wakening light,*
> *And showed the names whom love of God had blessed,*
> *And, lo! Ben Adhem's name led all the rest!*

By Leigh Hunt (1784–1859, English writer)

Billy at the Haskell Indian
Nations University in Kansas

What was the ultimate message of your father?

"He told me that the Lord, the Creator, would bless the one who loved his fellow man. He was also, at that time, giving me the strength that would ultimately help me win a gold medal at the Olympic Games. This was the gift of the seven virtues of our people. I'll give you four right now. Bravery, fortitude, wisdom, generosity. You can take bravery and fortitude and go on a journey to the center of your soul, and that's where you find wisdom. Use the virtue of wisdom to make the right choices for yourself."

What happens when you make the right choices?

"The right choices will empower you and that's where you can express the virtue of generosity as you empower others. That sets you on the path of becoming a virtuous warrior. So, again, you take the first two virtues and go on a journey to the center of your soul, and there you find the virtue of wisdom. Make the right choices for yourself. With generosity, you empower others. And there you become an emerging virtuous warrior, learning what a warrior means for you. Number one for a warrior is self responsibility with accountability. The second trait a warrior develops is incredible balance and harmony. Then humility."

(I'd like to add that Billy is from the time before political correctness. The recent widespread awareness of the ridiculous warring postures of mankind have caused some to take the word "war" and "warrior" out of certain contexts—not without reason. His use of warrior could be likened to "evolving spiritual and honorable person." The seven virtues are listed in a variety of ways. Additional virtues are often listed as love, honesty, prayer, respect, and compassion. Adding them up to seven is likewise handled in a variety of ways.)

Billy running in the Marine Corps, 1962

What did your father tell you to do with the message from the poem?

"He wanted me to be blessed, like Abou Ben Adhem, whom the Lord blessed for loving his fellow man. My dad would take the Lakota people's most powerful prayer which said 'We are all related.' And he would relate that with this poem."

What did he tell you about your people?

"We're no different as people from one another. Perceptions make us think we are. We are to give love and compassion to others. The warrior seeks to fulfill four spiritual steps. My dad warned, 'If you are an atheist or agnostic, don't get hung up with the word spiritual, call them human steps.'"

Billy after his 1964 Gold Medal "upset" race, Tokyo Olympics

What were those steps?

"To be unique, finding that special gift inside of you. Develop that strength, that positive, constructive strength. As it empowers you, go to the community and empower the community. Then the community empowers you. From that dual empowerment, you are making a creative difference to society. That creative difference brings understanding. From this dual empowerment comes global unity, dignity, and character, and the beauty of global diversity. And then unity through diversity. Not only to me, the theme of the Olympic Games is far more important than winning. That theme is for the future of human kind."

§ § §

An important part in the Olympian's journey is bridging political and cultural gaps to allow for understanding and befriending people around the globe. Billy has continued to promote that.

At a time of sadness, he received a gift in the very special poem his dad read to him. This gave him hope and drive.

Hearing Billy recite the poem moved me. That plus his touching life story gave me a new spark and, if you can imagine, this moment was followed by a bit of melancholy. Honoring one's fellow man—man, that was a deep message. Now, in 2013, I was a tourist in my former town. I got back in a car a friend had lent me, pulled out of the Mills' driveway, and made it to Fair Oaks Boulevard—a street that marked my beginning in California 26 years before. Driving alone in my thoughts back to my friend's—at 105 degrees—certainly helped put perspective on my own life. Things were heating up.

An aging Olympian had given me an extraordinary gift. I had to do something with it—both for myself and the global village. On that drive, I thought about all of my former friends and acquaintances in a place where I had lived for 16 years. Had I honored them as I knew in my heart that I should? Had we honored each other? The intentions were always there, but had we stuck with the plan?

Melancholy and loneliness often goes hand in hand with the writer's task. To really dig deep, you may have to spend long spans of time alone with your thoughts. Spending this time, sometimes 10 hours per day, often breeds loneliness. I shook off that questioning, the melancholic chatter in my head, and decided to honor the day. I knew that I had captured Billy on camera and in my mind. This man was able to pull it together and make his mark. He did it. He was born poor and was later orphaned. If he could work on his honor and bring it to the world, so could I.

Billy tapped into the wisdom and love—the spiritual bounty—his predecessors left for him. That's where Billy was most successful: in allowing the great spirits to speak through him. As quoted by Padraic Duffy, in the Rapid City Journal online: "Kevin Poor Bear, one of Billy's tribe's people in South Dakota shared this: 'He's an icon down here. He's almost like Jesus to people here. He's the person I looked up to the most growing up and the person who made the biggest impact on me. I think he's the greatest Oglala since Crazy Horse.'"

Billy has put on some pounds since his days as an elite distance runner, but his mind and heart have grown far faster. The low-blood sugar cravings and energy fluctuations are something many of us have had to deal with. Arthritis hit me in my late 30s (1998) when I was doing jiu-jitsu, twisting and mangling my hands on my opponent's kimono or gi. I never associated my own history of hypoglycemia with arthritis until I read an old book from Billy's era called "Low Blood Sugar and You." After almost a year of arthritis, I happened to find the 1967 edition of this book by Carlton Fredericks, PhD, and Herman Goodman, M.D. I then tried the high-protein diet which was not very difficult to implement.

Everything seemed to improve: energy, attention span, attitude, and physique. Most important, the diet adjusted my pancreas, almost completely eliminating the arthritis in about two weeks. I'm not suggesting that will work for everyone, but it has worked for me. I have since gone to a low simple carb diet. Almost none of my drinks are sugary besides an occasional bit of honey in some herbal tea. This year I've probably had less than three bottles of wine total. "How boring," you might say. Well, what if I said, "They were all at the same time ..."

Just kidding, only three-quarters of one was at the same time, and I wasn't driving. "Boring," you say. Well, how boring is it to feel euphoria every morning as I watch the sun rise? How boring is it to feel maybe not like a million bucks, but perhaps $100,000? How boring is it to do fitness 364 days with your sweetheart (unless intimacy counts, then add a day), meet with more than 20 aging athletes (including being on the receiving end of a highly hazardous leg lock from a ripped, 235-pound former UFC heavyweight champion), complete two books, spend two-and-a-half months travelling Europe and America, and spend three wonderful conversations with an Indian Nation elder statesman who took me not only to the 1964 Tokyo Olympics, but to the center of his soul? If you think your soul is boring, I suggest digging deeper and reading Billy's books and attending one of his talks.

As for fitness, there are many ways aging athletes (and you) can go about things. You can be super fit, like your old performance or high-school self, just older and perhaps a bit slower now. You might choose to focus on other things than fitness, and that's fine. You can be relatively physically active and relatively fit and still get the job done. For you that may mean endeavoring to complete your life's work and caring for your garden and other people. Billy is not trying to win any more races, instead he imparts his wisdom of how to tap into your own dreams so you can fulfill what you were put here to do.

What I got from him is that he was taking care of his body mainly for functionality. This way his partially broken body could serve him so he would then be able to keep up his schedule serving others. With the discipline to stick to his fitness and wellness plan, he has been able to do just that. Living a full life, Billy has stepped up as the figure for his people (and the global village) who would help heal their wounds and propel them to forgiveness, honor, and, ultimately, happiness. With knees and hip no longer fit enough for the impact that many sports impart, he has taken up active stretching, mixing in some weight training. With his schedule of constantly being in airports and hotels, it's not easy to find the perfect, natural foods at mealtime. But, as another flight awaits him, Billy strives on—traveling to the center of his soul, seeking out what will empower him to empower us.

Chapter 5

Better Than Flipping Channels

"Do not go gentle into that good night. Old age should burn and rave at close of day, rage, rage against the dying of the light. Though wise men at their end know dark is right, because their words had forked no lightning they do not go gentle into that good night. Good men, the last wave by, crying how bright their frail deeds might have danced in a green bay, rage, rage against the dying of the light. Wild men who caught and sang the sun in flight, and learn, too late, they grieved it on its way. Do not go gentle into that good night. Grave men, near death, who see with blinding sight Blind eyes could blaze like meteors and be gay, rage, rage against the dying of the light. And you, my father, there on the sad height, Curse, bless, me now with your fierce tears, I pray. Do not go gentle into that good night. Rage, rage against the dying of the light."

—Dylan Marlais Thomas

The poet Dylan Thomas was born in Wales on October 27, 1914, beginning his life with not an inkling of fame to come. In fact he never mastered Cymraeg, the language of Wales and who could blame him. He probably couldn't wrap his mouth around Cymraeg, to say nothing of his brain. The young Dylan did master English but not in high school. He dropped out at age 16. Four years later he published his first book of poetry and also picked up a taste for alcohol at the local pubs.

At first, he was hardly well received as a poet. He managed to eke out a living reading poetry, doing some acting, and as a critic for the BBC. He also did a lot of partying and got a reputation for offensive behavior. While in New York for a rehearsal of his famous poem "Under Milk Wood," which had been adapted for a play, he died of pneumonia on November 9, 1939. Dylan had been sickly most of his life. The alcohol, and some say drugs, didn't help. Hardly a role model for athletes but rather for what not to be. He did leave all of us the inspiring unnamed poem containing the famous line: "Do not go gentle into that good night."

It's unlikely that you've heard tell of Arrichion. He was an aging athlete who lived in the ancient Greek city of Phigalia, located in the mountains on the Peloponnesian peninsula in the south of Greece. At the 564 B.C. Olympics, Arrichion was the crown holder and the oldest athlete competing. As the story would have it, Arrichion was defending the title in the pankration, a chaotic no-holds-barred contest similar to the mixed martial arts competitions of today. Arrichion was tired and worn after having earlier fought some tough battles in the tournament. In his final match, he was pitted against a much younger, stronger, and quicker fighter who was out for blood and determined to take his crown. His opponent found an opening and, quick as a cat, got Arrichion in a choke hold. Arrichion retaliated with a foothold, took a twist and broke his opponent's foot, causing him to surrender. When the two were separated, Arrichion had won the match, but had choked to death in the process. Arrichion didn't die trying, he died winning.

Today's residents of countries in the region of the Mediterranean Sea have seen their diets tracked for the simple reason that they don't die as early as those an hour plane flight north. For years, some considered the Mediterranean diet as too oily or less than adequate for balanced nutrition. Later, some dietary critics held that those who ate such light fare were experiencing lower rates of heart attacks and strokes. If something works, and ain't broke ...

It always amazes me that we spend so much time dealing with big questions that were already answered by our ancestors. Even our distant ancestors merit a much closer look—not in the wars and politics as we tend to do in school, but in their social history, how they lived from day to day and meal to meal. The ancients had amassed wisdom about nutrition, exercise, and competition. Ancient cultures are generally thought to have avoided obesity epidemics. Instead of building upon that wisdom, vast numbers of modernities in the West have clamored for fad diets and quick fixes that have tallied failure rates in the high 90th percentile.

Ancient civilizations realized that a balanced diet was vital. Alexander the Great of the northern Greece state of Macedon was tutored in his childhood by Aristotle—"graduating" from his tutor's program at age 16. Alexander is considered one of the great military strategists of all time. How do we know about his battles? For many of them, he brought historians along to chronicle the events. In his quest for domination, Alexander was always on the lookout for new edible plants and herbs which might increase the strength and endurance of his troops.

Ancient athletic trainers were of course rewarded for the talents of their athletes just as leaders were rewarded for the skills of their fighting forces. Ancient trainers concocted special meals for their athletes. By the time Arrichion came to the forefront, physical competitors had developed a high-performance diet. Meat and other forms of protein had become the dietary trend for athletes and soldiers. They ate plenty of goat meat and cheese for protein, supplementing that with lots of figs, grapes, and cabbage. Soldiers who partook of too much wine the night before a battle are said to have utilized a high-performance diet to cure hangovers. Good nutrition must certainly have contributed to Arrichion's longevity and metaphoric victory over death. His example demonstrates that it might be hard for an omnivore to snap an ankle without chewing on one first.

How did ancient societies deal with changes in the food supply? Along the historical way, societies suffered famines. And there were other times where they had to get by on low-protein diets. You've probably heard of monocropping and the Irish potato famine. Those who relied on this high-starch staple were subject to a horrible death if they couldn't come up with enough nutrition to compensate for this failed crop. Whether driven by profit, by health concerns, or simply by good intentions, modern researchers, by the tens of thousands, have been studying and writing about nutrition, exercise, and aging. Not surprisingly, what tends to make an engaging headline is the surprise anomaly. Some young boy lifts his father over his head. Or a blind person scales a mountain. In this chapter, we'll spend a moment with an old man who comes in first when he does any endurance race with his very fit kids or even his very fit grand kids. But before starting in on his story, consider this one.

In the year 2000, a very special man stepped into his own—he was ready to test and show his mettle. He was a grey-haired, skinny guy in baggy clothes dressed for a jog in the park. He started out running a 60-meter dash in 27.29. A few minutes later he threw an 8-pound shot put 11 feet 6. Two years later, in an eight-day competition at the 2002 USA Track and Field Nationals, this same man set five indoor records. His name is Everett Hosack. Born on February 28, 1902, he was a former track star from the University of Florida whose amateur career was cut short by the Great Depression. He jump started his amateur track career at age 80, and was 100 years old at the time of the 2002 event. Shortly after that record breaking day he lost Elsa, his wife of 67 years. She died in November 2002. Everett passed away in July of 2004. In 1980, at an age when most people have already retired, Everett was just beginning. By 2002, he had set 50 career Masters world records, making Everett Hosack immortal.

When I began this book, I had set the intention to locate and interview a famous World War II veteran who would also happen to be an athlete or a fitness person. In my file folder, I had a cut out of a NY Times Magazine article on some World War II airmen who had been honored for their exploits as part of Lt. Colonel Jimmy Doolittle's squadron. My father, an avid reader of the Times, had sent that to me. Instead of a WW II ace who did some athletics, I wound up with a WWII unknown who became one of the best elder endurance athletes of the 20th and 21st century. This man has won five Masters World Cups for cross-country skiing, is a five-time ITU Triathlon World Champion, and was the United States Cycling Federation National record holder in 1987. He was also the first man to race with aero bars at the 1986 Ironman Hawaii.

Adding brains to brawn, he is the engineer who built and tested the now-famous aerodynamic handlebars with ski racing coach and inventor Boone Lennon. To clarify a debated topic, Boone holds a patent on these lean-on-me handlebars. That modern, ergonomic improvement helped Greg LeMond win the 1989 Tour De France by eight seconds, the closest finish in the history of the tour. As luck would have it, a friend of mine had a connection to this particular aging engineer-athlete and shared that his contact had competed in over 200 triathlons and was still going at age 87. That aging wonder is Charley French. It is my good fortune to have this conversation with Charley for this book.

Charley, age 27 in 1953, working in a sporting goods store while going to college

Tale of The Tape
Charles "Charley" French

Engineer and Champion Triathlete

World War II veteran aboard the U.S. Navy ship that transported U.S. Army General Douglas MacArthur to the Battle of Borneo in 1945.

August 3, 1926, born in Glendale, suburb of St. Louis, Missouri.

Engineer/machinist behind the fabrication of the first aero handlebars invented by Boone Lennon. Nearly undefeated in his age group in triathlons since his first one at age 60. Also competed in other endurance events on foot, on bike, and on skis. Former avid downhill skier and mogul lover.

At age 17: 5'7", 135 pounds. Was always into sports. Involved in competitive swimming and competitive speed skating as a kid.

Late bloomer. Grew to 5'9" by age 21.

Now in his late 80s, he says he's shrunken a bit to 5'6". Current weight: 146 pounds.

Trains 10 hours per week, including weights and machines. In his 80s, he had to be convinced that strength training would help him and it has.

At age 17 he had no aspirations, except to go into the military service during World War II.

In high school, Charley majored in auto shop, woodshop, and machine shop.

Mother, Mary Whitemore, born early 1900s in St. Louis. She worked in a department store. Died in San Diego in her early 60s.

Father, Charles Sale French, born 1890s in Huntsville, Alabama. Was a salesman for a wholesale paper company. Died in a rest home in his 80s.

Observation by Charley:

"At this age, everything I do gets slower. For a time I thought I wasn't training correctly. I kept reading all this stuff, 'you've got to lift weights when you get older,' and I kept thinking, 'no way, I'll train myself into shape, I'll ride myself into shape. So about five years ago at age 82, I signed myself up at a gym. I had never been to a gym in my life. The trainer at the gym set me up with a program. And after two years, my times went down by 10 percent so I thought, 'oh shit,' I've got to keep doing this."

We connected on Skype and had a bit of trouble making the connection work.

Charley, I'm glad you can hear me, how are you, sir?
"I'm great, how are you, sir?"

Good, I'm in Cannes where it is about 95 degrees and 9:52 at night.
"What are you doing over there?"

I'm working on my book, I am training my cycling, and maintaining my fluency in French. Having spent some 20 years studying the language, I find it helpful not to lose it.
"I go about once per year to visit a friend who owns a house in Uzes, but I can't speak a word of French."

I'd guess that if you stayed here for three years on the senior tour you would have to learn it. I know Greg LeMond once picked up some ability in French.
"Yeah, probably." (Laughs)

How about in World War II. If you had got shipwrecked somewhere in the Philippines, you would have eventually learned something when you were 18, right?
"Yeah, I probably would have. Actually in college, I was a physics major and I found out I'd have to take a language so I switched to engineering." (Laughs)

Too much fear of the left brain. (Laughs all around) That's not very daring.

So, the idea of this book: You, Charley, are in the minority of people who are athletes who are still performing fitness late in life. If you look at the 1940s photos of people going into World War II, and then you look at them five and seven decades later, you see that many of them were 150, 160 pounds going into the war and now they're 250 pounds and use a walker. Along the way, something happened. I'm trying to chronicle what happened to regular people and to athletes after they left their physically demanding career. Out of the folks who are former military and former athletes, about 90 percent are not fit because they are no longer pursuing fitness. Basically, I am asking each person I interview how and why they are fit, and why they think the rest of the people they know are either driven or not driven to pursue fitness?

We even see children these days leaving the playground's climbing apparatuses, which are structures that require high agility and strength, and moving to the lesser demanding exercises. Then, with increasing caloric intake—especially junk food—they experience what's known as creeping obesity. They may gain a pound a month and soon they're obese. This problem has become a pandemic. This didn't really happen in the old days.

"No, not at all."

Do you have any kids?

"I had two kids and my wife had two kids from a previous marriage. I first got married at 23. And the second time I got married I was in my 40s. Both of my own kids were born in the 1950s. My wife is a former competitive tennis player. She was diagnosed with nerve damage in her back and after several unsuccessful surgeries, she is alive but not well. She spends most of her time in pain or in numbness in the bedroom."

That's got to be the hardest existence, for an athlete or for anyone.

"She's been that way for 15 years. It's the hardest thing. She wants to do things but when she does venture up, the pain is excruciating and she pays the price. Still, she stays up walking around more than she should just to help her mind."

That's a tough situation. My gosh ... I'll say a prayer for her ...

Now, I've got to ask something about your age and how it relates to your kids. Your kids are all middle age and you're a senior. Can any of your kids beat you in any of your sports?

"Nope. They're both fit. My son is a good athlete and he surfs a lot. He's a house painter. When the surf's up, the paint brush goes down. Same thing for snow in the hills. None of my kids can outdo me in my endurance sports."

Let me ask you about your ancestors. Were any of your grandparents fit?

"The grandparents on my mother's side were fairly active and in shape. They lived into their 80s and 90s. They lived in St. Louis and eventually moved to San Diego in their retirement."

What were you like as a kid?

"I was very independent. My mother, who was single at the time, had had enough of me. When I signed up for the Navy at age 17, I had to get my mother's signature. When I brought her the form, she said, 'Where do I sign?' She was happy to get rid of me. At that time, at least in the United States, everybody wanted to be in the war. Many wanted to be in the service to go kill the enemy. When I was trying to get into the Navy, you had to take a test because they had more people signing up than they had room for. At the time, I had very little money. In Santa Monica, California, where I was at the time, my job was setting pins at a bowling alley. I also worked in a gas station while I was going to high school. I wanted to be in the war ... be part of it."

Are any of your siblings still with us?

"My oldest sister, Mary Falzone, died about two years ago. She was about 86. I have another sister, Barbara Trough, who is still alive, living in Laguna, California—she's 89. And she's still pretty active."

Charley at age 60, his sister Barbara Traugh
(now 89), and her daughter

What social status was your family when you grew up?

"I guess we were lower-middle class. We had a big home in Glendale, Missouri and both of my parents had cars. In those days, people didn't travel or go to Europe or anything, but we were always comfortable. We were never hungry for clothes or food or anything like that."

Do you remember any hardships that you heard about either through extended family or through friends' families during the Depression?

"No, I was too young. By the time I started figuring out life at all, it was in the '30s. My father had quite a bit of money and lost it all in the Depression. He was sort of on the way back up in the '30s as I grew up."

Did your father ever give you advice about finances and investments as you grew up?

"No, he was the typical Willy Lowman of the sales people. He just loved to sell and that's all there was to him." (Laughs)

How about any advice about life?

"No, I never got any advice from him and my mother … there was no advice, there was just guidance. She was the one who was athletic and liked to swim and speed skate and be involved in physical activities. There were really never any talks, she just led by example."

Where did you speed skate?

"In St. Louis. They had an indoor rink that specialized in speed skating. And we'd go there three of four days per week. And in the winter, we'd also go to races outdoors on frozen lakes. This was my two sisters, me, and my mother. My mother wasn't competing, just her kids were."

Were there any photos or stories of your father doing sports when he was young?

"No sports that I can recall. My father was in World War I, and he used to tell me bedtime stories when I was very young. He'd tell me stories of being in the Navy and in the war, and things like that."

Was there any smoking or drinking in your family?

"Yeah, both of them. My father was an alcoholic. He took the cure a couple of times then for the last 20 years of his life he was dry. My mother wasn't always an alcoholic, but she always drank. It probably had something to do with the early end of her life. She also smoked."

Did you smoke?

"Nah. My mother used to say, 'If you want to smoke, just come in and smoke with me.' Since there was no allure of getting away with anything, and I knew I could do it whenever I felt like it, it didn't appeal to me. I went into the Navy, and everybody smoked, and I think I smoked for two weeks and then decided it was dumb and haven't smoked since. I didn't stop for health reasons, I just thought I didn't need it."

I just spoke with a friend of mine and learned about how her father— who had recently died of lung problems—had originally become hooked on smoking. He was Algerian and wound up fighting with the French side in the war against Algeria. What happened is that when he was in training in France, they completed their very tough training and then had five weeks of stagnation before they were shipped out from where they were. They didn't have any books and this was before the popularity of TV. He said there was nothing to do so everybody just hung around. Someone had some cigarettes and then the military provided more. So they all smoked nonstop. If I were in a situation like that and I didn't have any books, I don't know what I would do.

"It's like when I was in the Navy, aboard ship. Nobody read books. Nobody. This was the summer of 1944 when I was assigned to a ship. There were 1,200 guys on ship and a lot of time there was nothing to do, and you didn't see anybody reading. When I went into the Navy, my job aboard ship was a machinist, so I worked in the machine shop and made all the parts the Navy wanted. I had no intellectual interests at all. When I came out of the service, I had to go back to junior college to take a couple of courses so I could graduate from high school. So, I started with that and just kept going. The more classes I took, the more immersed I got into books and learning."

When you were in the machine shop, was it loud?

"During the War, I was on a light cruiser—The USS Cleveland. Almost no matter where you are, you have air being pumped into all of the rooms so all you can hear are fans blowing. And that never stopped whether you were in port or at sea. And when you are underway, you can feel the propellers and you can feel the engine. After a couple of months, you don't even think about it anymore."

What type of personality are you?

"I've always been quiet. When I was younger, I was quite an introvert. I'd remember every person in that room and I would never say a word. As I got older, I gradually gained self-confidence. Now I have no inferiority complex at all and probably haven't had one for 20 or 30 years. That personality was perfect for my beginning as a machinist and later an engineer. I was into the mechanical side … I liked to create things and work on things."

Did you have a lot of energy?

"I've always had a lot of energy. Even though I'm slowing down, I still enjoy doing things and I still enjoy travelling … to a lesser extent than I used to. My outlook has been affected by aging—I'm more tolerant of things now. When I was younger, I saw no reason to be tolerant of anything. I don't think of how or why or where I came from, for me, I just think this life sort of happened. I certainly didn't have a lot of goals when I was 17."

Charley French
Age 86
World Champion
Asiago Italy

How did your direction come to you?

"When I got through with college, I sort of started having ideas that it would be nice to do something to make some money. Fortunately, I liked engineering and I like to build things and create things ... and improve things. Even today, the things I'm around, I want them to work, and I want them to be neat and orderly."

If you wound up tomorrow on an island, just like they were in World War II, with no modern anything, and all you had was a machete ... and they had tons of bamboo on the island and wild boar and other critters running around, do you think you could survive?

(Laughs) "Probably not. I could certainly build a lean-to to live in. And I could certainly kill animals and if I could have a fire to cook them I probably wouldn't starve to death. But I guess I could be able to get by in situations without a lot of amenities."

I had been picturing you chopping down some bamboo and building an igloo-looking thing within three days.

"Well, that could happen."

Could you share a bit of the triathlete handlebar genesis?

"When I was racing bicycles here in Ketchum, Idaho, one of the guys that was a bike racer had won the national championships a couple of times and was a very good racer. He also happened to be a ski coach for the Alpine ski team in Sun Valley, Idaho. His name was Boone Lennon. He recognized that when they took the Alpine ski racers and put them in a wind tunnel, he realized the importance of the tuck for the aerodynamics. So when he was racing, he started thinking about that. He thought, an Alpine ski racer goes into the wind tunnel for a 60-second race, and a cyclist is in a time trial for over an hour. So he started thinking about getting a bicyclist more aerodynamic.

(For bike racing, first came the low racing handlebars. Then the funny low-drag helmets came at about the same time as the aerobars Charley helped develop.)

"So he came up with the idea of making these aerobars which would drop your upper body horizontal to the ground to make a smaller envelope into the wind. He made a set of bars out of wood that almost looked like a toilet seat. And we'd take U-bolts and bolt them onto the handlebars. He and I got together and we went to this long downhill place. And we rolled down together, side by side, we were about the same height and weight. Without pedaling, we'd both wind up at the bottom at the same time. Then we put the bars on his bike and we did the experiment again, and he finished about six bike lengths ahead of me."

Presto, the bars are a success!

"Proof positive. Then we put the bars on my bike, and did the same thing, and I wound up six bike lengths ahead of him. And we said, 'Wow, this will work.' So that's how it started. We didn't have the money for a wind tunnel or anything like that so we just started making prototypes using conduit, EMT thin-wall conduit, and we'd take a conduit bender and we'd bend all these different shapes. And we bent up a couple sets of bars and I took one pair and rode in the Ironman Hawaii, and I gave another pair to a friend of mine and that was the first time they were used in competition. Luckily I happened to win my age group in the Ironman and set a new age-group record."

What year was that?

"1986. So, then, the next year, we started calling pro triathletes asking them if they wanted to try these bars, and we sent them all the data, all the tests we'd run, and we got one guy to try them. The next weekend they had another pro triathlon. And on the bike leg, the guy that had them beat four other guys he'd never beaten before. So the next Monday we got calls from three of those four triathletes—'Gotta have a pair.' Each Monday after a triathlon we'd get another call. By the end of the year, every pro had a pair on his bike. And that's when Dave Scott, the world champion at the time, started using them. That was in 1987."

What happened then?

"A couple of years later, Boone convinced Greg LeMond to try them in the Tour de France."

Riding up Mount Ventoux, France with a friend in 2012

This must have been for LeMond's 1989 win when he came back from the hunting accident and beat Laurent Fignon [in the final time trial to win the tour by eight seconds, again, the closest Tour de France victory in history]."

"Yep. That was it. Boone was over in France trying to get LeMond to use the bars and LeMond agreed to use them. So I bent up some bars and sent them over and Boone put them on Greg's bike and he won."

That's one of the best video clips in the history of the televised Tour de France … that final minute of Greg riding to victory, going all out.

"Yeah, I saw it the other night while watching the Tour on TV. Anyway, the next year we met Greg in a wind tunnel in Texas where we were doing some testing. And Lance Armstrong came down. He was a triathlete at the time. He of course lived in Texas. And he came to the wind tunnel and met Greg for the first time. That was before Armstrong became a pure cyclist and before he got cancer."

Was it harder to convince the pure cyclists to try things?

"It was. The triathletes would try anything new because they didn't have any history. But, at the time, bike racers wouldn't easily try anything new. It was as if the attitude was if it hadn't been in the industry for 20 years, they didn't want to look at it. Even when the triathletes were winning with the aerobars, the bike guys still wouldn't try them. When Greg LeMond won the tour, everything changed."

So you bent them. You mean just like conduit?

"Yeah, with a tube bender. We thought about using carbon fiber and other materials but then thought it would be too expensive so we stuck with aluminum. At that point, Boone agreed to sign everything over to Scott USA—the ski company. He got a patent and sold the patent rights to Scott and helped them in developing all the parts and helped in marketing—going to all the races and the Tour de France to get people to use the bars."

Sounds like a good business plan.

"It was. That patent was never voided. Everyone who wanted to make those bars had to pay Scott a royalty. There's the story of a patent that worked." (Laughs)

Where did you fit in to the invention?

"I just helped Boone. Boone had the idea and he had a lot more bike racing experience. So we would sort of jointly work on the details of the shapes and designs. And I would help him work out the better materials to use."

So you were more like a hired gun who was paid for your services with no royalties?

"Yeah. I think that over my time working at Scott USA, I had five or six patents on different things we did—on goggles, on ski poles, on boots—and I'd get a dollar for the patent. Most of them didn't make any money, but Boone's did. His agreement with Scott was that he'd get a royalty so he did okay."

So you're saying you got a dollar and that's it?

"Yeah, that's it. When you're working for a company, it's a company patent. They have put up all of the money for all of the expenses, that's how it goes. For me, it was just a job. Probably only one percent of the patents ever issued wind up making any money."

Jumping back to your family and your dad who was in sales, was your dad gone a lot?

"My parents separated when I was 10 years old. My dad moved to St. Louis, downtown, and we stayed in the house in Glendale. And we'd see him every week or two on the weekends. In the summer, my mother would take us to the river on the weekend where we could go swimming or canoeing—she was the motivator for being out doing things."

Was your father still drinking?

"At that time, during their separation, my father was drinking quite a bit. In the daytime, I suspect he was fine."

Do you recall having to ever restrain him or help him up?

"I remember one time my sisters were in a play in grammar school and he came to the play and he came into the theatre room and he was drunk and he essentially stopped the play."

Did he walk a lot and was he thin?

"I never saw him walking or doing any exercise. He was thin. In that day and age, basically everybody was thin. When he got into his 60s, he got a little bit of a pot belly. He never got fat; he was maybe 15 pounds overweight."

The subject of my first book—"Sedentary Nation"—has sections that discuss our spending too much time in chairs, how that causes us to slouch, and inevitably breaks us down. When you're working in your machine shop are you standing?

"Most of the time. At one point I was running a design group and all of the young guys would always sit at the drawing tables. The old guys always stood at the drawing tables. (Laughs) I guess since I never sat down while I was working, I never grew into doing it. The younger generation prefer to sit. It's just a different way they have."

I just finished reading a book called "Paleo Fantasy" by professor Marlene Zuk. She mentions that the pendulum has swung, incorrectly perhaps, a little too far in thinking a certain way about the hunter-gatherers. I agree with lots that she says. [But her book is itself slanted. She pulls miscellaneous quotes off blogs and basically tries to discount some of the more outlandish statements.] I like to emphasize that our current is evolution is perhaps a devolution like the Romans when they neared their collapse … illnesses of affluence and the like. They had so much wealth for a time that they stopped being strong, hardy people.

I tend to think the devolution merits a lot of prayers but I don't think, unless there is some drastic change of consciousness, that I or any other Jack LaLanne devotees can actually stop it.

"Yeah, I agree. For me it's not so much based on history but on observation. The hard part is the new lifestyle and working scenarios. Earlier, people didn't have the luxury of not having to go out and do things. If they wanted to work or eat, they had to go out and do things. They had to be active to survive. Every year, we can do less and less and still survive. We can sit and watch and email and we don't have to get up for much. How do you turn that around? With all of the conveniences we have, it gets harder and harder to get people off their rear ends to go do something. You and I who have the energy level to want to go do something, that's an energy level that you are given, you can't create it. You don't go out and buy it or decide, 'Tomorrow I am going to be energetic.' I don't think that the percentage of people who have that energy are going to change over time."

You've seen the aging cyclists, LeMond has put on a lot of weight, and Eddy Merckx [Belgian champion of five Tours de France] looks more like an ex-ruby player than a cyclist.

"It's interesting that you see some of these ex-famous athletes and some of them go to seed. A few of them hang in there, like Miguel Indurain who still looked pretty fit when I saw him recently. I have a friend who was a swim coach at Stanford for 20 years and he was also on the water polo Olympic team and he is still involved with a lot of swim stuff at Stanford. And we'd go to an alumni event and it's amazing the number of ex-swimmers who are still fit. Most of them seemed to stay active."

(As we continued the conversation, we learned that they were fit because they were still competing and training. We still don't know if aging former swimmers are maintaining fitness any better than other former athletes. My only guess is they would have fewer chronic injuries than any other major high school or college sport. Swimming is not an impact and shock sport. Even the racing dive is not a hard impact compared to a handspring or a sliding tackle in soccer or a slide into third base.)

When you go by a hospital, Charley, you see how many super-sized people work there. It's interesting that such a large number of obese people—perhaps even greater than the national average—work in what some consider wellness. I think it's more accurate to suggest that a hospital has more of a recent tradition of being better at handling sick patient care than prevention and wellness issues."

"Up here in the Sun Valley area, almost everyone is involved in sports. If you go to an evening event, it's all people talk about. You know, 'What did you do today? Where did you ride, where did you ski?' You almost don't see obese people. But when you go to the hospital in town, half the people working there are fully obese. One, you say, why would you hire people like that when you're in a health environment? In the cities nearby, you see the same things. You ask yourself, 'How can they do that?' So, for the most part, the only fat people we have up here, are all involved in the hospital." (Laughs)

Where do those people come from … out of the area?

"I don't know. Unfortunately, it's one of the areas where I don't have much tolerance. I just look at fat people and it bothers me that they could be that way. I can't understand how anybody could let themselves get in that kind of shape."

This leads to the line between political correctness and a live-and-let-live type of attitude Then there's the social contract of taking care of oneself, helping others, as well as not creating a burden for society and not modeling poor behavior for kids.

"We all realize what a problem it's becoming and it's only going to get worse. And you and I end up paying for it since they wind up requiring extra medical care and so on. You fly on an airplane and the amount of fuel is based on the amount of weight on board. So we're paying for fat people to fly."

Can you talk about your physicality?

"You know, I never developed big muscles. Some athletes don't look like anything special. My legs get developed because I do so much of that type of work—running and biking, but the rest of my body is just totally average."

Can you comment on the champion triathletes from the 1980s and '90s—Dave Scott and Mark Allen?

"They're both pretty lean builds. Similar builds, Dave probably had an extra seven or eight pounds on Mark. Talking about training, and pain and overcoming it, those guys, when they finish an Ironman, they're in the I.V. tent for hours getting pumped back up. I mean they can hurt their bodies to a substantial level ... and that's why they win. It's unbelievable how they can tolerate pain. And it's probably not doing their bodies a whole lot of good."

Yeah, free radicals, muscular damage, joint and tissue damage, etc. So, you're saying that Mark Allen pushed himself beyond the human limit?

"Yeah, Mark Allen was bleeding and had all kinds of stuff going on at the end of a couple of these races. And he was a guy who was really into the mental side of the sport, much more than Dave was. Mark was a Zen guy and he would just block stuff out and just kept going. It was almost scary. And, as far as I know, he is still healthy. I read that they're both still doing stuff, Dave and Mark. I used to know Dave's father and used to compete against him. He was one of the first triathletes and founders of the triathlon organization and helped organize the sport. I haven't spoken to him in about a year. The last I heard, Dave's father had moved to Reno and had started playing golf and quit competing in triathlons."

When you started competing in triathlons in your 60s, were you a champion?

"Yeah. When I turned 60 and went into the Ironman, I got in on the lottery and didn't have to qualify. I started training in April for the race in October. And I had every day written down … what I was going to do. And I trained really hard. I won my age group there. And in every triathlon since then, I've won my age group I think every time except three times."

How much do you think was your engineering planning of what to do versus just your perfect physique for the sport, endurance, and the way your process fluids, etc.?

"I think a lot of it was just the body you end up with and not screwing up in the training. The training for the Ironman that I did, nobody does today. I think I rode like 350 miles in my peak week and I ran 65 miles and swam … I don't know how many thousands of yards I swam. In those days it was mega miles for everything. And now guys are doing much lower volume but higher intensity. And they're going faster in the races." (We both laughed)

*Engineer and Elite Triathlete Charley French
with the handlebars he helped deisgn.
(Photo courtesy of Scott USA)*

You did a lot of pushing the envelope, you won, but you would have done it differently had you known ...

"Well, yeah. But that's when Scott Molina and Mike Pigg and Dave Scott and all these guys were the training gurus ... and it was all mega miles for everything. One thing I learned by doing three different sports is you have different pain levels for each sport. Because of bike racing, you have to learn to live with pain. Because in a bike race, you cannot afford to get dropped [left by the group you are with or the leaders]."

You can't just slow down and walk like you can with running. You could push the bike, but uphill pushing is no piece of cake. Pushing a bike in general is an uncomfortable position to be in.

"When the peloton [pack of riders] speeds up, no matter how tired you are, no matter how much you hurt, you gotta go, you gotta stay with 'em. Otherwise you're gonna be out there pedaling 60 miles by yourself. So, you learn to live with pain."

What about the other legs of the triathlon?

"Running and swimming. When it starts to hurt, I slow down. In triathlons, you see pure runners that can run through this pain level like I can do in biking. Ex- swimmers, the same thing. They can go through a huge amount of pain in the water. As you age, you learn what these levels are. Normally, you just can't get through 'em. When you're younger you can probably train yourself to go higher and higher into these uncomfortable levels. But at this point in my life and for the last 20 years, when it starts hurting in running and swimming, I slow down."

What lessons would you like to pass on to future generations about life in general, emotions, and family, and doing the right thing by mankind?

"For me, it's about if you have goals. And if you're lucky enough that your body is guided by goals. If it's to get up in the morning and have breakfast, to work out, to go to a movie at night, or go on a race, or go on a trip … you've always got something to look forward to. And you don't realize it, but there are a lot of people that have nothing to look forward to. They hate to go to work, they come home and turn on the T.V., and open a beer, you know, and the next day's the same. They have no reason to want to do anything. And I don't know how they begin, what starts that pattern. It's sort of like what body you end up with and what mind you end up with. You can only do so much with it. Fortunately, I've been born with this energy level that allows me to want to go out and keep doing stuff."

It's so good that your mind is set in that way. Some are programmed to stay sitting inside.

"Even when I'm hurt and can't do anything, I've got to go for a walk. I've got to do something. I can't just sit here. I can read for two or three hours, but I've got to get up and do something. I'm glad I have these attributes that are there. I don't think you can do a lot to create them or increase them. We know people we went to high school with and they're still living in the same town and working for the two weeks of vacation a year and we say, 'Phew, I'm glad I'm not them.' What made us relocate to where we are today? Some of it's not necessarily being smart but maybe having different curiosities, and energy levels, and being willing to take a chance."

There's nothing wrong with us praying for the current generation and the future generations and trying to create a positive energy out there in the world with every breath we take.

"Sure, that's good."

CHARLEY FRENCH
Age 78
WORLD CHAMPION TRIATHLETE
Tri World Championship
New Zealand

Are you going to donate your body to science?
   "If anybody wants it, they can have it."

So there it is, the end of the interview with the eldest aging athlete thus far interviewed for this project. He says,
   "… And dumb enough to still be doing it."

But, it's better than flipping channels.
   "True."

§ § §

   In terms of athletic drive towards victory, Charley's story has to be the most amazing single-person story of "The Aging Athlete." It's almost unfathomable what this aging athlete has been able to accomplish. Can you imagine finishing—and winning—extreme endurance events in your 80s? Can you imagine outdoing your kids and even your grandkids at some physical feats at that age?

   Charley is not only the most seasoned aging athlete thus far interviewed for the book, he's the most prolific. WWII, for many of Charley's era, was the defining moment of a lifetime. Charley started there and added on yearly battles, if you can call them that, more than six decades worth. They were mostly battles against himself. He got through the paved roads, through the Pacific waves, through the dusty trails, and through the snow-filled paths. And, as a true engineer, he always had a plan.

Chapter 6

The Civil Rights Game in Bama

"The old lessons (work, self-discipline, sacrifice, teamwork, fighting to achieve) aren't being taught by many people other than football coaches these days. The football coach has a captive audience and can teach these lessons because the communication lines between himself and his players are wider open than between kids and parents. We better teach these lessons or else the country's future population will be made up of a majority of crooks, drug addicts, or people on relief."

—Paul "Bear" Bryant, legendary Alabama Football Coach

When you think of someone nicknamed "Bear," what might come to mind is a big ole hairy lovable "aw shucks" type, that is to say, everyone but a somewhat serious type man on a mission that was Paul "Bear" Bryant. Though he benched and reprimanded his athletes for drinking and partying—most notably two elite athletes who at different times ran his on-field offense, Joe Namath and Kenny Stabler—he himself was an alcoholic who drank nearly every day and wound up dying a short 28 days after his retirement from coaching at age 69.

Alcoholism and being a drinker versus a drunk are interesting questions to consider. I include some pondering on this subject since alcoholism is a big part of the life of most families—especially the families of aging athletes. Some research has shown that athletes drink more than non athletes. Even when they're done with their competitive years, if they're still in pain, if they're depressed or bored, they may be drinking more than the general population. There is a tendency of people in pain to drink more to mask the pain.

Some people—as George Thorogood sings—like to "drink alone." At times, Bear Bryant had a drinking pal—a former jockey who hung out at the race tracks with Bear in the coach's off season. According to some, Bear was a functioning drinker—aka functioning alcoholic. His friend, Bill, was too for a time until it got to a point where everyone distanced themselves from Bill. That was because Bill had become a non-functioning alcoholic—aka a drunk.

I ran across an article by Bill's grandson—Spencer Hall. (Net search "College Coaches, Drinking, And The Two Men At The Rail," 2011, by Spencer Hall) In his well-written piece, Hall describes some of the real-world aspects of a "drinking man." He concludes by saying how Coach Bryant was a drinking man whose wishes mostly came true. I don't know how the coach's wife, Mary, felt about his comportment and serious drinking habit. Perhaps his children, his autobiography, or the film made about him will provide answers.

One question on drinks and drinkers is how do you put the last one down and then take yourself home? Perhaps I'll hear from Spencer, the grandson, on how Bear Bryant got home from his watering holes. It only takes one person who happens to be standing too close to where a car veers off the street—and into a sidewalk, front lawn, or café—and crushes a poor bastard who now happens to be one dead person ... Then, your entire life's legacy changes and they take your name off of buildings, fields, and maybe even remove your bronze statue. You also stand a good chance of getting early retirement in a striped suit or ball and chain or whatever they dress you in when they lock you up. Anyway, here's one absorbing part of Spencer Hall's article:

"Bear Bryant seemed to get more out of drinking than drinking got out of him, the best outcome a chronic drinker can hope for in the end if he's on the heavier end of the spectrum. [See: Winston Churchill.] He could have quit cold turkey and did for a while, but it seemed unnecessary to him. He still did his job, and the rest was an honest deal with time, his body, and mortality."

Bear was a poor kid from a poor town. So were most kids in the early 1900s. My father has often reminded me, things were different in the old days and not always better. Lots of kids were beaten and so were women. My parents saw it all in their own neighborhood of second and third generation families from the New York and New Jersey area. Fortunately for them, there were no beatings in their own nuclear families, but there was a bit of drinking in some of the family. And there was a fair amount of drinking in the neighborhoods and at social events.

In the old days, it was common to see drinking that never stopped. I had the pleasure of interviewing elite duathlon athlete Jack Bianchi. In his 70s, at the time of the interview, Jack mentioned how hard the conditions were and how workers—including some of Jack's uncles—often kept flasks of alcohol in their inside pockets. Is this more of a transgression than what we see today—popping prescription drugs and junk snacking for stress throughout the day?

Bear came from a tough place at a tough time. Kids tended to grow up early in his era. They knew they had to work, stake their claim, help their families, and do their best to get "unpoor." At age 13, he got his nom de plume by actually accepting a challenge to wrestle a bear at a traveling circus, for a dollar a minute. The young kid of English and Irish origins from the outskirts of a small town in southern Arkansas didn't get paid a dime for his trouble. The bear's muzzle came off and before the real furry fellow could take a mouthful of Bryant's hide, Paul did an end run out of the showground, leaving the bear hungry and the gangly kid forever associated with Bear. Another version of the story is the bear bit young Paul in the ear.

From then on this kid who grew into a football player of good size, and eventually a top coach and mentor, was forever known as Bear. With his trademark hound's-tooth hat reassuringly perched on his head (at times matching a blazer oft-associated with the used-car lot—eh hem, "pre-owned"), Bear became whom many sports writers consider the best coach in football history. He went on to win 14 SEC titles, six National Championships, 24 consecutive bowl games, spawned 67 All American Players, and, in 1970, a short seven years after Birmingham Commissioner of Public Safety Bull Conner's beatings and fire houses, integrated Alabama's football team. In that year, a black freshman named Wilbur Jackson began his 4-year record-setting tenure for the Crimson Tide and then went on to a career in the

NFL. Within a few years, one-third of the starters of the Bama team were black.

Football's integrated history takes us back in time to Shelby, Ohio, in 1904. Charles the "Black Cyclone" Folis signed a contract with the Shelby Athletic Club becoming the first African-American to play professional football. There's a lot more history between 1904 and 1973. This end point was the year another black player, Sam "Bam" Cunningham, signed a contract to play for the New England Patriots. A life-size bite of Sam's remarkable story is expressed in a single quote often attributed to Jerry Claiborne, an assistant coach under Bear Bryant at Alabama. In the 1970 Crimson Tide vs. USC game, Cunningham left his cleat marks all over the Alabama defense, running for 135 yards and two touchdowns, helping to crush the Tide 42 to 21. USC went through their second and third stringers in the later part of the game in what could have been an even bigger blowout. After the game, Coach Claiborne made this statement:

"Sam Cunningham did more to integrate Alabama in 60 minutes than Martin Luther King did in 20 years."

As rumor had it, after the game Bear Bryant invited Cunningham to the Alabama locker room and told his team players, "This is what a football player looks like." Although it sounds like typical Coach Bryant lore, Cunningham relates that the humbling story is entirely fiction. There is no doubt though that the inductee to the College Football Hall of Fame and the New England Patriots Hall of Fame, Samuel Lewis Cunningham made more of an impression than his cleat marks on the Alabama football team and its coach on that eventful day. I'm more than excited to have this conversation with Sam for this book.

Sam Cunningham at his Patriots Hall
of Fame induction. (Courtesy of M. Schickler)

Tale of The Tape
Sam "Bam" Cunningham

Football fullback and all-around football player.
Author. Currently runs a business in Longbeach, Calif.

Samuel Lewis Cunningham, born in Santa Barbara, California, on August 15, 1950.

Father: Samuel Cunningham, 1919–1982, worked for the railroads. The mother who raised him starting at age 3: Mabel Cunningham, 1926–1981, worked as a nurse. Wife: Francine was a dancer; daughters: Samandi and Jahmela.

All three of his brothers—A.C., Bruce, and Randall—played Division I college football. His youngest brother, Randall, is listed among the top pro quarterbacks of all time. Randall's wife, Felicity deJager Cunningham, danced ballet in the Dance Theatre of Harlem and is 6 feet tall.

Weight at age 63: 267

Height: 6'3"

Playing weight in the pros: first was 215, then went to 235.

Personality traits: A man of few words that mostly all come out with impact. Not generally subject to vacillating emotions. Goal oriented. Likeable. A smart coach of himself and a great, yet tough big brother for his three younger brothers.

Notable quote: Upon helping his parents retire: "I gave my dad and mom the opportunity to just hang out. I felt blessed to have had the chance to do that for them."

A Most Famous Moment: As third-string fullback in his first game as a sophomore at the collegiate level, USC Head Coach John McKay signaled for him to enter the now famous "Civil Rights Football Game" against Alabama in September of 1970.

Neill Wright, a former P.E. teacher, longtime Santa Barbara school and rec league umpire, and standout baseball player in his youth, was one of Sam's mentors. Neill connected me to Sam's brother, A.C., who connected me to Sam.

Most powerful attribute: "Sam can do a fingers-in-the-mouth whistle so loudly, it'll scare people." A.C. Cunningham.

Sam is a co-author of "Turning of the Tide: How One Game Changed the South." 2006, Center Street.

How does it feel right now being older than your father was when he was a young man, playing catch with you and your brothers?

"Actually it is a little different because I was more active with my kids then my dad was with us and with me. He just kind of watched us; he didn't really play catch with us. My brother Randall works out with his kids—not really works out with them, but he coaches them in football and in track. My dad never did anything like that for me. I got that kind of thing from Coach Bill Van Shack and other guys who watched out for us, and kind of made sure we stayed in line."

Tell me more about your dad?

"He worked for the railroad. He wasn't an athlete. [Sam's next-in-line brother A.C. told me that their dad was a good swimmer who was once known as *The Frog*.] My dad did give me my first two rules: one: never quit. Number two: once you start something, give it everything you have. So if you had a problem with the second rule you just thought about the first rule, so I never quit. Once you started, you couldn't quit, so if you didn't want to do it, don't start. I use the same rules with my kids today. They're pretty simple and they work."

Do you think those rules are as important as physical attributes?

"They are more important. They force you to commit. You could have all the talent in the world, but if you don't commit it won't make the difference. Those rules kept everything in play. Every athlete has to get to a certain point to where they question why they are doing what they are doing. If they never get to that point in their thinking, they frivolously give it away."

How easy would it have been for you to get mad one day when you were young, and just decided to pack it in?

"Well, I think that happened to me in basketball, in high school. At 6'3", I was a center. I was a good basketball player, but wasn't a great basketball player. I could weave around and play defense and had a little offensive game. I just wasn't having any fun, but I knew the rule. I had a choice. So I completed my sophomore season and that was it for me and basketball on an organized team. I loved football and track, but I only liked basketball. It wasn't that I was always having fun playing football, I enjoyed the physicality of it, and more than anything the competing, whatever the sport."

Sam Cunningham in High School

Where did that come from?

Just running around the neighborhood actually. We would run around in the streets and parks and compete. I was a little younger than most of the other guys. I looked up to them. I was trying really hard to keep up and always wanted to do really good. I just kept trying to compete and eventually I got to it."

It seems like you put these rules from your dad down in the level of your soul.

"Well, I mean whenever you enjoy something you remember the things about it and you remember to learn and pay attention to it. In elementary school, I played everything: kickball, basketball, volleyball, football, track, but I just couldn't wait for school to end so I could go do whatever I chose to do. At school and around the neighborhood, I learned a lot about competing. I also learned you had to have a certain nasty streak to you if you wanted to rise up a few more levels."

Did you have any friends you were close with who wanted you to cross the line with petty crime or graffiti?

"We didn't have any graffiti stuff, but I always knew if I got caught that my mom and dad were going to kill me. It was apparent early on that if you do something wrong you will suffer the consequences. They would just discipline me. Whenever I was confronted with something that was wrong, I knew in my heart it was wrong. I grew up not wanting to embarrass them, period."

Why do you think that the elite private college USC picked you when you were young?

"It may have been because I was a relatively nice kid. I wasn't overly disrespectful. I wasn't of that nature. I was taught well by my mom and dad, and my aunts and uncles and the many people at school and in the community who helped raise me."

Where was your family from?

"My dad, Samuel Lewis Cunningham, Sr., was born in Texas in 1919. He is not alive anymore. My mom was also born in Texas. She passed away when I was three. My step mom, Mabel Cunningham raised me. She was born in Chattanooga, Tennessee. A lot of who I am was instilled by her. My dad retired when I started playing pro ball. I felt blessed to have a chance to do that. It gave him and my mom the opportunity to just hang out."

Who else was around when you were growing up?

"My grandmother lived with us a bit at the end of her life. She lived well into her 90s. She was also from Texas."

Did your grandmother tell you anything about food or nutrition, or values from the old days?

"No, not really. But she was pretty tough as a person. I was pretty young. When you're young you don't really hold too much of a conversation with people. She was 97 years old. I just kind of listened and tried to obey, and pay attention."

What is your personality type?

"I'm definitely not a control freak. My brother Randall is a control freak which worked out well for him as a quarterback. My brother Bruce, if he could control anything, would be too, but he can't control anything or anyone. Anthony [also known as A.C.] and I are the most similar and I think it's because of our being close in age."

What was the money like when you went pro in 1973?

"Not very good. Forget that, let's say it was good for the times, but it was not like the money today. When he came in about 12 years after me, my brother Randall made more in one year than I did in my first three years being pro. They promised Steve Young, the quarterback that played after Joe Montana in Frisco, a gazillion dollars. Who knows, he probably got some of it but not all of it."

Young was probably one of the best and he was playing second string to Montana?

"Montana was great. Joe is one of the best finishers on the face of this planet. He and Walsh and that entire organization did something really special. Montana was at Notre Dame when I retired in 1982. He was a great quarterback then, but you didn't see all that was to come just yet. Good a player as I was in college, I had no conception of offense until I went to the pros."

How did you learn all of that stuff?

"I didn't have to worry about fundamentals. I got them at USC, so that was set. I would go to the meetings and tap into the playbook, and always talk with my lineman. So it's just communication. When you spend seven or eight months a year together it becomes a family. The so-so teams don't do that, the really good teams, they do."

Do you mean getting in a different zone, a different level of connection?

"Well, yeah, the best team I had ever played on was in 1972 at USC. Marv Goux was our offense's senior coach. He was born and raised in Santa Barbara and was a team captain during his time playing at USC. When he got into coaching, he brought in anybody from Santa Barbara who was a great prospect and was eligible. In my senior year in 1972, we were really good but not over the top physically. If everyone in our team played together, we were way better than anybody else. But, if we played as individuals, we weren't going to be very good."

How did you get your nickname?

"Two sports writers gave it to me. One gave me 'Sam the Bam' another one changed it to 'Sam Bam.' That was in college, as a freshman."

Did you ever have to be a leader with anything that you did?

"Yeah, with the Patriots, but I led more from behind, not necessarily by conversation. If I did say something, I'd talk to people individually. I was a mainly a leader in how hard I practiced and played. I would always teach the new guys on the team everything I knew. That is just how I grew up. In my subconscious it was always about playing and starting. Being a part of the team is great because everybody makes it happen but, if I'm going to put in all this work, I'm always going to make sure I'm one of the 22 people always out there playing."

Sam and his prized muscle car. This car made it more than a handful of times across the U.S. (courtesy of A.C. Cunningham)

I had the pleasure to interview one of the 20th century's most famous black bodybuilders, Robby Robinson, and he said that being as dark as he is was a problem for him in the '50s and '60s. He shared that most of his other siblings were lighter complected and that even separated him from them. Did you ever wrestle with those kinds of difficulties, things like skin color and people making things tough on you?

"I don't know how I could have lived like that, to have had to deal with what folks had to deal with in the big cities and in the Deep South. It was very fortunate for me not to have had to worry about racism. Even when I landed in the middle of things, in 1970, in Birmingham—things remained calm."

You're talking about the historic game—the first team with a good number of black players to play the University of Alabama at their home field?

"Yup."

Could you describe the scene, you guys got on a plane at LAX and flew to Birmingham?

"Yeah, we flew to Birmingham. It was two years after Dr. King was assassinated. The images of the South on TV were still the dogs and fire hoses. It could have really gone sideways. We had 16 or 17 African-Americans on our team. We went to a walk-thru at Legion Field, which was down the street from where four girls had been killed in a bombing at a black church. I couldn't believe it, but for our walk-thru, it became a big event. Something like 5,000 folks showed up to watch us practice—you know, mainly to see the black players on our team. Strange as it was people got to cheering for us."

In one picture of the game I saw, it looked like you're running through a field of bodies that are all over the place.

"Yeah, that's what it was like at some points. The Alabama players weren't very big or very good. We were a much better team. Our own coach wanted to recruit more African-American players to the team, but the powers that be at that time didn't want to do that. The same thing for Coach Bryant—he had one black freshman and he wanted more black athletes. That game in Alabama wasn't on TV, you had to listen to it on the radio. All I know is at the warm-up the night before, their fans were pretty sure they were going to beat us that next night. Their players felt the same way. Just listening to some of their conversation about the game, they were pretty confident. But, that didn't last for very long."

Did that give you ammunition for wanting to win?

"No, it didn't give me any ammunition because I was just looking at it as another football game. I was looking at it from a different perspective and there were a lot of other things going on in my mind. I wasn't looking at it like this is a black- and-white thing. Because freshmen weren't allowed to travel in those days, this was my first airplane travel and first away game while I was at USC. This was my first varsity football game. If I play and I make a mistake, I may not get to play anymore, so I had more important issues in my mind. Some people thought that we were going to be cannon fodder for the University of Alabama."

Set the stage for the game?

"There turned out to be 65,000 people in the coliseum that night. Football was like a religion in the South, so they asked to have the game played at night because they were actually playing somebody that was good. They figured if we come all the way from the West Coast and they beat us, everything is all fine and dandy in the South. It didn't look good for them at all from the get go. We started running the ball on them. I'm not sure why, but they put me in at fullback, and I only gained about five yards on the first play. The next time I carried the ball I went for 20 and a touchdown."

What was going through your mind after the TD?

"I was running the ball and thinking at the time, is it really supposed to be this easy? Then I got the ball again and kept moving it forward. We ended up winning 42 to 21, playing our second and third stringers for the latter part of the game. Because there wasn't any ESPN at the time, that game kind of laid dormant for almost 30 years before anybody started talking about it again."

Here's an excerpt from the book Sam co-authored with noted sports writer Don Yaeger and others: "USC ran twice off right tackle to get the ball to the four-yard line. Then Jones handed the ball to Cunningham, who bulled his way over from the four. Cunningham was met at the goal line by three Alabama defenders but used his brute strength to push his way in with 49 seconds left to go in the quarter."

Isn't this game the biggest story of your entire athletic career?

"No doubt, but it was just a football game. If I had been born in the Deep South, it would have had a different meaning for me. In Santa Barbara, California, I could always talk and eat with white folks. I had the freedom to be myself and be a kid. Anyway, we played that game, got on a bus, made it to the airport, and came home and started preparing to play for next week. We didn't dwell upon what happened that evening, we just wanted to win a football game."

So you didn't experience any racism? [Bull Conner was by this time in a wheelchair and no longer in public office. But racism was still alive and well in the South. I attended the University of Richmond, Virginia, in the early '80s. The majority of our black students, more than 98 percent, were scholarship athletes. Racism was apparent then and is still alive today.] In 1970, anything could have happened to the players of USC.

"Things could have really gotten out of hand, very easily. They could have mobbed up as we got on the bus. Or thrown things from the stands or yelled at us. But nothing like that happened. It was just a football game with two groups of athletes going at it."

Do you have any idea why things remained calm?

"I heard that the team's leader, Coach Bryant, put out the word for people to keep things under control. That this was a historic occasion and they should behave—not leave a further scar on the South and Alabama."

So what happened after that game laid dormant for all those years?

"Well, what happened is in the late '90s, I lived in Long Beach and Ducker Corey, who wrote for the Press Telegram, did a story on me. He was asking me about the NFL, and asked who the toughest defensive player I'd ever played against was. I said, John Papadakis. He said, 'Why, John didn't play the NFL?' I said because when I came to SC he was a fullback. They made me the fullback and moved him to linebacker, so he was like really, really pissed."

He wanted a piece of you.

"The first time we had to go against each other, John got me good. He busted my chin strap and my helmet slid down and busted a hole on my nose, tried to kill me. From that point on we did that shit to each other every day. We ended up with a profound respect for one another. John read the article by Ducker Corey, and it kind of tugged at his emotions. He was writing a screenplay about the Alabama game and he called me. The screenplay didn't work out so we co-wrote a book in 2006 instead."

So, in the realm of race integration, how did the Alabama-USC game affect football?

"Before that game Bear Bryant was not allowed to recruit more African-American players. After that game, he began recruiting them. Coach Bryant had to guarantee the parents of these young men that he was going to protect them, so it was all on him. The players and many of the people in Alabama ended up having more respect for Coach Bryant than they did for most politicians."

Do you remember when the news hit you that they integrated Alabama and college football?

"Yeah, when I got into the pros I got to meet a lot of players from around the United States that got to play with other black players. It really changed the face and color of the game."

That seems like a great time to be in college, with the draft and Vietnam looming over you, right?

"Yeah, but even then I got a letter from the draft court saying I needed to come down to L.A. and take a physical. I was reading the letter and I didn't have a student deferment. I took the letter to one of my coaches and I said, 'Coach, I'm worried about this letter. I know I'm going to pass this physical, and then I'm going to be gone.' I didn't hear anything for a long time and then in the mail I got a new draft card stating I was a student."

That was your belated student deferment.

"I didn't grow up with the expectation to get a scholarship and go to college. My mom always preached to me about going to college, but I never knew how it was going to happen."

You had good fortune with that. It could have gone the other way. Now, about luck, do football players have something they wear for luck, like baseball players who have their rally caps?

"No, I had a few superstitions though, more so in the pros. I would never polish my shoes. If they had scuffs and scratches on them then I wanted to keep the scuffs and scratches on them. Also, I would never let them clean or polish my helmet."

Could you provide a short summary of your time with the Patriots?

"We were probably the worst sports franchise in Boston during that time. The Boston Bruins had won one Stanley Cup and then won another two years later. The Celtics had won 11 championships and were a dominant force. We were the laggers. The previous year the Patriots were two and 12, so then we came in and lost three in a row. So that means you're terrible."

Did you ever get to meet [the greatest hockey player ever—in the opinion of many, me included, Boston's] Bobby Orr?

"I did. That was pretty cool."

What was Boston like at the time? You had already lived in Los Angeles and now you're on the East Coast, in another big city.

"Boston is a great sports city, but Boston had racial issues. In 1974, they passed Brown vs. Board of Education. I've never seen people go so buck wild in my whole life. That kind of shocked me. So, yeah, Boston was nice, but it was certainly an interesting time to have been there."

Sam and the Patriots gaining territory against the NY Giants (courtesy of A.C. Cunningham)

You mean a black guy from California living in Boston in the 1970s?
"Yeah, exactly. Then again, I came from Santa Barbara where I'd had always gone to school with every culture and had been accepting and whatever issues we had, we worked them out. It wasn't the parents working it out, it was we kids that worked it out. I mean, if you leave kids alone most kids will work it out. They may have some issues, but if the parents get involved it gets real ugly. So that kind of shocked me because here you were looking at where America was born, New England, and you see that it is not what you thought it was. It was a learning process—that's all that was."

[I pointed to a picture on the Web in which Sam looks sharp—in a red blazer. This is the photo in the beginning of the chapter.] What was this?
"That is the Patriots' Hall of Fame in 2010, yeah. I was inducted into that and the USC Hall of Fame all in the same year. At that point, I figured, 'I'm pretty much done now.'" (Laughs)

Who is this? (I pointed to another picture)
"That is Tom Brokaw and Bill Cosby, they were also honored at the College Hall of Fame."

Brokaw played football?
"I don't know if he played, but he was definitely a fan. This is Desmond Howard." (points at a picture). "He played for Michigan, a Heisman Trophy Winner, so he was inducted as well."

Do you have contact with any other interesting cats [I had to try some 1970's lingo] who would be good to interview for The Aging Athlete Project?
"My brother knows Hershel; they actually played together. I don't know Hershel, but I've met him. Randall will probably give

you a call eventually because right now he's running around with his kids and stuff. Hershel is one fit dude."

No doubt about it. He's done as many calisthenics per year as anyone I've read about. What does your current training consist of?

"I do a lot of low-impact activities, a lot of bicycle riding. Because of my knees I'm trying to do a lot of stuff that isn't as impactful on the body."

Inside your mind, do you still see the potential for you to be a slimmer dude?

"I do, but I don't dwell on it very long. But every now and then ..."

Being slim is easier on the bones.

"Yeah, it's hard on my wife. It's hard to convince her that we need to clean up our diet a little bit. She always has the sense that I need to eat, and no, I don't need to eat more."

Where did she come up with that?

"I don't know, she just ..."

Has she known you for a long time?

"We've been together for about 30 years."

Did she know you from your 220-pound days?

"No, she knew me from my 235 days, in the pros. But that was when I could eat what I wanted to eat and then burn it off. But I can't do that anymore. So now I take a little bit more control of it."

You know it's harder for surgery to get in?

"Yeah, because of the layers of fat."

And the recovery is tougher. And the other thing is that fat stores our toxins. A lot of our food is full of toxins.

"Yeah it's a whole different deal … I mean my brother Bruce, he's gotta be on a diet. He was also a top athlete and he's now a big guy. Bruce's son, who is 31, probably needs to be on a diet. He's a young man and I know I wasn't that big when I was his age."

It's not easy for some people to say no. Have you fasted before?

"I have, yeah."

Just for your own health reasons or religious …?

"Just because I wanted to do it—no religious impact. Although every now and then I talk about fasting for lent but that's like really long."

But you have done some things in your life that were harder than fasting. And most of those things have always been rewarding, weren't they?

"Yes, to a large extent."

Kids think life is so hard sometimes. And, without a doubt, it is hard on them—being cooped up in school all day, and then being in organized activities or being bossed around in the afternoon. They want a release. When I talk to junior high kids that are hinting about getting into that partying mood, I have a question I ask them. I say, "You really want to be messed up? You really want to lose all your inhibitions? Okay, here's what you do, stay up all night. It works, you'll laugh yourself silly.

"That's great. I love it. You didn't have to do any substances to get really lost. Some kids weren't really good leaders or smart followers. They would just follow and do whatever the group did. Fortunately, I wasn't one of those kids when I was young and still to this day. I kind of just did my own thing."

You didn't sneak out of the house or anything?

"If I did it's because I wanted to. (Laughs) It wasn't because someone else said to come out."

No peer pressure.

"Exactly, no peer pressure; I did things because I wanted to. I've always been able to be a little different, and then follow my own mind. With doing that, I was always ready to accept any consequences that came with that as well."

Now it brings us to Big Sam at age 63. He's a bit bigger than Sam "Bam," right?

"That's true."

Okay. This is where we get into the older Tale of The Tape. How heavy are you now?

"About 267."

So that's about 32 pounds over your final Sam "Bam" days. When is the last time you were in a state where you thought you were pretty darn fit?

"Probably when I was riding marathon distances on my bike. I'd take off and ride maybe 25 or 30 miles and I'd have to pace myself for a certain time and keep a certain speed. So that was probably the time I was the most fit. That was about three or four years ago. I haven't really been riding as much lately. There's no good reason for it. I've been trying to get my daughter to ride with me because she needs to lose some weight. So I'm trying to get her to just jump on a bike and ride with me. Once you get out there enough times it just becomes normal—a routine."

You know the word euphoria?

"Sure."

In Greek the word means healthy. So they associated health with feeling good or great. Like right now, I feel super. Because I was blessed to do a two-hour fitness thing this morning. I ran up Tunnel Road this morning at five A.M. in the fog. Not low fog, but there was a lot of fog in the trees and up higher. The cars could still easily see me. At the half-way point, I stopped and did one of my Maintenance Workouts—kind of like Jack LaLanne meets Bruce Lee. It was a very special morning.

"Sounds pretty cool."

It was. That's one of the main things that keeps me going—both mentally and physically. I get something like that in a few times per week. I used to be at Goleta Beach maybe four or five mornings per week when I lived out that way.

"Very cool."

Now, as I've mentioned, the body I got was basically Gilligan's. I've just put some more meat on it with good food and sleep and some hard work. The brain I have is wired for doing hard stuff. If I could have only had your body, I would have been like BAM!

(Smiles) "Then you'd have knees like me—messed up."

That's another thing to consider.

"Yeah, I have to also realize that my knees are not able to do a lot of the things I used to do. That's part of being a smart aging athlete."

Good point. I used to run a lot. I've been running less with each year. I told my sweetheart, a German nurse, that I'm going to start doing more biking because it's easier on the joints. I got her a nice bike, but she hasn't quite gotten used to it yet. Hopefully, with time ...

"I used to ride a long time up here in the Santa Barbara canyons and on Foothill Drive a lot. Biking is how I used to get ready for the NFL season. It was less wear and tear on my knees."

When you were a pro, where did you live in Santa Barbara?

"I lived in the L.A. area, but I'd come up here and stay with my family and bring my bike and I'd take off in the morning, then I'd come back later in that afternoon. I'd go catch up with some of my boys and we'd ride some more during the afternoon."

Were you single at the time?

"Yeah, I didn't get married until '83. So, yeah, I was single during that time."

You got married right after your pro career?

"Yeah, I was single my whole pro career."

And you focused like 80 percent on football?

"Yeah."

How about church?

"I was always spiritual, in my own way. I would go to church but I wasn't born again or anything like that. But I was always spiritual and I always knew that most of what I did was a blessing. I just felt like I was in the right position at the right time, and just blessed. That probably helped towards the end because when football became too serious and no longer any fun, I was at peace with not doing it anymore."

What year was this, you think? (I pointed at a picture of Sam in uniform, with helmet in his hand, with a bigger afro haircut. Not that big, not Dr. J big, but bigger than his normal look.)

"Probably '79 because I didn't play in '80. So that might have been '79, towards the winter, because I would always grow my hair out in the winter."

So as I told your brother A.C., the reason I started this book was because of a local surgeon here in Santa Barbara. He's a fourth-generation orthopedic surgeon, which means his ancestor was sewing up bodies in the Civil War era. His name is Dr. Bill Gallivan and he played Rugby at Temple University. He knew I wrote the book called "Sedentary Nation," about the history of movement in America and even before, all the way back to the hunters-gatherers.

What I said was that everybody was moving in the old days and even the industrial workers, like my ancestors who worked in the industries near New York City, were walking to the subway and sometimes to save a nickel they wouldn't take the streetcar, they would walk the entire distance home. Then all of a sudden in the '70s we really became sedentary, convenience stores and fast foods really became entrenched. To top it off, we got laced with corn syrup, which floods our systems and our brain responds without recognizing that our system is full. So not only are we drinking this high calorie stuff, but we're also thinking, Okay, I can eat another plateful. The plates when our grandparents were around were much smaller. In the '80s, plates became bigger, and food became a lot mushier and full of toxins. So think about how many extra calories our bodies are receiving in our era and then the fact that there are more people who are not moving as much. So it really just hit us like a baseball bat. And now we're super-sized and sedentary.

"Well, yeah, but it's also the computers, the cell phones, and the video games, and other things these days that you just sit and watch, like TV. My mom used to call the TV the 'idiot box.' She wouldn't force us, but we were always outside."

Agreed. Your mom was right. So, anyway, Dr. Gallivan gave me the idea to write a book on the subject of the aging athlete. You used to be the world's top at what you did and now you have to take care of yourself. Like many other football players who have injuries or have some other issues that resulted from all of their years of heavy-duty training and competition. They have problems to deal with.

"Yep."

How often do you stretch?

"Every day."

Stretching keeps us functional. It also keeps our bodies and minds ready to lift what we need to lift and help others lift what they need lifted ... Have you ever hit a roadblock?

"Yeah, I have. Sometimes it's me who gets in the way of myself."

Of yourself?

"Yeah. So sometimes, well, I have always looked at things spiritually. So I would try to get out of the way, and let it happen. If it happens, it happens. If it doesn't, it doesn't. But whenever I push too hard, that is when (troublesome) things start happening. So I kind of just let it work itself out."

Don't push too hard: That's a great line for an aging athlete to hear. Also, don't sit around too long.

"Yeah."

Our grandparents were always moving. Now, in the current generation, we're not moving much, how did that happen?

"Because cars, planes, gardeners, maids, are the accepted forms of affluence and everybody wants to be affluent. Nobody wants to work as hard as our grandparents worked. They will just pay somebody."

What is fun for you now?

"I like being outdoors. I gained that from just being in Santa Barbara. I still do and I appreciate that. It comes from growing up and having a very different upbringing here. I like to ride a bike, throw it on the bus, ride on the bus to a location, get off, and ride."

What would you do if you had a chance to speak at a Senate hearing that could change the way we do things?

"Well, I truly believe they are not taking care of the individuals or the citizens that have disabilities and health care issues. I've done a lot of work with disabled kids and diabetic kids, and cancer kids and stuff, and that tugs at my heart strings more than anything. There seems to be a ton of money being spent on a lot of different things, especially the wars. It may never end. There might always be a conflict somewhere. We seem to be always trying to be the big power abroad and we have our own issues here."

*Do people recognize you or know you now, like when you put your
bike on the front rack of the bus and you hop on, and take a bus ride
with them?*

"No, I'm just another big black guy who is on the bus with
them. (Laughs) I may have on something that says like USC or
Patriots or something, but they don't really know who I am. I wore
a face mask all of those years. And now I'm old."

*My friend and Sam's friend, Neill Wright, hugs Sam, who made the trip for Neill's
induction into the Santa Barbara High School Hall of Fame. Neill was a standout
baseball player in the '40s and '50s and was Santa Barbara High's first black
QB. He umpired in the area for over four decades. (courtesy of Neill Wright)*

Do you have some parting words for our readers?

"I would like to thank Sifu Slim for the opportunity to walk
down memory lane and just talk about some of the things that
I have had the extreme opportunity to have been a part of. As a
young kid I don't think I would have ever have known that my
journey would be this wonderful. I had the opportunity to grow
up with a lot of great people and live in a wonderful city and grow

into the person I am now, able to pass on my lessons and beliefs. It's been fun. It's been a lot of lessons learned. It's always great to be a part of something and be able to pass things on, because when you pass it on, it gives people the opportunity to put their own little spin on it. Thank you, Sifu, take it to the people and see what they think!"

Thank you, Sam, this conversation has been interesting and eye-opening. It has left me with a deep appreciation of what you were able to contribute to the integration of football in your humble, quiet way.

§ § §

What Jerry Claiborne is attributed with commenting after the Historic game between USC and Alabama in 1970 bears repeating: "Sam Cunningham did more to integrate Alabama in 60 minutes than Martin Luther King did in 20 years." Some may disagree, but none can question the impact that Sam "Bam" Cunningham had on the game of football. None who ever tackled him on the gridiron will ever forget the Bam.

Chapter 7

My Goal Was to Be a Pro Surfer, But ...

"Always assume that your opponent is going to be bigger, stronger and faster than you, so that you learn to rely on technique, timing and leverage rather than brute strength."

—Grandmaster Hélio Gracie (1913–2009),
co-founder of Brazilian Jiu-Jitsu

"Recognizing the influence of my subconscious mind over my power of will, I shall take care to submit to it a clear and definite picture of my major purpose in life and all minor purposes leading to my major purpose, and I shall keep this picture constantly before my subconscious mind by repeating it daily!"

—Bruce Lee (1940–1973),
founder of Jeet Kune Do

Luis got into jiu-jitsu in Rio de Janeiro, Brazil, when he realized that his big dream—being a pro surfer—wound up not being his professional calling. At age 14 he began training in Brazilian Jiu-Jitsu and eventually settled in a school founded by the famous Gracie family, known as the first family of Brazilian Jiu-Jitsu. Now, more than three decades later, he's still at it. From his spacious jiu-jitsu training center near the big waves on the north shore of Maui, he says, "It's about the love, the sweat, bonding with people of all backgrounds. In my gym, you might even find a reforming criminal grappling with a police officer. In here, we're all brothers and sisters in the aloha spirit."

Luis "Limao" Heredia, standing as his students do push-ups.

Tale of The Tape
Luis Fernando "Limao" Heredia

Jiu-Jitsu master instructor and top competitor

Born in Rio de Janeiro, December 22, 1962.
Age 18: 5'8", 150.
Age 48: 5'8", 160.

Lives on the north shore of Maui. Travels frequently for tournaments and seminars.

Mother: Maria Isabel, born 1946.

Father: Isidro Heredia, 1940–2012. Good soccer player in his youth. Salesman. First, machinery and construction parts. Later he got into real estate sales and did well.

Eldest of three children. Sister Alba lives in Charleston, South Carolina.

Sister Adriana lives in Sweden.

Both sisters are fit, perhaps influenced by their eldest brother.

First love as a kid and adolescent: soccer. Second love: surfing. He was very competitive by nature. Then, little by little, jiu-jitsu became his first priority. He also played basketball and water polo.

Children: Son, Kaile Heredia, age 19. Daughter, Luana Heredia, age six.

Has a daily fitness program: sim (Brazilian word for 'yes')

Does recreational fitness: surfing, and paddle surfing. Gardening helps keep things in perspective.

Personality traits: perseverance, philosophical, attractor of people, creates a dynamic of peace and love in his surroundings, wise beyond his years (learned a lot in his first two decades as an adult, sometimes the hard way).

Mild pain: left shoulder, perhaps rotator cuff. Still training, hoping it will go away.

Good Quote: "The supreme art of war is to subdue the enemy without fighting." Sun Tzu

Quote on Encouragement by Laird Hamilton, waterman, big-wave surfer who loves to surf Jaws, the famous big wave that breaks not far from Luis' Maui jiu-jitsu center:

"If I see my friend going into the next wave, I'm trying to encourage him to go. It's amazing how if you encourage somebody how much strength you give them. I think that's why they have big sports events in big arenas where people are screaming and cheering because it brings up your energy and, at times, this allows you to do things that are superhuman." April 2010

Website: MauiJiuJitsu.com

Luis started his life's adventure with a surfboard under his arm, running to the beaches in search of the next paddle out and the next great ride. "At one point," he shares, "I wanted to be a professional soccer player. Then I got involved in surfing. I must have signed up for at least 20 surfing tournaments. This is going to be a bit funny and embarrassing, but I never made it past the first round. And here I thought I was this super-nut surfer kid. Maybe if I had had blond hair," he jokes, "things would have been different."

At age 17, while still training as a jiu-jitsu blue belt, he got a call to fill in for a competitor in a tournament. All calls those days went to your home where your mother might have to take a message. "Rickson Gracie [his teacher] called me telling me he needed me for a tournament. The blue belt who was slated to be in the match at 140 pounds couldn't go. So I went to the tournament all scared, all afraid with a lot of issues on my mind, like performing well in front of Rickson, all of that. This was in 1980. Amazingly, I went through six people all in the same day and wound up winning my first jiu-jitsu tournament."

You could still hear the fear, anticipation, and relief when he recalled the pivotal day three decades later. "The final match was against a kid from Carlson Gracie's school which is the center where

I had originally begun my training. I remember very clearly that I could hear Rickson calling out to me from one corner and Carlson calling out to his student from the other. It was like an all-out gladiator match but with coaches. But, compared to today, the match was way different in terms of strategy. It's funny, Sifu, because back then we didn't have all of this technical way of understanding the art. It was like takedown, cross-over, mount, and finish. I remember that the six-minute fight ended without me making him tap, but I won on points. The other kid and I were bleeding everywhere."

I asked him if it was a case of finger nail cuts that each competitor gave to the other person. "Finger nail blood, elbow blood, everything ... it was a battle ... like a cat fight. This was on one of those old rough canvas surfaced mats that just rubbing your arm on the surface would take the skin off."

Luis is a fifth degree black belt and has won the *Pan American Championship five times*. Back in 1989, he became the first Brazilian Jiu-Jitsu practitioner in America at the rank of purple belt, which he got just before his departure from Rio. Luis brings a spiritual view—combined with technical mastery, and intuition—and the mind of a chess master to the art of jiu-jitsu.

Luis began his journey at age sixteen, eventually landing at the *Gracie Humaitá* School then run by *Grandmaster Helio Gracie*, and Helio's sons *Rickson and Royler*. Thus armed, his mission has long been to spread his passion for the art around the world. It was a joy and privilege to have shared time with him for this book.

The Backstory of the Interview

Maui, Christmastime, 2010. I was standing on the cliffs at Pe'ahi watching what's known as the world's biggest and most consistently big wave—Jaws. Jet skis were towing in surfers and carting around photographers. If you're a surfer, you almost have to get towed in because the distance is too great and the speed at which you'd have to paddle to catch one of these monsters is almost unfathomable.

Forty-foot waves and an occasional 50-footer were picking up and carrying daring big wave surfers for their relatively short rides. "It's not about long wave rides for the big-wave surfers here," an onlooker told me, "you want to take what you can get and get the heck out of Dodge before the waves crash. Big waves carry so much load, if you wind up underneath, you could be holding your breath for an uncomfortably long time. If you come up at the wrong time and can't get a few gulps of air, wave debris from the last one smothers you. Or a new wave comes and sends what's left of you tumbling. At that point, you become one with the fish—only you're no longer breathing."

I stood there on the edge of the world, taking it all in, watching surfers get the ultimate balance workout and speed rush also known as a free ride from God. The next day, still glowing from the cliffs at Jaws, I woke up before daybreak and started with a warm-up jog. As the sun began to throw sufficient light, I cut off the main road and headed down a sand and dirt road, out to Maui's North Shore cliffs. When I arrived at the coast, I was just one mile west of Jaws. There I set down my water and began what I call *The Maintenance Workout*, my daily staple to maintain functionality, tone, and mind-body connection.

This physical program oxygenates the brain and provides a grounded timeframe for a relationship with the spiritual side. The workout uses the principal of body as gym and uses whatever the land and terrain provide. Stumps and rocks provide a place to park your hands during incline push-ups and bench dips, and a place to park your feet during decline push-ups and hamstring stretches. If they are flat, you can also use such raised surfaces for posture-improving and moves to strengthen the thighs and hips called step-ups. A tree provided just a bit of shade about 25 feet from the last jump you would ever take. The beach one hundred feet below wasn't a beach, it was a parking place for large boulders. I threw my long and sturdy jiu-jitsu belt over a tree branch for leaning exercises like chin-ups (aka modified chin-ups) and isotonic abdomen crunches.

The jiu-jitsu belt foreshadowed what was to come later that day. After a day of writing, I rode my bike up the hill to the small shopping area in the town of Haiku, stepped off, and wandered into Maui Jiu-Jitsu, a large jiu-jitsu center housed in a humongous sheet metal building reminiscent of an aircraft hangar. I knew about its resident master teacher by reputation and from the Internet. Over the days I spent at the center, I would come to learn that Luis Heredia, a Brazilian transplant my age (48 in 2010), was not only dedicated to his practice, but that emotion poured out of him so that everyone in his martial arts school were uplifted by his presence.

He was standing at the front counter, greeting some of his students as they entered the center for evening class. *Ah, he's more of a business person perhaps*, I thought. One of his younger black belt student teachers will probably teach the class. I introduced myself.

"I'm conducting interviews for a book called 'The Aging Athlete.' I'm a jiu-jitsu student from California. I wonder if you might be willing to share your story about the mindset for lifetime fitness?"

"I'd like to know more," he said as he excused himself to head to his locker room.

When he returned, he was wearing his white jiu-jitsu kimono, aka gi. "I have to teach a class right now. We can talk afterwards."

"Sure, do you mind if I film a bit and shoot some photos?" I asked, showing him the small camera I had at the time.

"No problem," he told me. "Shoot as much as you like."

Twenty-some students lined up for the initial salutation and then began their warm-ups: running, lunges, rolls, shrimping (jiu-jitsu escape moves done while on your back and side), and calisthenics most of us will recall from high school P.E.

Similar to the jiu-jitsu schools I had been part of in California, after a 15 to 25 minute warm-up period, the instructor leads the students through a jiu-jitsu move—perhaps an escape, a reversal, a passing-the-guard move, and maybe, eventually, a submission. Then each pair of students practices the move with roving supervision from one or a number of instructors. This typically happens three times, that is, three moves are taught and practiced. Then the students do some real-effort practice using those moves or the positions at which those moves are initiated.

After 40 minutes to an hour, students are offered the chance to do some free rolling also known as sparring. Here they get to do some competitive practice in three-to-five-minute rounds. In Brazilian jiu-jitsu, this no-punching or kicking sparring is how one gets to test the ability of their grappling art as they attempt to submit their opponent. After one round, grapplers often switch opponents and do another round. This sparring time sometimes goes on for 20 to 40 minutes. For serious students of the art in search of mastery, some do this two or three times per day. I've heard of dedicated grapplers sparring for an hour or two at a time.

I don't know if you realize how hard that is, but it's right up there with trying to go out into the waves by paddling a board against the onslaught of rough surf. It's exhausting, to say the least. The good news is, the better you get at the art, the less muscle and cardio you use. When you get it, your touch becomes lighter and lighter. You use slight changes in position and pressure to generate the leverage needed to move, control, and submit your opponent. Think anaconda on a goat—measured and steady constriction.

When Master Luis had finished his class, he stepped up to the bleachers where I was sitting.

"Do you feel euphoric?" I asked him.

"What I feel is ... it's excellent. It's very, very, very good."

"Is this why you are still at the art?"

"That's part of it, do you want to hear the rest?"

"Let's do it," I answered.

Here are the broad strokes and key bits of dialogue from our interviews over the course of three days. Let's start with the biggest moment. Of course, these often come from the heart. This bit was from the very last part of our three separate interviews:

Ous (probably from Japanese osu, which has a number of meanings, including respect and patience with myself) was uttered by all who were bowing to end the adult evening class on the grappling mat. Master Luis told his students, "I am grateful for the training, I am grateful for your friendship." Master Luis had just finished a one-and-a-half-hour teaching and training session bowing to all of his students. Lots of hugs of thanks and respect were shared by the entire class. Full of endorphins and sweating just a little bit (again, the more advanced you get, the less energy you use), he approached the bleachers.

Master Luis motioned to the camera. "Is that on?"

Yes.

"It's about coming back. Persistence, what was the word I told you?"

Determination.

"Aloha ... Besides that word, determination, there is nothing that can be done if you don't open your heart for love, for understanding, for observing your weakness and other people's weakness. Like we say in Hawaii, aloha ... live with happiness."

A man with a clean haircut and a nice clean gi—
and an ample laundry bill—surveys his students.

His presence is such that when he travels, class attendance often drops 30 to 40 percent.

I suggested he could try an experiment to counteract the attendance drop: let them know what is expected in his absence. That his spirit would still be watching over them, encouraging them to keep attending and sharing in the art.

Since these interviews had surpassed what I think of as going deep, I knew I (a New Jersey-born lover of comedy and levity) had to press for the fun times in his past. In 1989, Luis left Brazil and joined Rickson Gracie and some of his brothers in the Los Angeles area. They were a small band of age 20-something Brazilian athletes, mostly all good surfers, and of course advanced belts in Gracie Jiu-Jitsu. They were living in the garage of the eldest Gracie brother Rorion's home in Hermosa Beach, Calif. In 1978, Rorian (pron. Horian), got on a flight for southern California and became one of the first of the Gracie Jiu-Jitsu clan to set up residence in America. His relative, Carley Gracie, had started in New York in 1972. Ten years later, other brothers came to California and expanded the jiu-jitsu school. With Rorian at the helm, this skinny, hungry, and ambitious band of Brazilians was teaching students, training with each other, and challenging all comers in submission wrestling and submission fights. Since our interview went deep immediately, I went for the lighter side which Luis was happy to share.

Did anything funny happen to you and your band of jiu-jitsu instructors in those early days in California?

"A lot of funny things happened when we were in Los Angeles. For instance, my first ever seminar experience, like one week in Los Angeles, Rorian tells us, 'Hey, we've got a seminar to do in Coronado Bay,' which is a Naval Base in San Diego. And I'll tell you what, man, I never got my neck squeezed so tight, so hard ... We all piled into a van and drove down there. We go through the security checkpoint which was pretty funny because these armed Marines were checking out a bunch of unarmed guys wearing martial arts outfits. When you're inside the place, there were like 200 Marines waiting for us. They were all dressed up in fatigues and ready to kill. They were looking over at us as we entered—a bunch of Brazilian scrubs wearing white kimonos, right? And their look said, *What are these guys doing here in our territory?* Rorian spoke English. So when he heard them talking, he said they were pretty much being sarcastic about the whole thing."

They were undoubtedly licking their chops. After all, they had been through boot camp and were trained to kill.

"They looked ready to hit the beaches and invade some place. Back then, the most typical way of proving the point of the story, proving that we skinny dudes could escape, is we'd let them get a headlock from the side, and then drop to the ground—the judo immobilization."

That's the type of thing I saw on the playgrounds back when kids used to grapple more. A street brawl move.

"Yeah, street brawl. To prove the point, the Brazilians picked the skinniest, smallest guy in the room to escape. Guess who that was—me? And they said to this big Marine, 'Squeeze as hard as you can this kid's neck and see if he can escape.' I'll tell you what, man, it was good that I didn't know how to speak English. I didn't know how to say NO, STOP. So I fought for my breath and to get blood to my brain and I kept going and, when the guy ran down on his energy, I escaped. I got the scars today on my ears [touching his ears] to prove it. It was a pretty funny, pretty crazy moment, you know? We had to take on so many of those Marines. They all wanted to try their luck."

Did any of them have any luck?

"Their luck was only temporary. Eventually we all wound up reversing them or tapping them out."

That formula is a great way to get your name out. Putting out a challenge to all comers. Is that the Gracie way?

"Well, Rorion started in Los Angeles with almost no money. The money he had, like a few hundred bucks, was stolen from his locker at the YMCA by the beach. He didn't want to call home and ask for a bailout. He had to make his mark. Then he just started training people, giving away free lessons to anyone who would bring a friend. He had to do things to survive, make a name for himself. His gym—which was the same garage where I first lived in Hermosa Beach—got so popular that he brought one of his brothers over to help teach. That was in 1985."

Wish I knew about you guys and your gym. I moved to northern California in 1986. I would have loved to have seen that, those early days.

"It was an unbelievably cool time. It was like the Brazilian invasion. Then, he opened his first official gym in Torrance and they needed even more instructors. That was back in 1989 and that's when I came over with the second group of crazy Brazilians. Still jiu-jitsu was so unknown and unseen, so unusual. We set up these challenge matches. A lot of like super heroes came to our center and tried their luck. Everybody that tried, failed. Many of these guys were 'known' people—martial artists, boxers, wrestlers, and just real street fighters. And we were pretty scrawny guys, not that big."

Amazing. That must have left people, these other super heroes, shaking their heads and then spreading the word about how these little guys were dominating them. I'm sure some of them wanted to learn the art.

"Yep. That's how it happened. Then, in 1993, Rorion and his business partner set up the UFC. [The highly watched Ultimate

Fighter Challenge, which was held in an arena where the fighters fought in a fenced-in octagon with one referee.] Out of the first four years, Rorion's younger brother, Royce, won three tournaments. He was skinny too."

First UFC, 1993, Denver, Colo. Notable in photo: Proud father third from left with white hair, Helio Gracie, winner Royce Gracie (black belt) standing, to his immediate left is his brother Rickson Gracie. Luis Heredia farthest on right. (courtesy of L. Heredia)

(This is called mixed martial arts or MMA. There are rules but it's basically a combination of kickboxing, punching on the ground, and jiu-jitsu. Eventually Rorion and his partners reportedly went on to sell the UFC for a tidy sum. Today, it's a multimillion-dollar company with a strong record of pay-per-view sales. It has been growing in fans while boxing, the combat sport with more rules, has been losing its popularity. Apparently people want to see the real deal. Once, I asked a friend who knows the world of boxing as well as the MMA, "What would happen if one of these skinny, grappling guys went against a boxer with great footwork and power, like a Mike Tyson?" He responded, "These MMA guys who know takedowns can come in so low and so

quick that they can likely avoid the punches. Then the boxer is on the ground and he has no power from there." The moral of the story is, you have to know how to attack and defend from all positions, standing and from the ground.)

Luis, let's talk about the mindset you need for this type of physical training and competition, whether just the jiu-jitsu or the mixed martial arts combats.

"The training is about having a strong mind and body. The right way to train is to develop the highest level of strength—psychologically and physically. And then there's your spiritual side. Nothing can be done if you don't have your spiritual side awake, aware."

Amen to that. How do you say that in Brazil?

"Amém. Yeah, I see a lot of strong people succeed for a little bit, relying on their intelligence for a while or relying on their body strength and their body conditioning. They keep their title for a very long time. After that they disappear. If you don't develop, if you don't motivate, or if you don't understand that this is just a mission, this is just a journey ... We came to life to help others. We came to this life to serve. If you don't connect yourself to your spiritual side, none of those lasting good things can be reached or done."

What keeps you going?

"I was so focused on succeeding for such a long time. From being the first purple-belt student in North America to hosting probably the best jiu-jitsu school in all the state of Hawaii. But, now I'm older and I've had some success. Things are different now."

What do you mean?

"Well, it's the sharing in the art in a whole new way. Age can do that if you let it. One of the reasons I'm so stoked again on this new phase is because I'm attracting people from all over the world to come and train with me right now.

"I forgot for so long this connection, this spiritual connection with life. I was so focused on building my schools that I lost some of myself. It was from too much pride. I went from one school with a few students to three schools and over 300 students in Hawaii. I'm not blaming myself and I'm not disappointed with the course of life for me through those years, because I reached somewhere. Professionally I am in a happy place. But I had to realize that it's not about all the ego stuff. God gave me another chance at centering myself, finding myself. He allowed me to come back to a place where I could reconnect to my spiritual side and my mission."

(Two-and-a-half years after the original in-person interviews, when I spoke with Luis on Skype in the summer of 2013, we were both 50, and I was the only one with gray hair. He was wearing glasses. I did mention to him that his glasses made him look the intellectual in our conversation. Professor Luis was up to four schools and 500 students, all on the relatively small island of Maui. I joked to him that he was becoming the jiu-jitsu evangelist, the MLK of grappling and group bonding on the island. My memories of that mind-opening trip in 2010–2011 were of an island strongly in need of a theme of fitness and spirituality, as well as reminders of old-school sweating.

Among the residents you could see the obesity epidemic in full force—from old folks to young. Residents had shared that drug addiction and alcoholism levels were high, and old and young were spending way too much time sitting around in front of digital devices. Even finding an affordable, healthful meal was a challenge in some parts of Maui. In the downtown area of Kahului, your choices were the oil and grizzle franchises at the mall and things like franchise sandwich places.)

What is the message of that mission, Luis?

"It's to live the right way. Share what others taught me. And to all the ones who are not here with me anymore, I feel they are around me, helping me with this journey. I do this for my friends, my family. It is so amazing that this is developing so fast inside of me. It's so amazing right now, because I think I came back to my younger days, the young man's journey. That's what it is."

That's the discovery of life. It never leaves us. It's always there for us to tap into. Being a kid was pretty cool in many respects, eh?

"Well, I've had kids, so I got to live that all over again. Do you remember when you asked me if I ever failed? It wasn't only based on my physical abilities. I did fail for a time, with life, with God, and the world, the mission, and helping others. I think for a long time I was naïve by choice. I was selfish by choice, to become something, to fight, to prove a point."

Mastery and self-mastery. They both deal with the ego. In self-mastery you move mostly without it. Winning is okay, so is not winning—being fulfilled just from taking part in the process.

"That's it. My old self, and all the big accomplishments and sacrifices for the ego ... this has all gone down the drain—there is no more ego. Okay, there is a little [he smiles]—but only to give me the confidence to go back to California and get my title. I agree with you about jiu-jitsu in the sense that jiu-jitsu is not about winning."

What is it about?

"One thing is easy ... this," he said, wiping his forehead in tropical Maui. "There's nothing wrong with sweating. The most physical attribute that I take from jiu-jitsu is how easy and how fast we can sweat. Sweating is a very natural condition. You can sweat working hard, or working hard under the sun, or working out. Every time you sweat, you release toxins. This is a process of renewal and regeneration of cells, and mind, and brain, and energy. It is one of the things that I praise when I go to teach my seminars and when I teach in my schools."

You sweat, your students sweat, in one big, friendly, healing sauna. (I held my smile and that broke him up which is a good thing to do with jiu-jitsu masters who may want to try a new move on you.)

"It is like I only praised what I believed and then what I do. I don't praise things that I don't do. I don't teach positions that I don't do, so I don't teach things I don't do. I stand by these students in this big sauna as you called it. The reason I come to jiu-jitsu these days, I have many reasons, but the most important is because it feels good to sweat, feels good to see the students sweating."

What about the group dynamic? You know, bonding.

"I enjoy the spiritual part of martial arts, and the bonding between all kinds of different people, from all kinds of different backgrounds. I have classes with troublemakers, criminals, police, rich people and poor people. But in here we are all equal. It all becomes such an equal thing. This levels us all out. [He laughs] We laugh so much here, especially when guys go to sleep. [That means they get choked to sleep due to lack of oxygen.]"

I've been there a few times. The first time I rolled with someone, they got the mata-leon choke on me. [This was what Tarzan did to the lions to kill them.] I didn't know about tapping out in submission. I was in a tae kwon do class and my instructor thought I knew to tap. That was nearly a jaw breaker. My instructor, A.W., stopped just before he became the breaker.

"I've fallen asleep and that has made lots of people laugh too. Including me when I woke up. Yeah, I have a lot of fun here. We all do. The word 'stoked' that I mentioned before, stoked means fun. So if you come to this school with the purpose or the knowing that you're going to sweat, then you're going to have fun, you're going to learn. I think that the posture and the position teachers should take is like this is a family. We can have a conflict in a match, but it is all friendly. It is like in my school when a person taps [gives in] to someone else, and it's the sharing and the curiosity: How this was executed? The learning and the enjoyment in the submission comes from both sides. If you don't teach your training partner, they never improve. Then, you never improve. It's fun to help people improve and watch them use things you taught them as they take on other training partners."

The first time I went into a jiu-jitsu center was in 1997. Carlos Garcia, the teacher in Sacramento, California, pointed to a top student on the mat. Another guy was going after him. The teacher said the good student is a hunter, but he's also being hunted, which makes him the prey. If the other student learns a lot, and someday, months or years from now, eventually wins, he becomes hunted. For the others, he becomes the prey.

"That's the way it is. I use that relationship a lot—predator and prey. Because of my passion for animals and nature, my teachings have a lot in common with that—intuition, instinct. So many times in life or in training, I put myself in both worlds. When I put myself into the predator mode, I'm there to catch. When I put myself in prey mode, I love it because it is like a turtle going inside its shell. It is a very intelligent, bright, creative lifestyle."

Luis, can you give me a short version of your background to put your life in context here?

"I have been living on Maui for 10 years and I have been doing jiu-jitsu for 32 years. I'm 48 and I enjoy the spiritual part of martial arts. Jiu-jitsu is about bonding between different people from different backgrounds. Jiu-Jitsu is about respect, it is about courage, it's about a laugh."

Can't put it any shorter and sweeter than that.

"I'm trying to bring that message to the young people of the world. What I'm trying to communicate to the new generation is: nothing is going to be built without its ups and downs. When you are spiritually and physically aware, you know when you've hit the bottom. You can only come up. Now, it's like I'm leaving my teenage years older and wiser. I think the spiritual connection that I am having with God and the spiritual cleansing I'm undergoing right now have a lot to do with the way I discipline myself. I have screwed up many times, we all do. The point here is to learn from your mistakes, and I made so many of them."

Did your parents, or anyone, tell you that you had more energy or anything special, that you were different in some way?

"I don't remember many people saying that I was special. I don't think of it that way. Not to be naïve or cocky, I do have a special feeling and energy about me. I think I am special because I have a good idea of what my mission on Earth is."

Were you a rebel when you were young kid?

"A little bit, yeah."

What did you do with your energy, how did you focus that energy?

"Soccer, I played a lot of sports, mostly soccer. I'm Brazilian. So if you don't play soccer you're an outcast. Everybody has to play soccer in Brazil. So I used to play soccer pretty steady, pretty consistently. I ran all the time, playing on the sand, boogie and body boarding. Then from the age of 11, I started surfing. Pretty much I have been involved in sports as far back as I can remember."

When do you consciously remember first beginning to train as a young person, and what did you do?

"I started to focus on my fitness at the age of 13 and 14. A lot of times I was alone. I started to develop this way. I would run on the sand at Copacabana Beach. I would swim as much as I could and tried water polo for a while. I also started off by running in the hills and then in the mountains."

When you were a kid, do you remember telling a lie that kept eating at you all the time?

"Did I lie before? Yes, we all do. I am far and away from considering myself perfect. However, I do have a perfect life. I try hard as I can to speak and practice the truth. I don't remember faking the truth or being fake to people. I just remember as a kid saying a lot of lies. I remember lying about things that I knew would get me into trouble. I don't remember the last time I had to lie or had to hide the truth. But I think the question is integrity and loyalty to self, to love, and loyalty to God."

When you were a young guy training in Brazil, did you have anyone come into your gym that changed the way that you thought about jiu-jitsu, or that motivated you?

"There were a lot of very impressive guys back then and some of their students were impressive. There were many others but here are a few: Sergio Pena, Paulo Barrozo, Marcel Behring, Pedro Sauer, Mauricio Motta Gomes. Again there were many who inspired me with their talent and their ethics."

Being a part of martial arts centers you have seen a lot of different personal circumstances. Did you regularly encounter young people going through difficult and painful life changes?

"I have seen a lot of those circumstances. People were regularly going through tough times. Even me dealing with my own set of problems, even trying and sometimes being unable to help my own son. It cannot be more painful and difficult than that. At the same time I went through my own demons and problems, but I had people who trusted me and helped me."

How did you come out of it? Could you give one example of an early demon in your life and how the process went for you and how you came through that?

"Sometimes you get confused, hang out with the wrong crowd. Sometimes you get hurt, or hurt someone. I was popular amongst my friends, so I was exposed to and experienced many different environments and lifestyles. I would say most of them were not always proper for me, so I disassociated myself. Jiu-jitsu was a lifesaver."

What do you think the reason was that you were destined to go through a few phases?

"It's just because I got involved. I sense that everyone that came into my life learned from me, and I learned much from them."

Luis and his son, Kaile, 1997. Teaching students who sign up is one thing, teaching family can often be another thing altogether. "Patience, a good sense of humor, and more patience," are the secrets according to Luis. Age 12 and 13, son Kaile was the state champion in jiu-jitsu. At age 14, Kaile decided to take a break from jiu-jitsu. Luis admits to putting a bit too much pressure on his son. At the time of this interview, his son had taken up hunting and playing basketball and was living in Oregon.

Do you have enemies and if so, would you want to straighten it out, apologize if you offended anyone?

"I probably do have enemies, not that I know of, though. Apology—that is easy for me. Apology is the strength of a warrior. That is the same as saying thank you. That is how I am approaching life."

(Rickson Gracie, see Rickson.com, is often considered the 'purest expression of Gracie Jiu-Jitsu.' Born in 1958, he is an eight-degree black belt and red belt. In competitions, he has reportedly never been defeated. In one weekend, he is said to have tapped out—submitted—a few hundred America wrestlers who tried their luck, one after the other. Rickson was one of Luis' first master teachers.)

Luis, what would you like to say about your teacher, brother, Rickson Gracie?

"Out of all of the jiu-jitsu fighters I have seen, like 100,000 or some huge number, there were maybe 1,000 that were at the top. Out of them, the only one I saw that came closest to perfecting the art was Rickson Gracie. And, thankfully, he adopted me as like his little brother. Rickson's teachings have given me the capacity to make honesty, creativity, friendship, courage, balance, faith, health, and respect the foundation of my character. For this I owe Rickson all the respect, devotion and loyalty …"

Why is his jiu-jitsu so special? Is it the way he sees things?

"I would say so, he sees things differently. He sees jiu-jitsu pretty differently than most people I have known."

Were you around during those Zulu challenges? (Rei Zulu was a 220-pound, heavily muscled, black fighter who challenged all comers. Born in 1948, he was still fighting in his early 60s.)

"Yeah, I was around and I was pretty impressed by the skill of the performers."

Were you a part of that inner group?

"I wasn't training at Rickson's family's school then; I was training in jiu-jitsu at his cousins' place—this was at the Carlson

Gracie School. But we all defended the jiu-jitsu flag and so I was always rooting for him. The guy [Rickson] was my idol back then."

I got a tape lent to me by a friend in 1998—the video called "Gracie Jiu-Jitsu in Action." Whose idea was it to make lions a part of the video?

(The video opening showed lions taking down wildebeests and zebras using their four legs as weapons to hold onto their prey. They then used their mouth in a suffocation technique ... similar to parts of jiu-jitsu fighting. Luis told me the video was developed by the eldest Gracie brother.)

"That was Rorion's idea. I liked it."

Let's talk about where you are now, your training and life as an athlete and coach. What is your routine morning to evening?

"Right now the thing is to change, not what I do, but how I do it. For instance, before I became a professional I was waking up at 6:00 or 7:00 in the morning to work out. I eventually had to stop this because of teaching. I broke the routine. Now I'm up at 6:30 every morning again. I eat a little bit in the morning, then work out usually an hour doing heart conditioning and training, then have a second meal. Because of the upcoming Pan American Championship in California, I'm also working out four times a week with a personal trainer on strengthening, agility, cardio, flexibility, and nutrition. Because of my routine for the last month, I'm leaner, like I was as a teenager. After this competition I'm going to try to keep it that way."

How do you do your cardio?

"I do cardio throughout the day. I ride a bike and do a lot of jiu-jitsu. I am working out every morning and getting stronger every day … much more than I was a month ago. Amazing how a little bit of effort makes a whole world of difference."

What are the training techniques that you are using right now?

"I'm using cross training. My training consists of different phases, the first, stability and flexibility, and then flexibility and strength. In a couple weeks I am going from flexibility-strength, to strength and power, which is a lot of explosive exercises. I'm just very excited and I'm looking forward to this work."

Another Pan-American win for Luis.

Luckily he didn't have to face off against the ref who looks like he has these middle weights by about 60 pounds. The ref is none other than eighth-degree red and black belt Rigan Machado, also from the Gracie schools in Brazil.

Luis' opponent, Colin Oyama, became the trainer for top MMA fighter Quinton "Rampage" Jackson. What Luis remembers most about these Pan American battles was that he and his opponents were not fighting for money. "We fought for pride."

Luis winning the Pan American Games in the following year in California.

He said, "This one was an all-out war." When I asked him how he compared today's ability to the Luis from 16 years prior, he responded, "The Luis from today could beat the Luis from back then ... as long as I had the gas." He added that he was a more relaxed fighter today. The other fighter "disappeared" after this fight, which may have been his last fight.

I'm guessing there are substantial responsibilities when one is a top, committed athlete-teacher. Are honesty and integrity the most obvious of those?

"Yes, I think so., and you know, it's important to just be yourself, speak the truth. It might hurt at the time, but in the long run you will be considered a hero."

What other things have you learned about the life as a champion?

"One of the most important things that I seem to have developed is intuition. I sense that people are losing this ability."

Why are they losing it?

"People are living too much of their lives in a big city. They put their shoes on, they turn their alarm clock on, and they walk and behave like ants. Going this way, and commuting that way, going here and coming back, so they barely have any time to stop and appreciate nature. It's important to develop a strong intuition. I started to lose it while living in Los Angeles. I lived in Los Angeles for 13 years."

Los Angeles must be similar to Rio in some ways, isn't it?

"Well, except that Rio is way more panoramic. It is a city surrounded by mountains and ocean. As opposed to Los Angeles where it is kind of a flat place, where a lot of people only think about money, cars, and clothing. I don't want to say too much or label, because I have had good experiences there too. I did learn a lot in that city and have a lot of friends there. But it's just not my type of city, not my type of life. So, when I felt like I was losing my energy and my intuition, I moved to Hawaii."

You traveled to a small island and wound up starting your life in a remote part of that island.

"Exactly. Here I started living only in the country. I live on a farm. The place where I live, at six o'clock in the winter evenings, you don't see any more light. You just see the stars, and the lights of your neighbors, who are miles away. I needed that. I needed to stay connected with the stars, the moon, the wind, the clouds, the trees, the green, the colors, the flowers, the earth, the smell of the earth, the plants, the fruit trees, the ocean, the salt of the ocean."

That's one of the reasons I moved to Santa Barbara. When I was living in Sacramento, the medium-sized city I had moved to in 1986 eventually turned into a sprawling place like Orange County by Los Angeles. Because of its popularity, job market, and cheap real estate, it took less than a decade. In the late '90s. It just became too big for me.

"So this is why I moved here. What I told you just now is it. That is the connection. This is my life. That is how I have kept the intuition. I do believe I am continuing to develop a very strong intuition. I sense that my jiu-jitsu schools will continue to grow. At the same time, I know I will grow even more connected with my spiritual side."

What does your intuition say about where humanity is heading?

"I think humanity is walking through to brighter times. I think kids of today have a better chance of being better athletes than any generation before. I think the information we have access to today, as far as data, as far as supplements, as far as exercising, psychology, etc., is more abundant than 10 or 20 years ago. It is conditioning and habit."

Athletes always seem to break the old records.

"They develop and advance their skills. You get into a habit where you are sleeping good, eating better, and your training is more productive, and everything is responding brighter, faster, cleaner. That is how I have changed in the past year. Time has been teaching me. Before, it seemed like a year to me was like an eternity. But now, putting things together, a year is just the blink of an eye. I already turned 48 and boom it's the blink of an eye. And so it goes so fast, the last three months, for example, went by so much quicker than I had thought. I look back and I think I can put in another three years more than what I had originally thought it would take, for what I wanted to attain."

Are there limitations?

"There are no limitations for how high you want to go. It is only in the mind. The mind can bring you down, not the circumstances of life. Life itself is something you are supposed to deal with. Things are not designed to be good or bad. You might not agree with certain things, and you may agree with other things. The ones you don't agree with are beyond your control. Realizing this has made me understand life better."

How does this happen?

"It happens in the mind. There is no space for accepting in your mind that you are going down. You are the one who puts space on the mind with: 'I think I'm going down because of this, this, and this.' You have to learn how to accept things. You have to take care of a lot of stuff, things that are happening all day long in your life. If you do that, nothing changes. It's not easy. I'm still dealing with feelings from other people, relatives, from kids that are in unhappy or in uncertain situations. But like I said before, that is their life. I cannot see a step for me to go down. From here I can only go up. The higher I go, the more helpful I can become for the ones who have not found their path."

Today, you are better able to accept, learn, and be blissful—perhaps this relates to enlightenment?

"I think so."

("Choke" is a famous jiu-jitsu and no-holds barred documentary about the training and competitions of Rickson Gracie in 1995 in Japan.)

You have watched the documentary "Choke" at least five or 10 times. Now, let's say you and I are putting out our own mini version of "Choke." What would you entitle what we are doing here—about Luis Heredia in 2011?

"There are a lot of words that flash, but the first word that comes to my mind is determination. That was the first word that came to me. Without determination we will reach no air. A journey with a thousand steps starts with the first one. It is about determination, it is about discipline, it is about integrity, it is about patience and intuition."

You keep mentioning the importance of intuition. Is this how we find our paths in this life?

"That's part of it. Do not forget about intuition. Stay connected with life. Stay connected with self ... You know, as a matter of fact, before my 48th birthday, instead of putting my age into a calendar date, I changed my mind because I pictured not a year. I turned my mind to the thought that I have been around or have rotated around the sun 48 times, without getting hurt, so healthy, so thankful to God, so I just hope to continue spinning around the sun."

The journey of learning and enjoying and putting back.

"Yes, enjoy going around the sun. I'm not seeing one day after the other day, I'm just seeing that this is all in movement. This is another good point to put down. I just think that life moves that way because I have related myself with this motion of going around the sun and actually feeling the Earth going around its axis 24 hours every day. So we go around the axis and we go around the sun. It is a lot of movement."

You emphasize that cosmic movement, why do you intuitively find it important?

"What happens to people is they forget they are moving, so they get stuck in the lousy or bad moment that they are in and they think the world is going to end right there. It is not, and every single second the Earth is changing. Look out there to the jiu-jitsu mat and you can see right now my students are straining, but every single second the positions are changing. Life is changing. Life is like jiu-jitsu, bro."

(That made me smile, a Brazilian mixed with a Hawaiian was calling me "bro.")

"When life is changing and you are in a good position, stop and enjoy it. When I am in predator mode on the mat, I love being on top, using the gravity. When I am in the prey mode on the bottom, I also enjoy. It doesn't matter the phase or the mode because life is changing, moving, every moment. Because it moves, it changes. It is not moving because it is changing. Things are changing all the time because everything is moving all the time. However, because of gravity it doesn't seem like it all the time, but we are moving right now at a very high speed."

(With that, Luis headed back to the mat to roll with his students.)

After he finished another class with some live sparring, grappling, at the end, he came over to where I was sitting. I asked him, "What other word comes to mind, besides determination?"

"Besides determination nothing can be done until you open your heart, for love, for understanding, for observing your own weakness and other people's weakness. Without that it is nothing. Like we say in Hawaii, aloha."

Are you high from work-out euphoria right now?

"No, the feeling for me is being happy. I think one of the secrets for now is leaving the euphoria aside and just live with happiness."

Do you want to leave us with any last thoughts before we end the conversation?

"Yes, I want to thank Sifu Slim for bringing up such an honorable and good idea, and writing about people, making a difference in the world. And also coming up with such good questions. Thank you so much, it was wonderful to know you and to help you anyway I can and aloha."

§ § §

Here's a quote from Master Luis on the spiritual side of his martial arts practice:

"Today, jiu-jitsu is part of my blood. I teach jiu-jitsu with passion. It is my way of giving back to God by helping God make people uncover the positive aspects of the human spirit."

Jiu-jitsu is a game of millimeters—so many sports are. Think of the positioning footwork in basketball, football, fencing, and tennis. Jiu-jitsu has the same story, but instead of footwork, think of bodywork. The body moves to create the perfect position. Since a jiu-jitsu practitioner often operates from a seated position, some of this millimetric movement is generated by repositioning the butt.

Shrimping is a move that allows you to gain distance or close the distance on your opponent. This is done by repositioning yourself with a crawling, shimmying movement which you do when lying on the mat. Gaining distance via shrimping is a jiu-jitsu escape move done while on your back and side. It's not crawling exactly but it's in the crawling family. If you can, imagine yourself under your house, working on your back in close proximity to the floor above you. In order to go backwards, you probably have to shimmy your body and press off of whatever is touching the ground. Snaking backwards like this is shrimping. So is snaking forwards.

In jiu-jitsu, you change your position, often ever so slightly, to effect a change in your opponent's posture. You set up your body position in relation to your opponent just like you would set up your surfboard to catch the next selected wave. Surfing is another game of millimeters. Atop a waxed board gliding down the angles of breaking waves, your body adjusts, and if you do it where and when you're supposed to, you get a free ride from God. Sometimes you even catch the perfect wave. Luis has lived a life of board time and mat time. He has shrimped his way across the mat so many times that his millimeters have turned into tens of thousands of kilometers.

For Luis and his students, a clean gi means one won't be literally stinking up the place. It also means the student will be keeping the pride and honoring the art that originally came from India, then through ancient Japan, and was then brought to South America. The seed of the style known as Brazilian Jiu-Jitsu was planted back in 1914, when a famous judo instructor—Mitsuyo Maeda—came to demonstrate his art in Brazil. In ancient times, jiu-jitsu was used in one-on-one combat (often in warfare) until death or incapacitation. The winning warriors basically strangled or broke their opponent to death. The modern version—sport jiu-jitsu—finds its winner by points or by tap out. Such a win by finalization is earned by having one's opponent give up in total surrender. The Brazilian-born version of this art grew out of Maeda's initial instruction to a family of Brazilians whose recent ancestors came from Scotland—the Gracie family.

Since several of the founders of the Gracie schools were slender or of smaller stature, their main adaptations worked on leverage and technique, as well as fatiguing the opponent to set up the submission technique. Think of a jaguar that sucks the life out of a deer by biting the throat and suffocating it. The jiu-jitsu choke works in the very same fashion. Then there are the arm bars, leg bars, and locks that put pressure on the joints, immobilizing the recipient who is taught to tap out before injury.

The advanced practitioners and most honored masters of modern-day Brazilian Jiu-Jitsu are skilled in energy conservation and keeping their breath and heart rates under control. That skill doesn't mean they are able to cruise effortlessly as they grapple against a competitor of superior strength or equal or superior skills. As with animals on the hunt or the defense, it's common that substantial energy is expended in a normal combat or in a fight or flight response. Breath and heart rate pick up, the combative movement heats up, and sweat is produced.

Another grappling art, wrestling, requires its practitioners to wear a spandex/lycra singlet. Despite the scant attire, wrestling produces a lot of sweat. Now turn to jiu-jitsu. The no-gi version typically uses spandex/lycra jiu-jitsu shorts and a spandex/lycra long-sleeve shirt called a rash guard. The gi version often uses the no-gi clothes as undergarments. Then, over that goes long cotton gi pants, and a thick jiu-jitsu gi or kimono, tied closed by a strong cotton belt matching the artist's rank.

That's quite a bundle of clothing to wear. Things do get hot on a jiu-jitsu mat and inside the gi. You sweat, your opponents sweat, and the cotton absorbs what passes through the lycra or comes straight off the skin and scalp. It's literally a sauna inside the gi (and the gym often heats up) during a training session.

To avoid staph infections and other bacterial contamination, the mat and the garments are washed frequently, sometimes after each use. For any type of building construction—especially gyms, schools, medical centers, and locker rooms—fresh air, cross ventilation, and sunlight are helpful in preventing a situation in which microbes flourish.

Clothes are helped by the same airing out and solar rays. After a session of jiu-jitsu, if the weather cooperated, I would leave my exterior jiu-jitsu clothes and headgear out in the sun, flipping them over to make sure the sun made contact with all sides. Then I would wash them after a few uses. The lycra undergarments I washed after each use.

The sun is one of the most powerful antimicrobials we have. Spraying a white gi (or your linens) with vinegar or lemon juice and then leaving it in the sun is a wonderfully natural way to bleach out stains or to bleach the entire fabric.

One of my instructors described to us students that he washes his gi in the washing machine using nothing but vinegar. This is one of the most healthful ways to care for these close-contact sports clothes. I can't tell you how many times I have dreaded grappling with opponents who used chemical-smelling detergents and fabric softeners that hadn't been properly rinsed out and dried. When the gi gets sweaty, all of those chemical odors make their exit from the fabric. As you are gasping for air trying to survive your training partner's dominant position, you are sometimes forced to breathe in these chemicals, which are only slightly better than mildew.

Suffice it to say, if you added up all the students Luis works with at his jiu-jitsu centers, laundry usage is up there with that of a busy boutique hotel. A jiu-jitsu man is a man (women too) who first and foremost needs a good washing machine and a good clothes line to dry the garments. Besides his frequent travel to give seminars, Master Luis has spent most of his life in Rio, Los Angeles, and Hawaii. So, Luis' personal clothes cleaning bills can't be as bad as someone in, say, Canada. Luis has spent most of his life in a pair of beach shorts.

The important thing, he reminds us, is, "It's no matter if you're on the surfboard, or going for a take-down on a grappling mat, the truest expression of the art is when you land softly. If no one gets hurt on the mat, if your board lives on to ride another day, you have made it."

Jiu-jitsu—the gentle art—works its magic whether you're running through big swells in the Blue Pacific, or running through practice drills with a bunch of dedicated martial artists. The key is to go with the flow.

Chapter 8

The Little Hard Ass

"You can keep going and your legs might hurt for a week, or you can quit and your mind will hurt for a lifetime."

—Mark Allen–Ironman

Mark Allen is a former all-American swimmer and a six-time Ironman Triathlon champ with a degree in biology and a deep connection with shamanism. His quote above says it all. Aside from things like hand-to-hand combat and extended-delivery childbirth, triathlon is perhaps the most mind bending, body breaking one-day event ever conceived.

Leave it to the Gaulois psyche to push the human limits. The descendants of the ancient Gaules founded the Tour de France, the 24-hour auto race at Le Mans, and stuck it out in trench warfare against the Germans for the better part of the Great War. Some hold that this punishing three-sport event was invented in France about 1902 and included running, cycling, and canoeing. Scott Tinley, a triathlon historian, has a differing point of view about the date. Scott claims the first real triathlon was indeed held in France, but rather in the 1920s near Joinville-le-Pont. It was called—whichever one you can pronounce: Les trois sports, La Course des Débrouillards (the Can-Do or Adapters Race), or La course des Touche à Tout (the Well-Rounded Race).

Sacramento, California, claims July 27th, 1974 as the first modern "no swim" triathlon. Known as Eppie's Great Race, the event hasn't missed a year since it began and features a 5.82-mile run, a 12.5-mile bike and a 6.35-mile paddle held along the scenic American River Parkway on the outskirts of downtown Sacramento. Modern swim, bike, run triathlon was the hobby horse of two limit pushers—Jack Johnston and Don Shanahan. These wild and crazy guys snake-talked the San Diego Track Club into sponsoring the first one on Mission Bay in San Diego in September of 1974. Triathlon is a race of miles, lots of miles, 140.6 to be exact. If that isn't badass enough, it begins with an invigorating swim of 2.4 miles, then a break to change into your cycling duds, drink a revitalizing drink, and then jump on your bike and put the feet to the pedals for 112 excruciating miles. Ticktocking along, change into running shorts and shoes, chug a glug of a glucose drink. A custom in this event is downing some pale ale and nibbling a few pretzels. If you're still standing after that, it's off for a 26.2-mile heartbreaking run.

The average transition time between lower-level events is under two minutes. For the best competitors, the transition time between events is counted in seconds. Of course, times depend on location and terrain. For the average triathlete it takes 12 hours and 35 minutes and includes the time-out for pale ale and pretzels. The best time recorded in the 2013 Ironman Kona was just over eight hours. Of course, just to finish one is a tremendous feat for any level athlete.

This sets the table for a highly-motivated endurance athlete to make his entrée. David "Mac" McCluskey is a nine-time Ironman triathlon finisher, and 2001 Ultraman World Championship finisher. Mac is also a National Academy of Sports Medicine certified personal trainer, National Academy of Strength and Fitness Certified track and field and cross country coach, United States Ski and Snowboard Association alpine skiing coach, and a PSIA ski instructor, all rolled up into one tough iron enchilada. With the table set, let's chew the fat with big Mac.

With his students and with himself,
Coach McCluskey strives for the patience to hang in there.

Tale of The Tape
David "Mac" McCluskey

Endurance Athlete and All-Around Athlete

Born June 19, 1954 on Ryukus Army Base, Naha Okinawa, Japan.

Started out as the all-American kid who proved himself in athletics—notably in football and track. Mac became an endurance athlete on a dare. He started in Connecticut in the early days of triathlons. Now also does ultra-distance running and ski coaching. He achieved 3rd degree black belt in karate.

The son of a tough truck driver and grandson of a hard-nosed coal miner, he is also the son of an equally tough mother. He is the little brother of a bigger, faster, and stronger athlete who used to kick his butt.

Age 59: 5'9", 170 lbs.

At 18: 5'9.5", 185.

Personality traits: Silly, friendly, driven. Likes to prove himself every day.

Website: MonkeyRaces.com

Notable quote from his father: "We're McCluskey's, we don't quit—it's just not what we do."

Most famous moments: When he was baby in Okinawa, a nurse threw him down (yes, threw, in frustration) and broke his ankle. Some thought he'd never be able to walk.

He proved them wrong and became a star athlete. Right in his prime, playing semi-pro football and getting into acting and modeling, Mac was hit by a drunk driver on Halloween night in 1980 and got his face crushed.

After multiple plastic surgeries on the face, he left Akron, Ohio, where he was living at the time, and headed to California. While trying to find himself in Los Angeles, he happened into the car of the "Godfather of Fitness." He was telling the man who picked him up while hitchhiking, how depressed he had become. The man gave him some needed advice. When he turned to thank the man, he saw it was Jack LaLanne. Jack's advice helped get Mac back on track emotionally in a short pep talk that took about four years to fully work its magic. Patience is a virtue.

Mac, it is a pleasure to have this conversation with you. Tell me about your start in this world.

"My father was in the Army and was stationed in Okinawa with me, my older brother, and my little sister. It was a sort of unusual type of place to be born."

Do you remember anything about Okinawa?

"I don't really remember much about that time except that when I was a baby in Okinawa, something big happened. I guess I was cocky or something. A nurse threw me to the floor because I was crying so much. This broke my ankle. The Army doctors put a cast on my leg. A month later when they removed it they also had to remove my Achilles tendon, which had been eaten away because they had not used any gauze to protect my skin. My mother was told I'd probably never walk. My father walked around holding me up and took the attitude: This is my son. I know he can walk. I feel like that is very much where I am now—never say quit. This ancient injury sometimes hurts but I don't let it bother me. I just keep going."

So your dad was all about self-salvation and self-determination?

"Dad kept reminding me, 'You're a McCluskey and we don't quit.' Even when I was a kid and trying out for little league, or other things that were hard, he'd say, 'We don't quit, it's just not what we do.' It's an attitude that I grew up with. Thanks to my father, it was the only one I was allowed to have."

If you have it, use it?

"Exactly, I've always been blessed by being in shape and having a great body. Dad passed it down to me. If you have a really good brain, and you have some talent, use it. Do everything you can with it. I think it's important that whatever your strength is—go towards it, and whatever your weakness is—work on it!"

Did you ever have a competitive thing going on with your older brother?

"Yup, it's kind of funny my brother was 358 days older than me, so there was one week per year in our lives where we were the exact same chronological age. 'It'd be like I'm 13 and your 13 ha-ha.' That pissed him off so much he'd be like, yeah, let me show you what 13 means, and he'd beat the shit out of me for a whole week. He was the big brother and that is how it went, me tagging along, always the unwanted, tag-along little brother. He was much bigger and stronger."

Tell me a bit about your grandfather.

"He was an old Pennsylvania coal miner with solid muscles from digging coal all day. He had a hard-joking, hard-nosed, don't-quit attitude. He died in his early 60s of black lung disease."

Was your dad still in the military during that time?

"Dad got out of the military, came home, and went to work at a lumberyard, then became a truck-driver. That is when my mom came in. My mom was just as tough as my dad was. She had to be, with two sons, a daughter—and living in a home by herself most of the time."

Now here in Park City, Utah, you have a large home with all the modern fixings. When you were 13, could you imagine living a more luxurious lifestyle?

"When I was 13, I don't think I thought about these things. I believed that I'd probably have gone to work as a truck driver, or at the steel or coal mines. I smile all the time now because earlier in life I wasn't allowed to smile. Life has been very good to me."

Take us through some pivotal moments of being a small kid. Were you intimidated by bigger athletes?

"Well, when I was a kid my father put us into baseball and football. Even though I was the smallest kid, the thing that I was most proud of was a moment that I really feel defined me. My brother has always been much bigger than me, but he never let up versus the small guy. My coaches at the time would say this is one tough-ass small kid. When I heard that, I felt like I knew what my calling was—be tough."

Mac determined to make his mark. Pittsburgh, PA. 1965

Mac McCluskey (glasses), his older brother (33) who he says, "Used to kick my butt," and his cousin back in Pittsburgh, Pennsylvania in the year 1970.

Tell me about your time as the little man.

"I was 80 pounds and I was playing nose-guard on defense, because I was just vicious. My brother, even though he was almost twice my size—and still is today—was brutal to me. This pushed me hard and pushed me over the top. This meant that when I played football, I was known as the little hard ass. This truly gave me something to be proud of. That really made me want to continue to be the little hard ass (Laughs). I played football then and I never looked back. I played football all the way until the late '70s. I was also very proud of my track and field record. I was a sprinter and I was one of the fastest guys in high school. I played football in college because a coach in high school vouched for me. He was also my track coach. The joke was always that I ran so fast because my brother ran fast. My brother was also a tremendous athlete. He became an all-American when he played for West Virginia as a middle linebacker."

Where did you go to college and what did you study?

"I attended the University of Arizona and studied criminology. Besides football, I ran track and field there. I kind of had it easy in college. As a football player you could take easy classes to get you by."

It's interesting that you say that. These days and even for the last decade or so, I gather there really are no easy majors. Criminology courses are demanding. When I was in school, the toughest class I heard about was a night class in religious studies. You've probably heard that even a P.E. degree can be one of the toughest these days at our universities. Some years ago, I was looking into applying for a program toward a physical therapy degree. One school only accepted eight applicants per year. The prerequisites were quite demanding. It was like, okay, you want to be in this program—then go out and do three to five years of this type of stuff and we'll think about you. The backgrounds of the people getting accepted were impressive. I drew a parallel to getting in to be a firefighter in a popular town—it's sometimes next to impossible. At the time I was considering it, it was especially difficult if you were not ethnically a minority.

"I hear ya. Getting on to be a firefighter in Park City would be a prayer answered. Everyone wants to work 24 hours and then ski for three days. Point well made. When I was in my major, I wanted to be an FBI agent, but I was too small. You had to be six feet during that time. They didn't have stretching machines back then." (Laughs)

We were both laughing pretty heartily at this point.

Mac, with your size and build today, would you still go out for high school and college football?

"Actually, football has changed. I think in respect that it's a little easier for a smaller guy to be more successful. I think I could be a more productive player today than I was back then. Anyway, after college in Phoenix, I played semi-pro football in Pittsburgh. I played an exchange position at wide receiver for the Pittsburg Steelers."

If you played semi-pro football, that means you had a day job and practiced football at night?

"During that time I worked full-time as a factory worker at Westinghouse Electric. At that time, I assumed that this would be my career. I used to play for the Pythons and the Wolfpack between June and November. I was a receiver on our first team. Then we had a vacancy at quarterback. I went from wide receiver over to quarterback because I was good at pass-routes. But it was pretty apparent that I was a horrible quarterback. But I stepped in and took ownership of the position and played there for a few years. Afterwards I went to another team and went back to wide-receiver."

How did you manage a balance of being productive at your day job, then the practices while playing semi-pro football?

"That was a lot to manage, but I worked the 4 a.m. to 12 p.m. shift at Westinghouse. I'm not really sure how, I just did. It was like when school was over and you wanted to play. It was the same thing with playing football. I made very good friends with people that I hung out with and we all just kind of did the same thing, growing up having fun and working hard all night."

Did you ever get to practice with the Steelers during the exchange?

"No I was on a semi-pro team. We didn't get to practice with the Steelers. We were off to the side a lot, although I had tried out for the pro team in Cleveland."

Let's talk about some of the mentors, were they mostly coaches?

"I'd say it was probably one of my first coaches, an ex-Navy guy named Bob Olanger. Bob was my coach as a kid He was a very intellectual guy. He always encouraged me. Kind of later in life, it was Eric Houska, a tremendous athlete. He was probably one of the best coaches I have ever had. Eric was a training friend of mine. He was incredible and a very motivational type of guy. Eric has been to Hawaii [for Ironman] every year since he has made the attempt to qualify—he's that good. He is also very encouraging to everyone around him. He is one of those guys who could have had a huge ego or a huge head, but doesn't."

That's always refreshing.

"Yeah. Back in the late '80s, Eric and I used to make a joke that we were only two of five triathletes in all of Connecticut. He was years ahead of me in his training and we traveled a lot together. During our travels and time together he was very motivational. We spent a lot of time in different triathlons across the world. I was always happy to have a chat with him. As coaches go, he was probably the one who stood out most for me."

What was happening in your life back in the '50s and '60s?

"I got into organized sports. It was one of the only things they had for kids to do back then. We played Little League Baseball. Our fathers literally dug it out of an open space right next to the railroad tracks. I think it's important to be a part of something, even if it's not sports, just to be a part of something. Later, in my 30s there was a guy in my neighborhood, Christopher Ciletti, who worked at a bank. He challenged me. He said, 'You run 5k, then bicycle for 20 miles and then run 5k again. And, I bet I can beat you.'"

Nothing like a dare.

"Yep. This race was the Derby Connecticut Triathlon. At that point, I'm thinking there is no way you're beating me. He wound up beating me by about five minutes. You might as well have just beaten me over the head with a sledgehammer. That snapped me into life. Then I decided to do another triathlon. To this day, I credit triathlons for saving my life. Thanks for kicking my ass, Christopher Ciletti. It's the best thing you ever did!"

Sounds like you're a competitor. How did you keep the well-rounded side going when you're training, considering other activities, family, etc.?

"We were both happy. My first wife, Helen, and I were getting life in order. But, I think, in some respects, some of that suffers along the way. Especially when you've decided you're going to compete. What I think is important is that you say okay, I have to move all of this non-essential stuff off to the side. You really have to pay attention."

What can you take from your experience that relates to the mindset needed to live a healthy life?

"I think it just takes some discipline and a type of commitment to wanting to have that and be generally concerned about that.

Get yourself on the daily routine schedule. Get yourself up at 6 o'clock every morning. Eat what you have to. Do what is necessary. Get your commitment done and the rest of the day is yours. Get yourself into the habit. Instead of it just becoming a task, it has to become your life."

Does it make you better in relation to tension and negative energy doing your morning routines?

"Absolutely. I'm the kind of person, I take it you may be too, if I'm not doing something constructive, I'm doing something destructive. Do you want to make something, or do you want to break something."

I believe in staying busy on projects. While I like to socialize, I prefer getting into deep conversations where we both may learn something and get something special from it—even if that's some good, hearty laughs. I don't like hanging out in bars—I never have liked that. Always felt like a waste of time to pay good money for mostly sugar and chemicals and have to be 'cool' or have to keep coming up with something to say when you meet someone new. I'd rather do that type of socializing at an outdoor café or at a social gathering. But, then again, there were those nights of girls' nights out …

"I hear ya."

What would you say was pivotal in overcoming obstacles, and learning about yourself?

"I think what is probably most enlightening to me is how you treat yourself. Growing up in the family I grew up in, we knew how to treat other people—aside from my brother kicking my ass. (Laughs) We learned this from my father. He taught us to give everyone an equal chance. Don't draw any conclusions about a person by what you think they are. We tried to see people for who they really are. I often present myself to people differently than I really am. I have doubts and I worry about things and I have nagging problems. Everyone has a closet full of crackers. I'm just like everybody else in that respect. But I don't sit around and complain. I keep it to myself. Every person is an ocean, and all you see is the surface. Everyone has a Loch Ness Monster. I know it's in there."

People today who had dysfunctional relationships with their parents now have their kids living at home because the kids don't know how or somehow aren't able to survive. What do you think about that, Mac?

"I have some pretty strong opinions about what you just said. They have never really had the general opportunity to live. The parents have made all of the executive decisions, so there has never been an opportunity for the kids to make those choices. They don't know how to take charge, because in some fashion they think taking charge means they have to be a bully."

Can you think of an example where you've seen someone who has been coddled, who didn't know what to do in given situation?

"I recently coached an outdoor track team. I had four boys who were extremely talented, great kids everyone loved … they were very popular at school. But going beyond being in charge of running a warm-up, they have never known leadership skills. When it came to one of the other guys on the team having a problem with another kid, they'd run to me. I would say to them, 'You can solve these problems on your own, work it out amongst yourselves. You don't need me to step in there.' I try to give them some leeway so they can figure out how to do it on their own. But it just seems they are unable to. They don't have the training for that because they always run to mom, they always run to dad. Dad or mom always solves the problem and the problem is over. I didn't have to deal with that growing up. This background they have in running to mom and running to me, the coach, has really become a problem for me as a coach."

Would a program like Outward Bound or being on their own training programs away from the parents and coaches on the weekends—kind of running their own thing—help them make a change or transition into more of a leadership role?

"I'd say so. I think for me, I saw that the kids on my cross country team had the chance to do that. I hoped the captains would try to motivate their friends, and try to motivate the others. 'Okay, we're going to get up early and run.' They tried that tactic and the other kids just wouldn't show up."

I remember telling my dad to wake me up so I could start a summer running program. That was when I was 14. We were in Cape Cod near the beach on summer vacation. I was scrawny and had lousy endurance for running. I was the consummate 98-pound weakling. It was so hot and humid, plus I was dealing with my own growing up and into my body that I had trouble waking up. I had the motivation and the inspiration, but this wasn't coming to me at 6 or 7 a.m. I was so groggy I could barely get out of bed. Even for golf, a sport I really appreciated, it was hard to get myself going early at that time. I get what those kids may have been going through. It's so much easier for me as an adult—no growth spurts, no peer pressure, no huge sleep needs—to get up in the morning and go for a semi-hard workout. I also recently learned about how melatonin levels tend to keep adolescents up late at night and sleeping in the next morning.

"I hear ya. I'm teaching a class in August for cross country and there are rules for high school where you can't really go and train these kids during summer. So, depending on what the path is, the job is to try to motivate them to do it on their own. Because if you can't, they just won't participate on their own. They won't go on their own, and they won't participate with the captains, and it becomes a problem for you later when you get 40 or 50 kids in training camp and you're asking them what they did all summer. 'Oh, you know what, we went to the pool.'"

A bunch of slackers. (I say, laughing)

"Yep, we say to the captains, 'Did you try to motivate them to work on track?' And they say, 'Yeah we tried, nobody really listened, and nobody showed up.' So it's irritating to try to organize but not even the captains could get anyone to show up."

Speaking of kids, something close to your heart here, what was the secret to success with the kids that you've coached successfully?

"A lot of love. I loved them and they loved me back. Those kids really performed well and they just had fantastic attitudes. The successful thing to do is to let kids know how good they are, because the kids themselves often don't realize it. It isn't so much as them believing in themselves at that age, but having someone else who believes in them, they can do great things."

True, but talking about great things, look at Muhammad Ali, Diego Maradona, Greg LeMond, and many other athletes who did great things. They have other interests, don't need the performance anymore, and completely lose their fitness, why?

"I think you become weary of the daily grind, is all. And once you feel like it becomes a job, it goes into a completely different realm. I think the guys who love it are the ones who continue on. The guys who set out to make the money and fame are the ones who stop."

I think what separates athletes like John McEnroe, Jimmy Connors, and Björn Borg is not just their athleticism but their mindset. McEnroe was a super competitive person and he had a gift of moving his body effortlessly at times. I watched him close up when I worked as a ball boy at the 1981 French Open. He was amazing, simply amazing. He was by far the most captivating player I have ever seen mostly because he was so different. His perception was unlike any other I had ever seen. He seemed to know where the other person was going to hit it. He saw the game differently than the other players—kind of like Bobby Orr who saw things differently. But here's the kicker. I heard that John McEnroe has confessed that he hated tennis for years when he was the best in the world. His attitude may be part of something called fear-based narcissism. So I'm trying to figure out why he kept doing it. Was it the job and the money or was it because he had to do it, because he was good at it, and he just had to. What do you think?

"You never really want to think a guy like that would fail because he's making a lot of money doing it and he really hated it. I think it's just that McEnroe is the kind of guy who says things like that to get attention, but deep down he really liked it. Because if he really didn't like it, he'd have gone home, put the racquet in the bag. Something about it, even at the end when it's just a stadium full of people screaming and cheering for him, there's something there for him."

That sounds like able-minded reasoning.

"They are typically super talented people doing what they love, and in many cases making great money at the same time."

The term adrenaline junkie is tossed around a lot. Can you speak about how athleticism left you feeling high or competition left you in a different state?

"I think adrenaline junkie is a naked term for guys who like to do crazy stuff. But then there are some things that you see and then say, 'Damn, I want to try that!'"

You're putting a lot of deep thoughts together right now. I'm guessing that the same thing happens during your training. On a long run, long bike ride, long swim, a lot is going through your mind, right?

"With runners especially, because when you're out there running you're on your own and there is a lot of time to be cerebral. That is how you can lose, because so much of it is in your head, it becomes a distraction. If I were running in a 5k and thinking about every full step; how my foot, ankle, knee hurts, my hips are hurting, my lower-back, oh, shit! See how that defeats you? Tell me how long you can run fast thinking about being in agony."

Not very far. I've been there. That may be part of why I got into martial arts—less wear and tear than distance running. You mentioned martial arts in our first conversation. What era did you become involved in martial arts and what was your motivation in getting involved?

"During training for triathlons I noticed my muscles were getting too tight. So, I got involved in martial arts. I was thinking at the time of Jean-Claude Van Damme. He can stick it to these guys and is constantly in shape. Who is more flexible than a karate guy? So I just walked into a karate class and watched how they were stretching. It turned out there were hardly any stretches. It was the moves that did the stretching for us. I thought that was really cool!"

Mac, all the blood drained from his skin, being helped
to the recovery station after the Ultraman World Championships, 2001.

Was it an eye-opening thing to see how things you did in your own training program paid off in your endurance sports?

"What it really enlightened me to was what other people were struggling with. Sometimes you take for granted what you have. You kind of don't understand the majority of it. If you don't have the right mindset you can develop a bad attitude. I think that's where personal training and coaching helped me. You know, from being in martial arts that you are basically doing the same exact thing several hundred times over until you get it. You don't think, it just flows."

When you have either an emotional or physical breakdown or some-thing going on with your family, how do you rebound from that?

"I've got a good example. In 1980 when I was playing semi-pro football, I was also trying to get myself exposure in acting and modeling and started to get some breaks. Then, on Halloween night, I had a head-on crash with a drunk driver. 103 stitches in my face and a piece of the car through my leg. If I hadn't been in decent shape, plenty of football, I'm sure I'd have been dead. I wound up going to L.A. But that didn't work out. One of the reasons I left L.A. is nobody would hire me. I had these big scars and everyone thought I was a gang banger—couldn't find work in anything. Or even a place to live. So at one point, I'm just a college student in L.A., hitchhiking back to Akron, Ohio. This guy picks me up. I looked like Frankenstein. I'm like; I think I recognize this guy. He's giving me this really motivational talk. He says, 'You've got to keep going, keep doing what you're doing, never give up.' I got out of the car and realized it was Jack LaLanne [the Godfather of Fitness]. His voice and his advice just kept echoing in my head."

Could you talk from a personal point of view of what doing the right thing means?

"I think doing the right thing is discovering what makes you really happy, gives you genuine pride in yourself. Don't make excuses as to why you can't. Don't make up some kind of invisible barrier. The truth is nobody has ever put a barrier between me and what I wanted to do. When I'm 80 years old, ready to die, I don't want to be saying, I wish I had. Therefore, if there is anything I wish for now, I'm going to do it."

To wrap up what has been an inspiring conversation, what are the overall key points that helped you prevail in life, snatch victory from defeat, so to speak?

"I really feel like being the small kid helped me in life. It pushed me hard, and pushed me over the top. I was really proud to have made it as the little hard ass. My dad was the most important motivator and the most important person in my life. He set the example by his no-die attitude. There was no quitting or any backing off. It was pressure. He would say, look, this is the way life is going to go, and this is the way you have to handle it. What pulled me out of it was athletic failure. We just don't quit. Even though I may have let dad down, I just kept trying to pull myself out of it."

Mac (I was readying for a fitting mutual hug), thanks for taking the time from a full schedule to have this conversation. It has been an honor.

§ § §

What is the driver for all-around athletes like Mac? Is it only the values instilled in us by parents or the need to please? Is it rising to a challenge of overcoming size and strength limitations, overcoming those obstacles in order to run with the big guys and prevail? Is it setting up to compete and then finishing a grueling athletic contest such as triathlon?

What is it that makes some overcome all obstacles when others are more prone to quit? Where does that competitive force come from that will not allow one individual to give up? Hopefully, some light has been shed on those intriguing questions in this interview. Mac McCluskey may be small in stature, but inside the ribs lies a huge heart. Thank you, Mac; we are grateful for your candor and inspiration. As noted in the opening quote by Mark Allen, your mind will never hurt in your lifetime. There is no quit in you. If any lifetime athlete deserves a quiet stroll along a beach in Tahiti, it's you.

In his 40s, Mac receives congratulations from his hard-working, truck-driver father. "You, my son, are the top family endurance athlete."

Chapter 9
Mayhem on the Field

In August of 2013, the NFL, a $10 billion industry, reached a tentative 20-year agreement to pay out $765 million to former players who have suffered cognitive injuries and to the families of players who committed suicide as a result of the concussion-related trauma they experienced. That is the good news. The bad news is what money generally can't buy back is a working brain and positive outlook.

Enough is never enough, or at least the bar continues to move. That bar is the bar of propriety or decency or tolerance—an even better expression is "devastation turn on." Old customs die hard. And football's big smashes and upending, somersault tackles, together with some high-stepping celebration dance moves wind up being watched in highlight films and Internet videos for years. "People want to see mayhem," I've been told ... "and even blood." Hence the term: "They're out for blood." The players themselves know the custom. They grew up in a pattern of being rewarded, patted on the back or helmet, for good hits. So, just what is a good hit? What do you think of the criteria I list here?

You stop the forward advance or offensive play of an opposing player by tackling him or blocking him.

You time your hit perfectly so your momentum violently outdoes the opponent's momentum.

You hit your opponent so hard they either get up slowly or can't get up at all.

A loud crack, thud, or utterance also helps sell the concussion of a good hit.

Is it any surprise that 3.3 years is the average career span of a player in the National Football League. That's all you get for those early years, almost two decades, of sweat equity, heat and ice treatments, visits to the doctor or surgeon, and lots of tweaks and tears. The average career span is worth considering. Since some careers last 14 years or more, that means some last a few months—or even one game. Or, no games at all. Maybe someone is a third stringer or rookie and they get injured in pre-season.

In the big picture of supportive and pumped-up fans watching from home or in the stands (some even wear funny hats and game-day face and body paint), and VIPs in private boxes, does the longevity of a player even matter? Sure, it matters. Everyone cares after the fact—after the big blast or slight twist that leaves collateral damage. It matters when you see a player hobbling or attempting to commit suicide. It matters when your child's favorite player winds up in a standoff with law enforcement or happens to kill his spouse, beat up a girlfriend, or throttle a neighbor or family member because they've completely lost it. It matters when a former elite athlete is shown using a walker (no matter their age) or admits to being unable to live without pain killers. It matters when a player dies in the line of duty or way before expected mortality. A big question is: are they expendable? If they sacrifice themselves and are easily replaced, the question is not one of lengthy debate, at least not as far as the for-profit game is concerned. Or maybe not. A new era could be coming about. Maybe fans and players want to change the game into highlighting athleticism and teamwork, while deemphasizing or even penalizing players for big hits from the blindsides. If you consider the rules changes related to late hits, spearing, and quarterback safety, the move to a tamer game is already afoot.

Let's take a sandal's step back in time—to Ancient Rome. Although some were praised for their longevity and became crowd favorites, Roman gladiators were generally considered expendable. These men fought it out for a living. Their living most of all meant they would live to fight another day. The citizen crowds got their fill and sometimes left the forum with a blood lust, which prompted more mayhem in the streets—fighting each other and wrecking structures in a display of hooliganism. In subsequent shows, and in subsequent years, the Roman event directors would alter the contests, finding some way to make them different, more appealing, more satisfying. This often meant that the event grew even more gory. Gore, the Romans learned, sells. Who else took up with this ethic?

Some Puritans liked a good burning at the stake, Parisians in the French Revolution liked a good beheading, American frontier townspeople liked a good hanging. Some of the most popular videos on the Internet show all-out fights between non-professional fighters like students on playgrounds or disgruntled people at

McDonald's. Sometimes these fights are filmed by bystanders with smartphones; other times they're filmed by security cameras. But when does the animalistic brutality end? When is thug life no longer vogue? When does a fan's hanker become rancor?

Now the NFL, one of the closest mainstream sports to team gladiator bouts we have, is getting hit in the most painful region of all—the purse. Yes, the purse. It's long been okay for military officials to deal with the death and disability of service people since they are sworn into something quite different from being a mere civilian. Everyone gets that. The same consideration has long been suggested of people in any field who knew what they were getting themselves into. Prison guards know ahead of time about cavity searches and people flinging excrement at them. EMTs and firefighters realize they may be splattered with blood from infected people. Football players know the ropes. They know they'll be asked to play hard, run fast, hit people, and perhaps even take substances not commonly considered to provide healthful outcomes—uppers, cortisone, growth hormones, and pain killers. They're supposed to put themselves at risk, essentially "taking one for the team" as they play injured or with the flu.

The athlete in the following conversation told me how he had pulled his groin muscle in his senior year of college. A short while later, now in the pros, he reinjured it. Since the team doctor was "looking out" for his future, he told the star-defensive end, "Let me give you an injection." Down came the padded paints. With a sizable needle, the physician gave the rookie a shot of Novocain directly into the site of the pain. As the player grew numb, the doctor said to him, "This is a big day. You should go out there and do something." The coach and the team doctor had some words.

Then, with a nod to the coach, the player put on his helmet and headed out onto the field. Four steps later, the 250-pound athlete's right side gave out and he went down like a darted rhino. He told the trainer and doctor, "I have no feeling at all." To this day, he posits the needle may have hit a nerve. "Yeah," the doctor responded, "I may have sent you out there too soon ..."

Tale of The Tape
Randy Beisler

NFL offensive and defensive tackle
Has run businesses

As a defensive end, he was selected the fourth draft pick of the 1966 draft.

Born Randall Lee Beisler, October 10, 1944, Gary, Indiana, a company town which grew up with the U.S. Steel plant.

Age 18: 6'5", 218.

In high school: Ran track, played football, and basketball. Jumping ability and agility got better with age and improved in college. Could dunk in high school. Kept in shape during the NFL offseason via gym workouts and playing some 70 fundraising basketball games per year.

Age 25: 255 pounds.

Age 68: 6'5", 235.

Notable quotes: "I haven't shrunk in size or height like many do—my weight training regimen keeps my bones strong and healthy."

"I use fitness as recreation. I'm in the gym five days per week with weights and machines and I play tennis a few days per week."

Father: Edward Charles Beisler, 6'3", 210 pounds, not an athlete. Over a 36-year career, worked his way up at U.S. Steel from manual jobs to management. His nickname was Easy Ed. Very easy going, soft spoken.

Mother: Katherine Sikora, 5'5", 115 pounds. Both her parents were from the Ukraine. Athletic—played basketball into her 30s, swimmer and fitness person for life.

Mother's brother, Mike Sikora, born 1926, 6'2", 240, played professional football for the Chicago Cardinals, 1952–1954.

Randy is the former professional athlete who kick-started this Aging Athlete Project. As previously mentioned, I had been given the book idea by surgeon and athlete Bill Gallivan, M.D. But, I had yet to get started on the project since I was immersed in my lengthy project "Sedentary Nation." In 2009 I was visiting my sister Heidi in Tiburon, California. During a workout at her fitness and tennis center, she introduced me to Randy. Here's what I asked him: "When you go to the reunions with the retired players from your era, how many of them are still in shape?" "Less than 10 percent."

For four years subsequent to that meeting, I asked other aging athletes, ex-military personnel, and former dancers and stage performers the same question. While this was an anecdotal rather than scientific study, the answers were generally the same: less than 10 percent.

For football players, years of pushing their weight around was generally not followed by pushing their weight around. In some of the cases of aged football players, others now had to push them around—in wheel chairs.

So you hail from Gary, Indiana, home of the Jackson 5?

"Yeah, there's talk of building a museum there in their honor and to attract people to Gary. Gary has really declined since U.S. Steel closed down a lot of their plants. When that happened, about half the population left. A lot of the iconic buildings that were there when I left have subsequently gone back to nature—trees are growing through the middle of them. U.S. Steel brought everyone there. It's a company town."

Is that how your family got there?

"Yeah, my father wound up working at U.S. Steel in Gary. He worked his way up over the years and did shift work—you'd work one month at one shift, perhaps working all night, and then the next month you'd change to another shift, perhaps days. For that reason, it was very difficult for him to have any kind of a recreational program outside of work."

Did he start off on the physical side and then move to the desk side?

"Yeah, he started out in labor and ended up in management. He was there for 36 years."

How did your family get to that area?

"Both of my parents were born in the area—my mom was from Hammond and my dad from Hobart. One side of my grandparents—the Beislers—came from Germany, the other side came from the Ukraine. The Beisler grandparents died when I was very young, and the Ukrainian-side grandfather, his family name was Sikora, died when I was in high school. He also worked at one of the steel mills. My grandparents all spoke with thick, European accents. And the Sikoras didn't speak any English. My grandfather Sikora would pat me on the head and say, 'Big boy, big boy.'"

Where do you think your athletic side came from?

"My mother was the athlete. She was a swimmer and a basketball player. And she ran track … she did it all. She was athletic, still swimming and doing exercises, right up until she passed away. My dad was supportive of mom's physical activity. She became a tax appraiser and later cut women's hair in our basement. Because it was the local gossip mill, I couldn't get away with anything growing up."

Did your mom drag you to her athletic endeavors?

"She did indeed. I can remember going to her basketball games as a little kid. She not only played, later she coached. She played with the CYO—the Catholic Youth Organization, and played people in her own age group."

How did she start?

"I know she played in high school for the team. And later the CYO, which was a club league. She played into her 30s and coached into her 40s."

What was your height and weight in senior year of high school?

"I was 6'5", 218."

That has to be in the top one percent of size athletes from the 1960s. When you were 18, were you your most able-bodied in terms of running athleticism or did you make gains from there?

"I ran track when I was in high school, but not in college. I think I improved as an athlete—my jumping ability got better and my speed improved."

Randy already determined as a high school student-athlete in 1962

How about your agility?

"Oh, yeah. I think it definitely did improve with age."

How do you think that happened? Just growing into your body, doing better drills, or just time?

"I think it was a combination of all that. As you get a little more mature, you grow into your body. And the training, of course. I could dunk a basketball when I was in high school, with two hands standing under the basket. By the way, my uncle, my mother's brother, was a professional football player. He played for the Chicago Cardinals. His name was Mike Sikora. He played for about three years in the early '50s."

In the old days, wasn't it common to play only one to three years of professional football?

"It was and it still is. Today the average years of service is three-and-a-half years."

When do you think it was more brutal, or was it always the same level of brutality?

"Do you mean my era versus now?"

Even your Mike Sikora relative's days. I've seen the old games with the limited helmets, maybe playing both ways—offense and defense, not having chiropractors, personal trainers, Epsom salt baths, perhaps not having ambulances at the site.

"Yeah, people playing for the love of the game. My uncle, of course, had another job when he was playing. He passed down his helmet to me, several helmets, and with those helmets I started my own team. This was in our neighborhood. We played against other neighborhoods. We were the Maple Street Rams."

Could you give us your take on the helmet evolution?

"Sure, those old pro helmets weren't as good as the ones I wore as a college player or in the pros, and mine weren't as good as the ones they're using today. And with the evolution of helmets, with the improvements, that resulted in the more frequent tactic of using your head as a weapon. That made things more violent with time. The helmets are so good, you can ram people. Or, at least you think you can."

What was your weight at age 25?
"255."

And now?
    "235."

What was your weight when I met you in 2009?
    "Probably 248."

Are you slimming down on purpose?
    "Yes, on purpose."

Are you losing any height with age?
    "No, same height."

Wouldn't you say that's rare for a person who is aging?
    "I think it is, but you know I'm still lifting weights. I think that really helps. It keeps you straighter, adds to the bone density. I think what happens to older athletes is they stop lifting weights, and you have to do that to keep the bone growth. You have to have density in your bones."

Back when you were in high school, I mean we've all had somebody who wanted to get a piece of us. Did you ever run into that?
    "Yeah, older kids would confront me because I was big for my age. Boys wanted to take me on and that concerned me for awhile."

So what did you do?
    "In grade school, I avoided them. Then it stopped. Then, when I got into high school, I got into a couple of confrontations ... the usual stuff that happens with boys."

Did you have to go to the office?
    "First you had to go behind the boiler room. That's where you had the fights. And it's funny, word would spread throughout the school and it would draw a big crowd."

Do you have any snippets from an event that you could share?

"There was a kid in my class, he had the ducktail hair and wore leathers. And we just didn't get along. And we eventually ended up behind the boiler room, but it took a few weeks to set up the event. He had challenged me at my locker. At the time, I had a broken finger, I had a cast. I told him, 'Well, when I get my cast off.' And he would show up every day and say, 'How about today?' So finally I get my cast off, so that was the day. The whole school was waiting … So behind the boiler room we have our fisticuffs, and he ends up at the doctor's office. And my mom happened to be there at the doctor's the same day. And she came home and she was so mad at me because I gave him a couple of good ones and he had a broken nose, black eyes, all that stuff. I didn't need to get sent to the principal's office because my mom confronted me."

Was the other kid an athlete?

"No, and I can't remember his name, but I think he wound up being a cop." (That drew laughter from both sides.)

You said your mother was a basketball player. What was her height and approximate weight?

"My mom was 5'6" and weighed probably 115 pounds."

Do you have any idea where you got your size from? I know your father was not a small person.

"My dad was tall. And my uncle, my mother's brother, was 6'2", and he probably played at 240 pounds. And my other uncles, his brothers, were all stout."

Did you know anything about proper diet in the '50s and '60s?

"I didn't know anything about diet until, I think, I got to the pros."

Was your mother cooking up meat on a regular basis?

"Yeah, my father would buy a cow with a couple of neighbors. And they'd have a butcher cut it up and we had a big freezer in the basement. You know, full of meat. We went through a lot of meat. I have two other brothers. My mom had to feed four pretty big people."

Were your siblings athletes?

"My older brother, Gerald, played on the same basketball team in high school. He was a senior when I was a sophomore. I was taller and weighed more than he did. We hung out together a bit. We both went to Indiana University. He wasn't an athlete at that point, as I was. My younger brother Edward was six years younger. He was a basketball and football player in high school—good athlete. Edward died of a rare form of leukemia, and my older brother Gerald is still alive."

Did you have any coaches or mentors other than your parents?

"There was an assistant coach in high school who took me under his wing. He also became friends of my parents and would travel to see me play in college. His name was Jack Owens, and he had played at a small school in college."

What position did you play in high school?

"I was an end on both offense and defense. My preference was offense because I loved catching the ball."

What did Jack Owens teach you?

"He taught me the fundamentals of blocking and tackling. How to rush the passer, those kinds of things."

How would you characterize your youth up to college?

"Very carefree. I grew up on the shores of Lake Michigan. And our house was about a block from the beach. It was a beautiful white, sandy beach … sand dunes. The lake was fabulous at that time and it still is, I think. I was a lifeguard in high school, so a lot of my growing up was at the beach. It was pretty idyllic."

When you were looking out from your lifeguard station, were you looking north?

"We were looking north, and we had no sun protection. Everybody all got hit hard by the first hot day of the year, so you peeled. As a lifeguard I can remember sitting up there on the perch, no sun glasses, probably no hat. And one of my mentors was a college guy and one of his suggestions was, 'You've got to get as brown as you can, the girls love it.' (Lots of laughter.) So you put baby oil on, and that was it. Six or eight hours a day for several years, baking in the sun."

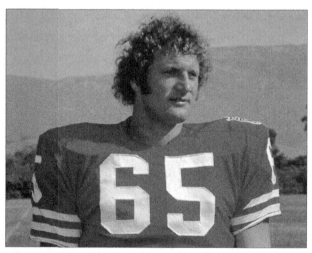

Randy as a rookie with the 49ers. (Athlete's personal collection.)

How did that bear out?

"I'm light-complected, blond hair and blue eyes. I had cataracts before I was 40 years old. That was probably mostly from the lifeguarding."

Do you recall a top moment growing up?

"I don't really have a best moment. As I say, it was pretty idyllic. We had bonfires at night, waterskiing during the day. We even played tackle football in the water, which was a lot of fun. The lake was a place to gather for everybody, it was unbelievable."

How about the best moment during your playing days in the pros?

"Well, when we were successful in San Francisco, we had three years in a row when we won our conference and went on and played in the playoffs. All three years we lost in the title game before the Super Bowl. Three years in a row we lost to Dallas. One particular year—1972—we were up by 12 points with a minute and 53 seconds to go and Roger Staubach came off the bench, he'd been hurt, and threw two touchdown passes, and beat us. I can remember how as a group our offensive line was standing on the sidelines and we were up by 12, our defense was on the field, and we were talking about how we were going to spend our bonus money."

(Mucho laughs.)

"And that evaporated pretty quickly."

So, were you jarred from your daydream with your cohorts when Staubach was throwing these touchdown passes?

"Yeah, he throws a touchdown pass and then they tried an onside kick and the ball squirts through one of our receiver's legs and the Cowboys jumped on it and Staubach throws another touchdown right away. It was unbelievable; it happened so fast. We had some time left but we didn't put it together. In football, even with time running down you're often not completely out of it. You've still got a glimmer of hope."

What would the bonus money have been in the early '70s?

"Ten grand maybe plus whatever you got for the win. I think I had something like that on my contract. Six to 10,000, something like that. But at the time it was a lot of money.

"You could have purchased a house in Indiana for that money back then." (Laughs from Randy)

And now, best moment, I'm thinking euphoric moments, of your life?

"The birth of my children is probably right up there. Both of my kids were high school athletes—soccer, tennis, and swim team—so I was pleased to have been able to watch them play sports. I actually coached their youth soccer league teams for five to eight years. Devon is my eldest daughter. My youngest daughter, Candice, was always the best one on the field so that was fun to watch. And now my grandkids are playing soccer and my youngest daughter is coaching them."

Are your daughters both maintaining their fitness to this day and, if so, did they get that from you?

"Yes. I believe it's because I was active in their lives and their sports. I led by example."

How did they learn about recreational sports and activities?

"We played volleyball in the pool and sometimes on the beach. Yeah, I just made sports as fun as they could be … never any pressure."

Randy, you seem like a level-headed individual, I'm guessing that you were not one of the guys grabbing people on the sidelines, banging helmets, trying to pump people up?

"No."

Did some people want to do that with you?

"Oh, sure."

What did you say, I'm not interested right now? (Laughing)

"No—you had to go along with it." (Laughs too)

When you were in your peak performance years, who was the motivator, borderline psychotic on your team and how did you handle that personality?

"Let's see, who would that be? Well, there was a guy named Frank Dudley who was a middle linebacker who was very enthusiastic and would try to pump us up. Offensive line is a little more cerebral than the defense. As an offensive line you have to be very cohesive, you have to know what everybody else is doing, you've got to work as a unit. And we did that well. Our offensive unit, as a line, we set a record for least amount of quarterback sacks in a season—eight sacks over the whole season. That was in 1970. We were nicknamed the Protectors."

I'm looking at the Protectors photo from Sports Illustrated, the cover from 1970. In the photo, you and your cohorts from the offensive line are all muddy. Next to you is the quarterback, John Brodie.

[Authors note: The caption says: "Along with right guard Woody Peoples, center Forrest Blue, and tackles Len Rohde and Cas Banaszek they were tagged the Protectors." See: http://posttrib.

suntimes.com/sports/19621476-556/mutka-garys-beisler-served-as
-brodies-protector.html]

The article says, "Frisco's best record in that stretch was 10-3-1 in
1970. Quarterbacked by John Brodie, they beat the Vikings 17-14 in
seven-below-zero weather."

Where Are They Now?

Here is the breakdown of the bios and what happened to the rest
of the people in the front-page photo after the 1970 season—a true tale
of the aging athlete—from Randy's recollection. The idea here is not
to belittle anyone or their condition, just to take a look at the outcome
over the decades:

"No. 75, center, Forrest Blue. From Auburn U. Ran the offensive
line. He was big for a center at the time: 6'6", 265 pounds. He died
a couple of years ago from something related to Alzheimer's. He
had a business career and then, in his early 50s, he started showing
some signs of dementia, and he didn't have a very good life from
that point on. About a year before he died, we all got together at a
restaurant in San Francisco. He was a beneficiary of what the union
and the league had put in place to aid players who had suffered
head injuries.

"Up above Forest is Len Rohde, who grew up on a farm in
Illinois. He said he went through high school in a one-room
classroom. And this was only 45 minutes outside of Chicago. He
was the tackle, played 17 years in pro football. He was the senior
member of the team and captain. He had some kind of record
for playing with the 49ers 200-plus games in a row. He and I stay
close. He is having some mental problems—he has no short-term
memory. He has some family members helping him live. His wife

and he and his son's family live in Los Altos. He can go back and remember names of people from way back, people whose names I have forgotten. But you can make a date with him and he'll ask you, "When are we going to get together again?" He is about seven years older than the rest of the players in the photo.

"I think his condition is probably from head injuries. A lot were probably just from hitting guys head-on-head in normal blocking."

A quick aside on head injuries, from Randy's point of view:

"In those days, concussions were no big deal. A coach who would see that you had your bell rung and they'd expect you to shake it off. One coach might say, 'Go see the trainer and tape an aspirin on the side of your helmet.' In our era the head slap was legal. The defensive lineman, the first thing he would do is take his forearm and whack you across the head. And that stung. They eventually outlawed that. That was a main weapon for a guy like Deacon Jones [Hall of Fame defensive end who died in 2013. He was huge and had quick hands.] That was how he made a name for himself and everyone mimicked it after his success."

[No. 58, African American] "Robert Hoskins, from Illinois and Wichita State U. He was a backup defensive tackle and guard who played a lot on special teams. He's still alive."

[No. 69, African American] "Woody Peoples, from the South, from Birmingham, Alabama. A real quiet person and very focused. He died in 2010, I think from a heart attack. Woody was not a fitness guy. He would show up to practice but didn't spend any time in the weight room or work out in the off season. It would take him a few weeks to get in sync when training camp started."

[No. 79, white guy behind Randy in photo] "Cas Banaszek, a Chicago guy, went to Northwestern. Started out as a tight end and they converted him to tackle. He told the coach in training camp, 'I can't get out and can't get open. I think I'm too slow for this game.' That's when they made him a tackle. And he was a good one, played for a long time, 10 or 12 years. He's alive and lives in NorCal. He's had some serious health issues—one is an incurable infection. He had a cut on his finger and went to the hospital. He picked up some infection there and once it got into his system, it went to his knee where he had to undergo a knee replacement. His body wound up attacking the foreign body—his replaced knee joint. Because of that infection, he had another knee replacement. After lying in the hospital for months, he lost 80 pounds. After football, he got way overweight. It's both hereditary and from being sedentary. His father was over 400 pounds. Now he's in trouble again because the infection came back."

[No. 66, white guy next to Cas who resembles the Brawny paper towel guy] "Elmer Collett. He grew up right here in San Francisco. He's a surfer, a beach boy, beach volleyball player, a hunter, fisherman. After football he became a fireman, retired from the force. I understand that he would ride his bike to work at the fire station over Mount Tam. So he is one of those fitness fanatics. He maintained his large size and muscles despite the onset of age. He's the only ex-49er who owns a real gold mining claim in the Sierra foothills."

[No. 12, white guy; bottom center of cover photo] "6'1", 200. John Brodie, Stanford guy, all-around athlete. Played as a professional senior golfer and won a few times. Retired as the third greatest career passer in the NFL. He had a stroke in 2000 and is still alive."

What are your memories of Candlestick Park?

"Candlestick in the fall was okay. During early baseball season it was not the place to be with all of the fog and wind. My first year, we played in Keyser Stadium in Golden Gate Park. The field was either at or below sea level so it was always soggy. Sometimes you'd get in your stance, you'd put your hand on the ground and there'd be a whole bunch of worms in the mud. When we left, the seagulls would converge on the field to feast on the worms."

I'm sure you ran across players using underhanded tactics like sticking Bengay on their fingers.

"Guys would resort to throwing dirt in your face. You know, a number of things, like wearing a cast or something that was hardened on their hand or elbow that they could use as a weapon. They finally outlawed that, probably mid '70s, and the referees would come and examine the armaments you had and make guys take them off."

You started in 1966?

"Yeah, I started out in Philadelphia. I was a starter at defensive end and did pretty well. I wound up getting knee surgery for a torn medial collateral ligament between my second and third year and had to stop for a year. I remember it was a goal-line stand and someone came crashing down on the side of my knee. When I came back the next year they had drafted another defensive end. Then I got traded to San Francisco who, at the time, needed an offensive guard."

Was that your first major injury?

"I had an 'almost torn' groin injury when I was in college that was pretty severe. And that came on again as a rookie in the pros, in the pre-season. The doctor came to me and said, 'You know the coaches really want to see you play, I know you have a strained groin. But you should really get out there and show them what you can do. In the locker room, he gave me a shot of Novocain in my groin. He must have hit a nerve with the shot because as I was running out on the field, I didn't have any feeling in my leg and I collapsed. He came up and said, 'I guess you're not going to be able to play, which is probably a good thing because if you had torn it any worse, you might have been gone for your career.' That's the kind of thing the doctors did back then, they did what the coaches were telling them. They had no independence. Anyway, my groin did heal. I never had any problem with it after that."

So you have no groin pain when you are lifting weights or playing tennis?

"No. I also got smacked upside the head and this broke the orbit under my eye. But that didn't keep me out. My eye completely closed, was black, and I got stitches and all that, but I played the next week. This was from a guy throwing a hard elbow to the side of the helmet and the impact did the damage and broke my facial bone. The helmet went into my bone."

I got to hear an interview of Dan Fouts and the San Diego Chargers' team physician. They went through all of Fouts' litany of injuries over the years, complete with his x-rays. And Fouts, as intelligent as he was, kept coming back to play again. What would make someone like that want to keep coming back?

"I have a lot of respect for Dan Fouts as a player and as a class human being. I got to attend one of his youth football camps one time up in Oregon. I think the answer is that he enjoyed the game so much it kept bringing him back. Everybody I know who plays the game is the same way. They would probably play the game for free. It's the competition, it's the camaraderie, it's everything all-inclusive. You never want it to end. It was a great life. Everything is taken care of for you—your team meals, your travel plans, your uniform, you get to see the same guys, you become friends. It's like an extension of college but without the final exams."

Is there a way to turn football into a less violent game—still keeping the athleticism, the speed, the artistry, the competition, etc.—but eliminating the cheap shots and the blindsided hits?

"It all gets back to television. What they want to show on television is the most violent hits. People love a train wreck, you know. That's what brings them back. I think the players do have respect for the other players and no one wants to see anybody get hurt. But they still want to deliver as devastating a blow as they can. And the average fan wants to see as much mayhem as possible."

So to bring this back to the original idea, Dr. Bill Gallivan, orthopedic surgeon, himself an aging athlete and not a small-framed person, told me to write a book about the aging athlete—a new field in orthopedic medicine. I imagine he was thinking I'd have brain scans, knee scans, and hip x-rays, but since that is not in my realm of expertise, I went after the topic based on mindset. And as you'll remember when we first met in 2009, I asked you how many of the aging athletes from your era were still fit all of these years later, you said, "Less than 10 percent." I was flabbergasted, but it made complete sense because the same thing has happened to many of the people I used to train fitness with back when I was in my 20s. And if you not only stop training, but you continue to drink beer while you're sedentary, your body doesn't like it and over time you turn into a completely different cat than you were in your athletic days. So, I started with the questions, among them these two: 1. What percentage of ex-performance athletes, military, and stage performers, etc. are still fit when they leave their performance days? After talking with a large number of people, that answer is still what you originally told me: less than 10 percent.

Randy Beisler, trimmed down to 234 pounds at age 70

Then, 2: Why did or would they stop?

One thing that I have learned over the course of the interviews is that somehow, someway many athletes, maybe in their subconscious mind, still believe they can get back what they used to have. Muhammad Ali in his early 30s is the classic example—he kept having comeback fights. Then, later, it was often a question of him needing the money. I believe this is no different than a Wall Street hedge-fund guy who made a million dollars last year and then this year, he takes some time off from full-time work, is dating a younger woman, living the high life. Somehow, in the back of his mind, he thinks he can always repeat that million dollar performance. And that being able to have a banner year will always be available to solve his problems. So a number of the aging athletes, they simply don't take care of themselves and don't get the maintenance part of it. They don't get that part of the aging process, but many somehow believe they are going to be able to get their health and some of their performance back when they need it.

"Speaking of football specifically, we would go through training sessions that were brutal. They were two-a-days in the summer, and it was hot and humid and the coaches wouldn't let you drink any water. There was no water out on the practice field. They thought it was part of getting in shape, and that you were going to be tougher if you didn't require any water. You'd go through the whole session with cotton mouth, you couldn't swallow, you couldn't do anything. Now you look back and it makes no sense. It was nuts. It was the same in high school, in college, and in my first few years as a pro. So they made it [training] an unpleasant experience for a lot of people. So, a lot of guys I know, as soon as their last year was over, that was it. They weren't going to go back to training for nothing. It was so unpleasant. But for myself, I managed to get to enjoy training. I like the endorphins, the excitement of whatever you've built up. You're stimulated. So that's why I continue. But most of the guys I know, they don't have that same feeling that I do. They'd just as soon sit on the couch and watch television. I just like a lot of activity. I get it from my mom, she was the same way. Until the last year of her life, she'd be sitting in front of the TV doing sit-ups."

So you had your mom modeling that type of behavior all along.

"Right."

Is there a way to teach that type of behavior to athletes in the off-season? I know they play golf and they do other things. But since so many are way out of shape, you'd have to think there is a better way to handle the off-season and later the post-performance life. Is there a way to teach people to be more like you—happy and well? Not just looking good but happy and well?

"There absolutely is. I mean I think there is now. In the locker room, the trainers are more versed in what it takes to live a lifestyle rather than just get ready for a season. At the early part of the time I was playing there was none of that. They just said, 'Enjoy the off-season, and come back in shape.' But nobody said, 'This is what you should be doing, what you should be eating.' There was no monitoring. Initially, most of the guys were barely in shape when they came back."

What changes, if any, happened in this regard?

"Well, it wasn't until I was a few years into my time with the 49ers that one doctor instituted a way to track our heart rate, blood pressure, speed in the mile and three-quarters. Before that, guys mostly just ignored working out in the off-season. So that test right there helped start everybody in getting into better shape."

§ § §

Randy played some 70 fundraising basketball games in the off-season. This kept him in shape, well, happy, and engaged in positive pursuits all year long. Towards the end of his playing career, Randy and one of the 49er trainers looked at how quickly Randy and other players who did weight training, machine exercises, and agility training tended to bounce back from injuries. Quite simply, their minor and medium severity injuries healed while other players often faced a slow healing process for their injuries. Sounds highly scientific for the 1970s and sounds pretty scientific for today. Active healing works. That's what physical therapy and Rolfing is largely about. But, let's not forget how functional, strength, and agility fitness creates a healthy organism that stands up better against injuries and illness and heals better.

That said, Randy's career ended—as so many do—with a major injury. Before this incident, Randy had been traded to Kansas City. While playing in 1977 for his new team—the Chiefs—there was an interception. While making a tackle on the cornerback who had picked off the pass, one of Randy's teammates—a 290-pound offensive tackle named Jim Nicholson—flew into the play late and they clanged helmets together, resulting in a broken neck for Randy and two more injuries to the others. The big player who came flying in and hit him was put out of the game as was the cornerback who made the interception. Sounds like a three-car pileup ...

As always, the tough and dedicated Randy did his best to rehabilitate himself. When he came back the next training camp, he was no longer playing at his full capacity, so he retired. Guess what his first endeavor was? During his playing days, he and the 49ers' trainer became involved in a high-end fitness business. They opened up a sports training facility in Cupertino near Apple. (Apple eventually bought this rehab-fitness center for their employees.) This fitness center had opened right before the time of the neck injury. Randy and his partner had decided that athletes and the public should be able to come and get proper training using the latest equipment. What they had in mind was not only fitness but overall wellness—and health promotion, injury prevention, and a good, solid, invigorating workout. They ultimately decided to make it a rehab/fitness center and brought in two orthopedic surgeons as partners. "We had 100 patients on our first day in business."

Eventually they had a couple thousand members and were using state-of-the-art equipment, mostly by Nautilus.

"I went down to Florida and trained with Arthur Jones," Randy shared, "the developer of Nautilus. He trained me in a few weeks and then we had some of our staff trained on the equipment."

While he ran this venture, Randy worked on healing his neck and staying in shape. He also owned a successful sports bar with some other members of the Protectors, including the one they protected—QB John Brodie. That business also did well. After hearing about Randy's business acumen, I was ready to put down my pen and go into business with him.

At age 68, Randy still gets tingling from his shoulder down into his arm—results from the broken neck in his late 20s. "There are some positions I can't be in when I'm lying down. I also have one knee that's not so good. I can't play singles in tennis."

I also asked him about his hands. I had noticed them at our first meeting in 2009. "Yeah, my knuckles aren't so good—they go in different directions."

Fitness played a big part in making Randy the stellar player he was. Sure he had size and ability, but so do a lot of young athletes. Fitness and recreation kept Randy level in demeanor and gave him the edge he needed at each stage of his athleticism. And this dedicated athlete did it all without the juice—performance-enhancing substances that became more and more prevalent in sports. Now, still active in the business world—he's a busy commercial Realtor in Mill Valley, California—Randy embraces his practice, fitness as recreation. He hasn't lost as big a step as so many of his colleagues in the world of aging athletes and the world of regular aging folks. He is still big and strong and mentally with it.

Despite the mayhem on the field, the man who learned much of his physical drive from his mother, did physical things well, and is still doing a daily regimen. Randy has expressed no sour grapes about his time in football. He said, "Most of the people I played with loved the game so much they would have played the game for free."

"Despite the injuries that lasted a lifetime?" I asked him.

He answered, "Most would say they'd do it again starting tomorrow."

Today, Randy's fitness mindset is driving his spirit and his wellness. Randy has passed on this gift to his daughters and now his grandkids. And this story of active aging athletes is now passing it on to you.

The fit former lineman at Machu Picchu in Peru age 67

"I do it as a therapy. I do it as something to keep me alive. We all need a little discipline. Exercise is my discipline."

—Jack LaLanne
the Godfather of Fitness

Performance Training vs. Wellness Training

Physical training for a certain sport could be called "end-use-directed physical activity" or performance training. Competitive sports provide an obvious example of what the participation in performance training can do or not do for someone's athletic stardom and wealth prospects. Some get mansions for their performances while other less funded performance athletes get free T-shirts and non-leaching sports bottles. And it's not just college and pro athletes who engage in performance training. High school and even pre-high-school athletes are known to spend time with highly skilled personal trainers and coaches. Everyone wants the edge.

An edge helps us get ahead. In the case of a world-class athlete, it can lead to fame and fortune, or at least a better deal on what has become a very expensive college education. I have met college athletes whose drive to make the college sports team was based on the college scholarship it provided. Although they assuredly must exist, I have yet to meet a pro athlete who did it solely for the money. These particular college athletes who personally shared their motivations for making the team admitted to me they would have stopped playing after high school. But, they disclosed, an education in exchange for playing a sport is "an incredible deal."

Randy Beisler is a former college scholarship athlete and professional football player who played on the offensive line of the record-setting, lowest-sacks-allowed, 1970 San Francisco 49ers. The information he related helped kick off this aging athlete book project. Randy told me that all of his close confidants of the gridiron loved the game so much they would have played pro football free. Though they are mostly all in various states of repair or infirmity, "they would do it all again starting tomorrow."

Performance sports training is obviously geared to provide better results in a game or competition. But there can be a steep price with this type of training. Injury is the normal result of physical impact and repetition of movement. A team of pro basketball players was interviewed in the late 1990s. Each player ran through their own personal pain and injury list. Not one person was without some condition that was a bother to them. Instead of stopping the training or performing to heal or to find another life activity, the performance minded often receive injections or take pain killers and NSAIDs (non-steroidal anti-inflammatories) to allow them to continue.

Wellness is not a direct offshoot of sports performance. In general terms, wellness can be provided by wellness-oriented movement programs which might include jogging, running intervals, swimming, calisthenics, stretching, yoga, chi gong, fitness center training, and lifetime sports like golf, tennis, and ping pong. All of these programs can assist the performance athlete and many of these activities can be part of an athlete's normal week of performance training. Though yoga is often a challenge for many of us, watching a competitive boxer's workout reveals just how intense and lengthy it is compared to a maintenance-oriented Hatha yoga class or the standard training required in high school physical education classes.

A given is that performance training is harder, more intense, and more subject to overloading the body and mind. Experience shows how rare it is to see someone do performance training for a lifetime. A famous actor, himself a fitness nut, once wrote a film about a boxer. He wrote that he would not have been able to do certain overbearing parts of his training without large quantities of coffee. He talks about this in his biography, which also mentioned some banned performance enhancing drugs (he was apprehended with them at a checkpoint). Heavy-duty performance training is simply too hard on the system and it tends to break things down if continued ad infinitum.

What's more, any training breaks down parts of our human system on a cellular level. All of those cells and the areas they make up need to be repaired. The more difficult the training, the more one goes to exhaustion or past that point, the more repair is needed.

Heavy-duty training—and proper rest, diet, and state of mind—can put an athlete in peak form. How you grow an athlete for top productivity can almost be compared to growing the winning pumpkin. As someone who has spent a fair amount of time in the garden and a bit of time around greenhouses, I'll offer this observation: a faster than normal growing vegetable plot generally needs a steady supply of nutrients, more heat (like found inside a greenhouse), more sun, and the ideal amount of water.

In the same way, some will suggest that a harder training athlete generally needs performance enhancing substances to repair the damage of heavy-duty training. These substances can be natural, or they may be synthesized and unapproved by athletic oversight organizations.

Far more often than not—and this comes from athletes themselves, including one from this book—people at the top of their athletic disciplines have used at least some banned substances. The primary reason they do so is to repair their bodies. They go so hard so frequently that the only easy way to heal—many seem to believe—is with hormones, steroids, and perhaps even blood transfusions. Others swear by acupressure massage, Epsom salt baths, elixirs, and acupuncture. Significant numbers of athletes use both banned and therapeutic healing techniques.

So, yes, performance takes its toll. Athletes who wish to continue performing generally have to deal with pain. A large number of retired athletes also have to deal with pain, often from injuries suffered decades ago. A key discovery that surfaced during The Aging Athlete Project is how performance activities don't necessarily lead to recreational activities. In this case, movement doesn't necessarily beget movement. Performance training does, however, often generate a dislike or even loathing of performance training. The story of the aging athlete can be extremely poignant. Things like pain, letdown, apathy, and broken relationships are not uncommon. In his interview, mixed martial arts fighter and former UFC heavyweight champion Ken Shamrock suggests that athletes who come to the end of their career don't realize that life goes on. "And once we're done with what we do," he says, "then we basically come down to everybody else's level."

I added, "And then you're signing autographs as the former Ken Shamrock."

He agreed. "You almost go below what normal respect is, because people don't look at that same level anymore."

Not every athlete signs up for or is dealt the downbeat retirement plan. Some aren't injured beyond repair. Some don't have debilitating hip injuries or brain trauma but do have the awareness to keep the active mindset which carries over to recreational activities, family raising, and spending time in rewarding pursuits. Those who plot a course of physical activity and proper lifestyle don't fill up the fridge—and themselves—with too much food.

Let's look at some positive outcomes from some athletes who were extremely fit during their youthful years. The combative cast members of the "Rocky" films illustrate how some elite performance fitness people were able to continue on in healthful physical pursuits. Stallone is still fit looking and considers himself proficient in his muscle training programs. Considering his opponents in over three decades of fight films, here's the breakdown of what seems to have occurred in their health and longevity: Carl Weathers (Rocky I, II; b. 1948) is still fit; Mr. T (Rocky III; b. 1952) is still fit; Dolph Lundgren (Rocky IV; b. 1957) is still fit and has professed to training 6 days per week; Tommy "The Duke" Morrison (Rocky V; b. 1969), who was a top-notch professional boxer, was a partier who was not maintaining fitness or wellness and died at age 44, of, as rumored, the result of AIDS; Antonio Tarver (Rocky Balboa; b. 1968) was still fighting as a professional boxer at the time of this book's publication.

If I would have had to guess who of these film stars would stop maintaining fitness, it would have been the long-term performance athletes. Tommy Morrison, who had an incredibly long amateur boxing career and noteworthy pro career, maintained a partying lifestyle and admittedly was his own worst enemy. The poor guy was sick for a lengthy period leading up to his end. Maintenance was not how he was wired. Antonio Tarver fought the best and trained hard for more than 25 years in amateur and professional boxing. According to what I gained in writing this book, out of all of these living Rocky athletes, Tarver would be the least likely to take up retirement from the ring as a practitioner of maintenance fitness. One hopes he proves that statistic wrong.

There are always exceptions to the rule, but I'd suggest the number is less than one percent of aging athletes who continue to do heavy-duty training all the way until late in life. And it's nearly unheard of for them to continue heavy-duty training until the time of late senior-hood infirmity or old-age death. Elder athletes I have met led me to this conclusion. Their opinions were of course well informed. Athletes tend to associate with other athletes and many keep in touch or stay up to date about those they spent time with.

Charley French, the eldest athlete featured in the book, can go down his own personal list with you. I'd wager that of those he served with in the U.S. military in WWII and of those he skied with in his 20s and 30s, he's the loner who is still training for triathlons. This activity is such an extreme endurance event, especially for someone in his late 80s. Continuing to train for and compete in such event can easily result in debilitation. Taking a stride back to when he was 50, I'd also wager he was one of the few of his formerly fit peers from his 20s and 30s who was still doing that type of extreme training post mid-age.

I write this passage seated on my "soapbox" with arms and back pumped up from a horizontal bar workout of pull-ups, chin-ups, knee ups, and glute squeezes. I've added a new intensity to my maintenance plan at age 51. These five sets of bodyweight bearing training are what I've done three days per week for the past six weeks. Some motivation comes from the fact that I've been doing these training sessions with a workout partner—a 17-year-old natural athlete who cycles most every day. By natural athlete, I mean that he has balance, quickness, and coordination and most sports come naturally to him. We complement each other, but we're not competing for some end prize, unless of course reality TV wants to sponsor a free trip to the Andes for the winner and his girlfriend. Have them send us all. Let me emphasize, I'm not pre-wired with an aspiration for entering an age-group chin-up contest. I'm not trying to outdo other people who are 51. As far as my training goes, I'm mostly in a friendly competition with myself and my desk potato lifestyle. Most of my day is spent working on a laptop.

It's good to keep maintaining fitness at mid age. The bar isn't really "kid stuff" as some may suggest. And if it is, what's wrong with youthful playtime and the ability to lift your own body? As any Marine drill sergeant and fitness expert will agree, the bar is *the* great determinant of overall fitness and suitable weight. If your all-around health is decent and you can't hold yourself from a bar, what does that say about your fitness level?

A Short Essay About the Total-Minutes Theory of Energy and Performance

An idea that has some currency in sports psychology holds that performance athletes have only so many total minutes of emotional and physical energy to draw upon. As that thinking goes, once the minutes are used up, the machine stops or its driver is simply unwilling to go on. Unlike a recreational athlete who may carry on for ages like a Toyota, according to this particular theory, a performance athlete's days are numbered, at least in terms of the drive for high performance physical operation. In this instance, it might be helpful to think of performance athletes more like the stereotypical Jaguar automobile—lots of performance, but a short career using the original parts and brain center. (No offense to Jags, they were the mark I longed for my entire youth.) As an example, some top-finishing triathletes have been known to pass bloody urine at the end of Ironman contests.

How many years could a competitor's body and mind tolerate that?

Football linebacker Brian Bosworth retired from the NFL due to injury. During the athlete's physical, the team physician flunked him due to Brian's being age 25 with the shoulder joints of a 60-year-old.

This total-minutes scenario may parallel why many staffers in the corporate world or other jobs can only take so much of the monotony or overly taxing workloads. They may leave the job or be asked to leave when they're unable to perform as before. Domestic relationships may fit here as well. Do you think their breaking points may in part have to do with a formula of total minutes? In a time of short-lived relationships, is it possible we are *time-limited* in our ability to endure differences, remain attentive, express love, or handle relationship stress?

According to the total-minutes theory, even without painful injuries, a performance athlete could simply run out of steam, concentration energy, and other parts of their emotional and physical performance capabilities. Consider why the out-of-retirement comebacks of athletes rarely produce stellar results. It takes a major effort and an incredible number of hours for most athletes to reach peak performance.

When they're no longer training, or are simply no longer capable of remaining in the zone for their sport, high-caliber performances diminish. And, once retired, some of the skills disappear astonishingly quickly. When they leave their competition days, athletes instantly face the same problems as the rest of the population in the sedentary world. But why do large numbers of these former peak movers become as sedentary or more sedentary than the general population? Are they simply out of energy? Are their minutes all used up? Or, are they still thinking their former fitness level can protect them indefinitely or can return with the flick of a switch?

It's possible to compare our modern era's denatured, disharmonious, potentially unenduring lifestyle with the millions of years of existence of the hunter-gatherers who survived by being peak performers, well acclimated to their changing surroundings. One reason hunter-gatherers may have survived so long is because living in relative harmony with nature and each other has a better track record for rejuvenation. Up to a point, certain survival skills tended to get better with age. Imagine how important it was to know if water could be consumed just by what your senses told you. In this example, skills acquisition equals strengthening. Adapting to nature's offerings and requests increases our chances for survival.

If tribal people contaminated their spaces or depleted their attainable resources, they perished. Climate changes and things that fell from the skies also acted to depopulate the planet. In a communal situation, when individuals could no longer do their jobs or take care of themselves, others would have to help them or they perished. The idea of lingering in incapacitated states is not favorable to tribal living where each person had vital responsibilities.

For the true hunter-gatherers who were not unendingly threatened by rival tribes, the physical life of movement and cooperation, accompanied by a natural diet, and a life that may have been more conducive to downtime and better sleep, meant hunter-gatherers had the chance to thrive. Prior to industry, they also had less exposure to harmful chemicals (things like volcanoes and naturally occurring asbestos may have provided some exposure) and a significantly reduced bombardment by electromagnetic frequencies. They also lived at most times electrically grounded to the earth. Their bare feet or leather footwear allowed for the balancing effect of electron transfer with the ground.

Of course they had problems along the way—infection, starvation, attack, and weather to name a few. But, as their bones generally testify, their lifestyle often left the survivors with fewer of the type of ailments that we suffer. Heart attacks and diabetes are unheard of in true hunter-gather populations. We may imagine a life in the wild that was simply too tough. Since upright walkers of the Homo species have handled it for perhaps 2.3 million years and since wild animals do it every day, obviously there's a way to thrive in nature.

Like evolving animals, evolving humans also became acclimated to their surroundings. Today's high incidence of ailments and disease suggests we are not acclimated to our modern surroundings. In tribal living, acclimation meant locomotion, which kept bodily functions optimized. Proper movement and posture during travel and hunting made people stronger, provided fulfillment, and reduced their stresses. Conscious and unconscious proprioception, the body's posture and awareness through movement, fires the nerves, linking brainpower with brawn power. But if a hunter wants to make the long trek for food, the brawn has to be efficient. The more efficient, the fewer calories burned and the less wear on the body.

How many total minutes did a healthy hunter-gatherer have at peak performance? Their bones suggest that adults weren't dropping like flies in their 20s. Many more of them would have died off young if they lost the ability to hunt, gather, and defend as they ran out of total minutes. Because caregiving is so taxing, it would have been simply too difficult to care for significant numbers of a tribe's members who were not performing, yet still consuming. Certainly there is a limit to how many undercontributors or people needing care a group can support.

More importantly, who is caring for the aging athletes who have broken down? Would a mother or wife be able to handle a 300-pound ex football player who needs help toileting or who experiences fits of rage? The anecdotal evidence provided for The Aging Athlete Project suggests that only 10 percent of retired performance athletes (including military and physical performers like dancers) take up a life of physical activity.

Because of a drive for success in performance activities, such athletes and physical performers have ostensibly rewired any programming that once may have had them doing friendly kids' play. They suffer a complete disconnect from any former front porch and neighborhood recreation. A retired competition athlete may completely forget how enriching it was to perhaps have done fitness and movement activities in their primary schooling. In many cases, the retired athlete—whether a gymnast at age 15 or a former U.S. Marine at age 22—might step into the next phase of life with a sigh of relief. "I don't have to do that hardcore training anymore and I don't have to listen to that task master ever again." Who becomes the task master of the recently "unshackled" athlete? Who teaches the retired athlete about transitioning back into maintenance fitness, recreation, and wellness?

At once, the performance-retired body tells its end user how good it feels to take a break. The mind too presumably welcomes such a period of calming down. But how long should a recent retiree relish in this physically unstructured calm zone? As the athletes themselves have attested, it only takes one day of being complacently immobile to create a whole new type of agony that comes with adopting a sedentary lifestyle. An unused physical body starts breaking down, characteristically causing pain and discomfort in mind, body, spirit, and relationships. And let's not forget how dietary rebellion is easily coupled with more time to wash down the stresses of inactivity with more food and drink. Together these practices often touch off the vicious cycle of unwanted additional fat with all of its potential negative health consequences from diabetes to diseases of the heart and other "favorite" organs.

The athletic performance total-minutes theory has athletes falling apart, or dipping way down from peak performance, or wanting out at a specific point. That seems like a theory worth pursuing. There's also the normal aging process and aggravated body abuse from the nature of their competition. But is this the reason many of them refrain from doing noncompetitive physical movement as they transition to a new side of life? Is this why so many become first sedentary, then unwell? Is there a way to circumvent the prevailing forces of the theory and prevent a state of diminishing health—both physical and emotional? Understanding recent trends is an initial step that can help lead us to a path of prevention. However, openly accepting a theoretical trend, without studying the history of human performance, seems limiting.

Despite stress, new responsibilities, and physical and emotional challenges (sometimes severe), a reported 10 percent of aging performance athletes decided to pursue physical movement for a lifetime. In "The Aging Athlete," a group of former performance athletes share how they have done it. Even though a number of the aging athletes in this book are still doing performance-oriented training and competition, a higher percentage of these featured athletes are doing functional movement and maintenance exercises. This book presents how a group of performance-oriented athletes have taken a perceived limitation (like the total-minutes theory) and overcome it. For those of us who are not beyond repair, we can follow their path and can keep moving for a lifetime of recreational enjoyment and wellness. This book provides aging athletes, as well as those with little or no athletic experience, the opportunity, inspiration, and motivation to adopt the wellness mindset.

I hashed out the subject matter of this essay and contemplated life sitting in a restaurant in tropical Florida. Finished, our discards found the trash and recycling and my friend and I walked out towards our rental car. Ahead of us were two large and "fit" college athletes who looked in need of some time off—they both had limped out of Chipotle and were both still limping in the parking lot. Ace bandages gripped one's right knee and the second's right knee and left ankle. To my friend, I mentioned The Aging Athlete Project and how these two fit in the paradigm. What memories, I asked, will these two fellows have of their pain and suffering, reminders of which could remain with them for life?

Definitions

athletic coaching: creating the paradigm of effective drills, diet, and attitude to promote the development of the athlete. An athletic coach tends to work towards performance goals which would be different than a wellness coach who concentrates on wellness issues. In the new millennium, athletic coaches have become much more wellness oriented. An injured or sick athlete cannot perform and may not have good things to say about the coach or program that was part of what caused the debilitating state. For several decades, trainers have been increasingly teaching about healthful lifestyles.

athletic industry: the conglomeration of products for sale and people whose personas and performances are monetized. The fitness industry is connected to the athletic industry. It could be argued that proper time, knowledge, good coaching, determination, and the ability to listen to the body are more important to athletics and fitness than the aggregate of products that have come to the marketplace in the past several decades.

fit: a person with an optimally functioning body and mind and who maintains both with a daily practice and irreverent indifference to anything that seemingly prohibits fitness, like a packed schedule in an over-programmed world or bars on a prison cell … which can be synonymous.

maintenance training: training the body and mind for general wellness. Daily or frequent and regular fitness to keep all parts of the body working optimally and not allowing inactivity to produce atrophy and dysfunction. Maintenance training may incorporate parts of performance training but its main focus is to stave off the results of a sedentary or imbalanced lifestyle. Maintenance training also helps prevent injuries that tend to result from high-intensity workouts and over training. This is arguably one of the easiest ways to maintain one's optimally maintainable physique and happy mind over a lifetime.

microtrauma: small tears in the muscles that result from strength training, aka overload or resistance training. This is the principal way muscles grow. Intensity and difficulty is useful in promoting muscle growth and tone. The author has done both overload training (heavier weights) and maintenance training (typically lighter weights and bodyweight exercises). The periods of overload training have produced the biggest muscle gains but have also produced the most soreness as well as more potential for injury and diminished coordination.

performance training: preparing the body and mind to achieve a specific performance goal, as in winning an athletic event. For many sports, this typically comes with its share of what is considered high-intensity training—tire flipping, weights and machines, interval training, field drill workouts, endurance training—which is often performed until muscle or cardio exhaustion or near exhaustion.

physical recreation: a physical activity that gives us something positive to do and promotes a sense of well-being. This is perhaps the most important aspect to teach in school. Over the history of modern scholastics, the sense of athletic competition has frequently overshadowed the importance and joy of physical movement. For aging athletes, hula hooping is a more important skill in promoting health and wellness than diving into a football blocking sled or diving for a dig in volleyball.

well: a fit person who takes care of themselves and doesn't suffer from disease. Those people who suffer from disease can still practice pursuits of fitness and wellness.

Summary of "Sedentary Nation"
Another Book by Sifu Slim

"Sedentary Nation" recalls pivotal moments of the history of physical movement. Despite modernism and the decreasing use of the physical body, the book shows how almost anyone can easily benefit from a program that has a payoff of improved health, youthful look and energy, better sleep, and clearer thinking without the physical toll and battle fatigue that often accompany other approaches to wellbeing and fitness.

Expanding on that, the author details how, as Chinese philosophy explains, you can change your thinking and the body will follow. By sharing knowledge and practices from those he respects the most and cites throughout the book, including Jack LaLanne and Bruce Lee, Sifu Slim describes his own journey of self-mastery. "Sedentary Nation" is the result of several hundred interviews and over a decade of research. It stands as both wellness guide for the busy, modern era and humorous memoir of a life spent living the wellness walk.

Introduction to "Sedentary Nation"
by Gary Casaccio, M.D.

There's extensive, mounting evidence that supports what many people have intuitively known ... that we are sitting too much and not spending enough time outdoors for recreation and physical activity. The paths and fields we played on as children are inviting us, so why won't we reach out to take advantage of what nature offers us again?

We humans need to get moving, preferably outside, for optimal health. When done outdoors, our workouts may provide more mental, emotional, and physical benefits than those we do indoors. Even the color green, which is abundantly found in nature, may improve both mood and self-esteem.

Getting physical outdoors amidst the fresh air, sunshine, breeze, and negative ions found in nature against the background of blue skies and green foliage boosts mental and emotional wellbeing. Spending time outdoors, whether exercising, recreating, or even caring for the lawn and garden, has been linked to greater decreases in tension, anxiety, and depression. More benefits include improved levels of calmness, mental clarity, focus, vitality, and enthusiasm. Don't those sound like prescriptions for health and catalysts for great relationships at home and at work?

In addition, the benefit of increased vitamin D levels as a result of direct exposure to sunlight also contributes to improvements in mood and total overall health. Except for pollution, nuclear fallout, and other hazards, the research certainly isn't telling us to spend more time indoors. Aren't we listening?

I tell my patients that simple things, natural things, can provide wonderful health benefits. Focusing and even just gazing on the changing and varying terrain we see while we're outdoors has been found to stimulate our mind and senses. In an era where people complain of being bored and overwrought with repetition, who doesn't want more stimulation and a varying terrain?

Recreating and working out of doors has also been found to lower levels of cortisol (the body's stress hormone) to a greater degree than the same activities done indoors. This isn't to say we should avoid fitness centers and indoor yoga and martial arts centers, but that the outdoors needs to be where we spend at least some of our time. It's not a bad idea to spend some quality time outdoors every day. Even my grandparents knew this.

By experience, by passed down wisdom, and by positive results, my grandparents knew that it was healthful and joyful to walk to church on Sunday and go for walks after big meals. As immigrants who left their homeland in Italy, they loved getting out of the house and walking their adopted neighborhood in Chicago. They lived through the Depression and some very tough times. They knew enough to take care of their health and wellness. They understood that putting one foot in front of the other enhanced that and gave them a free activity to enjoy. Don't you have some lessons from your ancestors you can draw upon?

My grandparents even ate well. I can't tell you how much I longed for the big family meals that my grandmother and my mother cooked. Being Italian, the meals that bring the fondest memories were the pasta dishes. It always lifted my spirits and I somehow felt my grandmother's and mother's love more acutely as they lovingly prepared my favorite dish—spaghetti and meatballs.

Being young and having a high metabolism, I didn't have to worry about carbs back then.

Naturally for my era, those meals were typically followed by some physical movement. I would head outside and eventually locate my friends and we'd be choosing teams for another game of football, baseball, or pickle. Growing up, I would often take a walk with my dad after dinner and I was always active with baseball, wrestling, weight training, and martial arts. Later, in the overly sedentary world that was medical school, I did my utmost to keep moving. After studying for hours on end, I would clear my mind by going out in nature for a walk which helped to recharge my batteries and get me ready for another round of studying.

I regularly advise patients to take up walking to relieve stress and improve digestion. When we were young kids, our elders took us for frequent walks. That was a great way for both of us to spend some recreational time. Besides the benefits to the mind and the heart, the digestive processes are often enhanced when we don't just sit down on the couch right after a meal. Even our stomachs seem to like it when we stroll the sidewalks and paths. And, to help us through our busy schedules and daily challenges, this good digestive health and physical activity is associated with better sleep, often considered the best stress reliever of all.

There are a considerable number of long-term studies that directly associate stress with illnesses, including brain abnormalities, organ dysfunction, and cancer.

What can we do about that? We can de-stress by ensuring some good physical activity with enough sound sleep. Other studies have concluded that enjoyment levels and workout satisfaction are higher for those who train outdoors as opposed to those who train indoors. This suggests that individuals who train outdoors may be more likely to continue to not only engage in a consistent workout regimen due to the mental and emotional benefits, but may also find that their individual workouts last longer, are more focused, and tend to be more fulfilling. How much fulfillment do you feel after ending an entire afternoon flipping channels on the couch?

Sifu Slim makes the point that euphoria is what we all crave. He reminds us the term is derived from the Greek word euphorous which means "health." This book hits the mark when it enables us to consider the idea that we have an innate drive in seeking health. What you make of that will of course be for you to decide. How you get your health and euphoria is also for you to decide. What Sifu Slim has accomplished in "Sedentary Nation" is combining the knowledge we've gained from our ancestors stretching back over thousands of years with the latest research on achieving a healthy, active lifestyle. A true wellness approach.

His research enabled him to take a long look at tribal peoples who spent most of their time outdoors, frequently engaged in physical movement—some highly vigorous, some light, and often ending with the term that eludes so many of us today—Downtime. I can't disagree with this notion of finding useful answers in the past and I certainly am a big proponent of downtime. We need more of this as we age. That's not to say that today's kids have this in great supply—they're getting increasingly bombarded with sound and imagery, both of which are part of what's driving their decreasing mental and physical health. You will find this book steeped in history, philosophy, and common sense, yet with creative and actionable steps. A big piece of our modern medical knowledge is based on human history, as well as the millennia-old study of nature, especially botany. As a long-time student of health, I can support the book's emphasis that consistent exposure to natural sunlight may not only improve mood but also help to regulate your circadian rhythm which can help both improve and regulate sleep and boost energy levels.

My suggestion is not to simply take my word for it or Sifu Slim's word for it, but to see how some of this works for you. I like to think of myself as a caring physician who has dedicated a few decades of his life to learning as much as I can about the psychiatric components of human health. I see hundreds of patients per year and these folks all teach me a great deal. As a doctor who practices outdoor living and physical fitness, I may be somewhat different in this way—I normally only suggest lifestyle changes toward practices I myself would do or have done. I know what sedentary lifestyles and indoor living have done to me and I know the antidote, though sometimes elusive, is not that complicated.

Do you want to experience the increased oxygen levels found outdoors amongst oxygen generating trees and foliage? This can only enhance wellness, workout endurance, and workout recovery. Contrast this with the florescent lighting and air conditioning of most indoor gyms and workout facilities which may lead to increased fatigue and diminished muscular contractile strength. Working out indoors for extended periods of times on stationary equipment with unchanging environmental stimuli (i.e. staring at the same wall) often increases boredom which can lead to shorter workouts and decreased workout intensity and may result in reducing or eliminating the workout itself.

I suggest that nearly anything's better than perpetually staring at a blank wall. Having said that, we physicians learned long ago that having some outdoor, natural scenes artistically rendered on the clinic's inside walls—and even ceiling ... at least that's what some dentists do—furnishes our patients, our staff, and ourselves an inspiration for being out in nature. Actually sitting by a waterfall or a brook outdoors can generate the ultimate in soothing, relaxing, and even engaging experiences. Otherwise we'd never meet our sweethearts or write a poem ... down by the river.

Just like the water molecules running downstream through the river, we are a collection of individual and interrelated cells. When we are happy, our cells are happy. When we are stressed, so are our cells. Our human cells of course can heal themselves (and the structures they support) and reproduce better with proper diet, exercise, and rest. Moreover, without vitamin D—not easily obtained from the garden (it's found only in a mushrooms, fish oils, and vitamin pills)—the human physiology and brain chemistry deteriorate and we eventually wither away. To those who don't want to waste away like that, get outside a bit every day. Tell your employer and your spouse that your health simply mandates it, and that Dr. Gary prescribed the out of doors for the condition that so many suffer from today—lack of nature and lack of fresh air and sunshine.

In this wonderful life, I have spent decades as a student in sedentary, desk-bound positions, and also as an athlete, a fitness person, a recreational body builder, and martial artist. To some degree, I continue nearly all of the aforementioned activities to this day. Spending substantial amounts of time indoors and at the desk are part of what I must do to keep up my professional pursuits and tend to some of my home life responsibilities. But it will assuredly come as no surprise that long before I started studying medicine,

I knew that sitting in confining desks and chairs had noticeable downsides. During long bouts of sedentary postures, invigoration and focus were sometimes hard to come by and sleep and boredom were sometimes easily induced. I certainly wanted to have more joy in my life as well as a happier spinal column.

The remedies were apparent: Get moving and get exercising, outdoors whenever possible. Exercising's benefits, I found, lasted far longer than the post-workout hours. The benefits remained for days. Now in my profession as a practicing physician, I know that what I learned about the outdoors—recreation, exercising, and simple strolls through the neighborhood—are important things to share with patients, especially those whose health histories revealed some outdoor and recreational deficits. Many of my patients also admitted they were sitting too much. Together we determined just where they were missing out on some of the things our grandparents and prior generations had enjoyed just by living their routine way. My prescription—go back to the olden days. Get off the couch and out from behind the desk, get outside and get physical. Tell the green meadow or local park that Sifu Slim and Dr. Gary sent you.

Gary Casaccio, M.D., Psychiatrist.
Wheaton, Illinois

*The author's creed—no gym is needed for the
hunter-gatherer, martial arts workout.*

About the Author

Sifu Slim is a Fitness and Wellness Educator who has done a lifetime of intentional physical activity and is still built like Gilligan. "I may be skinny but I can fill out a shrunken, medium T-shirt like nobody's business!"

Sifu (Cantonese for Father-Teacher or Master) Slim is the Pioneer of MaintenanceWorkout.com and "The Business Traveler's Workout." With his mini workout DVDs and downloadable videos, which fill in while busy travelers are on the road, no longer can people use the "no-time" excuse. Instead of selling people dramatic transformation by showing them before-after photos of the program, Sifu promotes lifetime fitness. He is the after-after photo guy.

Consider Sifu as a resource for your group's wellness needs—in English, French, or Spanish. He is roadshow ready, webinar literate, and media ops fluent.

Sifu is also the author of "Sedentary Nation" a book that details the history and current status of physical activity and contains Sifu's well-researched wellness guide.

Honor life, honor it all.

Do you know any interesting aging male and female
former top athletes who are still maintaining their fitness
and who would be interested in sharing their story
for a future book?

Contact: TheAgingAthlete.com

Coupons

Coupon offers are subject to change. As discounts are available these offers may apply:

– Go to MaintenanceWorkout.com
– Click on DVDs
– Select a DVD
– Click on the order form.
– Type this into the CODE BOX:

> havingagreatdayofmovement

And you may be eligible for a percentage off your purchase of a fitness DVD.

To buy a discounted copy "Sedentary Nation":
– Go to SedentaryNation.com
– Type this into the CODE BOX:

> upandoffthecouch

And you may be eligible for a percentage off.

– Go To TheAgingAthlete.com
– Click on the order form.
– Type this into the CODE BOX:
– Whoisstillfitthesedays

All discounts are subject to change
and dependent on availability.

The Athletes Recovery Getaway

Sifu Slim and a number of his contacts in the health and wellness field have established *The Athletes Recovery Getaway*, aka TARGwell. Run as a cooperative of many different professionals, the group works with athletes of all ages who seek to get help in a variety of ways.

Sifu is the point person for the athletes who can call and schedule dates for their stays in Santa Barbara, home to world class training centers, medical facilities, and healing opportunities. The intentions: Prevention, Intervention, Rehabilitation, Performance Improvement, Coaching, Goal Setting, Skills Learning, and Rejoicing.

For more information, please email TARGwell@gmail.com.

www.TheAgingAthlete.com

www.SedentaryNation.com

Made in the USA
Las Vegas, NV
19 June 2022

50455945R00184